"Knowing Daisy Khan is to know what the future leaders will have to offer us. The wisdom of Daisy Khan becomes apparent as you read her excellent, moving book. Her life story is one of beauty and struggle, effectiveness and tension. She will be written about in history as one of the first Muslim women to give leadership to the United States. Daisy opens our eyes to the reality of the Muslim world in our time. She brings to us all a feminine gift marked by tenderness, passion, intelligence, and strength. She is a blessing to us all by virtue of her gift of faith."

—Rev. Dr. Joan Brown Campbell,
author of *Living into Hope*

"Daisy Khan's new book is a must-read for anyone who cares about women's rights. This memoir is a touching tale of growth and discovery that shows a side of Islam that is rarely seen today. She does not shy away from the darker side of a patriarchal faith, and she guides you through her journey of finding her own power inside that system. It is a beautiful story of spirituality and humanity."

—Anat Hoffman, chair of the board for the
Women of the Wall and executive director
of the Israel Religious Action Center

BORN WITH WINGS

BORN *with* WINGS

THE SPIRITUAL
JOURNEY
of a
MODERN MUSLIM
WOMAN

DAISY KHAN

SPIEGEL & GRAU

NEW YORK

Published in the United States by Spiegel & Grau,
an imprint of Random House, a division of
Penguin Random House LLC, New York.

SPIEGEL & GRAU and Design is a registered trademark
of Penguin Random House LLC.

Grateful acknowledgment is made to the following for permission
to reprint previously published material:
GULSHAN BOOKS: Excerpts from *Daughters of the Vitasta* by Prem
Nath Bazaz. Reprinted by permission of Gulshan Books, Kashmir.
KABIR HELMINSKI AND CAMILLE HELMINSKI: Excerpts from
three poems by Rumi, translated by Kabir Helminski and Camille
Helminski. Reprinted by permission of the translators.
BEHROOZ KARJOO: Translation of "Ruba'iyat" (Quatrain #1) by
Abū-Sa'īd Abul-Khayr by Behrooz Karjoo. Reprinted by
permission of the translator.
MARTHA POSTLETHWAITE: "Clearing" by Martha Postlethwaite.
Reprinted by permission of the author.

LIBRARY OF CONGRESS
CATALOGING-IN-PUBLICATION DATA
NAMES: Khan, Daisy, author.
TITLE: Born with wings: the spiritual journey of a modern
Muslim woman / by Daisy Khan.
DESCRIPTION: New York: Spiegel & Grau, 2018.`
IDENTIFIERS: LCCN 2017051900 | ISBN 9780812995268 |
ISBN 9780812995275 (ebook)
SUBJECTS: LCSH: Muslim women—Religious life. |
Islam. | Khan, Daisy.
CLASSIFICATION: LCC BP188.3.W6 K43 2018 | DDC 297.092
[B]—dc23 LC record available at https://lccn.loc.gov/2017051900

Printed in the United States of America on acid-free paper

randomhousebooks.com

spiegelandgrau.com

9 8 7 6 5 4 3 2 1

FIRST EDITION

Book design by Barbara M. Bachman

This book is meant for everyone:

PEOPLE OF FAITH AND NO FAITH, THE YOUNG AND OLD, MEN
AND WOMEN, SPIRITUAL ASPIRANTS AND COMMUNITY ACTIVISTS AND
THOSE TRYING TO DEEPEN THEIR UNDERSTANDING

For

Dadaji & Moji, Mummy, Papaji, Faroque Uncle, and Arfa Auntie

Feisal; his father, Muhammad Abdul Rauf; children; and grandchildren

*My siblings, extended family members and friends, scattered all
over the world*

The nuns of Presentation Convent, its teachers and its girls past and present

My Interfaith colleagues, true pioneers of upholding common human values

My American Muslim community, the MLTs and WISE, who give me hope

Muslim sisters around the world waging a quiet revolution

My special spiritual community that keeps me grounded

To

America, the land of the bold

Kashmir, exquisite in its inner and outer beauty

*Grandma Sarah, your green sparkly sandals allow me to walk
uncharted territories, and Pop, your red boxing gloves
will never be removed, they will be passed on to others who need them*

YOU WERE BORN WITH WINGS.

WHY PREFER TO CRAWL
THROUGH LIFE?

—*Rumi*

PROLOGUE

I AM ABOUT THREE YEARS OLD, AND MY FATHER IS TEACHING ME to box on the front lawn of our house in the shadow of the Himalayas. Yesterday, I ran home crying that I had been bullied by a bigger child. Now I am standing barefoot in boys' shorts as Papaji approaches me with a big smile, dangling a pair of shiny red boxing gloves with white laces. The gloves are almost as big as I am. He puts them on me and shows me how to punch:

"Left! Right! Jump up! Jump back! Duck! Lean into it! If anyone tries to bully you, stand up for yourself and, if necessary, punch them in the nose!" Papaji instructs as he pretends to be felled by my wobbly left hook.

My mother is scandalized at the idea of her daughter fighting or even fighting back. In Kashmir, girls do not pack punches. But Papaji says to her, "I'll turn her into a tomboy. She will always be a girl, but I can still have the boy I want."

I want to make my papaji proud. I struggle to put the gloves on and throw dutiful practice punches. I treasure the gloves, because they mean my father has confidence in me, and I keep them in a place of pride in my room. The thought of having a real fight and using the gloves as they were intended never occurs to me. But even as a very young girl, I know that the gloves are speaking to me. You are one thing, they say, but you have the potential to be something else. You need to be somebody else. Would throwing punches that please my papaji be the thing that could turn me into a greater, more powerful me? Or into someone else entirely? I peer into the mirror. A small brown-haired girl looks back. Then there is my mother, who frowns in her gentle way every time I put on the gloves.

And I do put on the red gloves. Yes, Papaji.

I wear them when I come to America for my education.

I wear them when I move out of the womb of my uncle's house to start my career.

I wear them when I write a protest letter to *Newsday* from my college campus.

I wear them when I refuse an arranged marriage to a prince and marry an imam instead.

I wear them when I feel the burden of what it means to be a Muslim woman.

I wear them when I challenge leaders who define our faith with archaic attitudes.

I wear them when I help convince an old woman to stop cutting girls on a filthy table and bring a new light into her life.

I wear them when I unite Muslim women to take back rights that have been stripped away over the centuries.

I wear them to convince imams to issue a fatwa against child marriage.

I wear them to honor my faith.

Finally, I wear them to fight the extremists among members of my own faith.

In fact, since that day in the yard in Kashmir, I have never taken off those red boxing gloves. I have quietly passed them along to my sisters around the world.

We are here; now we must reach there.

This book is about that journey.

BORN WITH

WINGS

WHEN I IMAGINE MY BIRTH, IN MY MIND'S EYE, IT IS A joyful occasion. I see a dark-haired newborn snuggled in her young mother's arms while her loving grandmother hovers over the birthing bed, cooing and strutting. Her father is proud, her mother beaming. Downstairs, the rest of the family is celebrating. The servants prepare a feast. In a trunk, there is a fine layette for the infant: There is a frock made of soft muslin cloth, fabric as delicate and transparent as butterflies' wings, with smocking tracing the fluttering hemline. There are hand-knitted booties, caps the size of flowers, and a blanket, along with a velvet box of jewels, gold coins, chains, and twenty-two-karat baby bracelets and earrings.

For a long time, that was how I believed it was. But on my tenth birthday, I learned the truth.

I had planned a big party. It would take place at teatime, and there would be samosas, *pakoras,* French pastries, and a cake from Ahdoos, the best bakery in Srinagar, Kashmir's summer capital, which was usually reserved for special occasions, such as Eid al-Fitr, which marked the end of Ramadan. As I busily blew up balloons and arranged the white hydrangeas and lilies in a vase, one of my aunts suddenly challenged me. Why did I celebrate my birth with such pomp and show? she asked me. Didn't I know what my real birthday had been like?

My real birthday.

My aunt went on to share, in hushed tones, the circumstances of my birth. She described a thin, pale, premature baby lying naked and alone and struggling to survive in a far corner of the birthing room while the midwives and my grandmother focused exclusively on my exhausted, feverish mother. I was the third girl in the family. In those days, half a century ago, in Kashmir, India, boys were assets while girls were considered burdens—bodies to clothe, feed, and marry off with substantial dowries. As my aunt continued speaking, it seemed as if every balloon in the room had suddenly been pricked. I was shocked. Why had I not heard this story before? I stormed off to find my mother.

"I was only nineteen years old," my mother explained when I pressed her to talk about it. "I was supposed to give birth to you, my third girl, at my mother's house, but my contractions had already begun, and I was barely conscious. Maryam, my sister-in-law, had given birth to three boys, and after I gave birth to you, my third girl, I was considered a failure for not managing to produce a boy. They kept you from me and your father.

"Your grandfather came home from work and was given the sad news that a third granddaughter had been born," my mother told me. "He rushed up the stairs and broke all traditions by barging into the birthing room. No door or lock could stop him. He found me lying in bed weeping. 'Where is the baby?' he demanded." Tears welled up in my mother's eyes as she spoke. "I was too weak to go to you, and the others would not bring me the baby—you were premature and fragile, and I was frightened you were going to die. All I could do was cry. I had no status, no power over even my own newborn child.

"But"—my mother brightened at this point in the story—"your grandfather scooped you up into his own Dussah shawl and announced, 'She is a gift from God—and she will be treated the same as everyone else in this household.'" Mummy told me that he handed me to her, and she held my face in her hands and assured me that I was her *dil* (heart) and her *jigger* (liver) and that she and my father loved me.

Then my mother told me the rest of the story. "When my mother, Moji, heard that I had given birth to a third daughter, after your grandfather had interfered and saved you, she rushed to be at my side. When Moji walked into the room, I began to sob. Moji rubbed her hand over my forehead. I had never felt anything so soothing. I was half out of my mind. 'But what will become of her?' I sobbed. I could not even imagine what the future held for yet another girl in the family.

"Moji lifted you and set you by her side while she bent down on her knees and pressed her head to the floor and then lifted her hands in prayer. She told me, 'I have prayed for you both, and you don't have to weep for this girl. Because, beloved daughter, she is destined to reach great heights.'

"I could hardly believe what she was saying. 'Can this be true?' I asked.

"'Yes,' Moji assured me. 'She will climb the sky! And you will never have to worry about her.'"

Mummy had found this confusing. What did that mean—"climb the sky," "never have to worry about her"? But her mind was at rest. My birth had been preordained. Perhaps her daughter would do well in school, become educated. Perhaps she would become a doctor, stand on her own two feet. This frail child might marry a man of great wealth or miraculously turn into a beauty, as Mummy herself was.

THE STORY MY MOTHER told me mystified me. On the one hand, I was thrilled by Moji's foretelling. At the age of ten, I already understood that my mother and her family put great faith in my grandmother's deep spiritual authority and took her predictions seriously. It was exciting to hear that I would have a successful future. At the same time, I wondered, What if Dadaji had not intervened? Would they have said it was God's will if the small baby girl had expired? What exactly, then, was God's will? Could we really know it in advance, or does human will enable us to create it for ourselves? In the faith of my family, cultural foreboding could have meant the difference between my life and my demise.

My near abandonment at birth is one of a long list of traditions that are impossible for me to accept at face value. To my harried grandmother, whom I called Dadiji, I was a burden on her young, struggling son; to my grandfather, whom I called Dadaji, I was a gift from God. It was like flipping the coin of faith. Learning my birth story was the startling beginning of a lifetime of consciously asking questions, of challenging the status quo. The questions I grappled with led me first to doubt and later to faith. For years, I lived the secular life of a modern American woman. In a sense, as surprising as it sounds, 9/11 changed that. Because though my life could have ended before it began, without my faith, I am not sure if my soul could have survived.

PROPHET'S DAUGHTERS
CARRIED OUT HIS LINEAGE

. . .

When Moji heard the raucous cawing of the ravens outside her window, she knew there was an important message being sent her way. As she flung the windows open, she saw dozens of frenzied birds flapping their wings, swooping, and swirling. Ravens are believed to bring messages from the other realm, and when they loudly caw, a person should give serious consideration to the message that is being conveyed.

As she looked around, she overheard her short-tempered stepson, Shafi, and his temperamental wife, Bashira, in a shouting match. The fight was serious. Moji was notified that Bashira was packing up and going back to her parents.

Moji's leadership was being tested, and she was resolute about providing a permanent solution to an unsettling family situation. She knew that marital problems are often exacerbated by meddling family members, so she insisted that the husband, the wife, and both her parents partake in a conflict-resolution session. When all of them gathered in her room, Moji queried the husband first. "So, Shafi jaan [dear], why are you always angry with your wife?" she began.

He replied, "She cannot give me what I want."

Moji dug deeper. "And what is that?" she asked.

"A son!" he replied.

She then turned to Shafi's parents. "What do you think of what your son just said?" she asked them.

Slightly flustered, they said, "We feel sorry for our son. In six years, Bashira has produced five girls. Everyone mocks him for not having a son. What are we to do?"

Shafi joined in. "When my brother suddenly died of a brain hemorrhage, I became the sole caretaker of my parents. If I don't have a son, who will take care of the family?" When he saw the disheartened look on Moji's face, he added, "Bodh Moji [Big Mother], don't misunderstand me. I love all my daughters, but when relatives minimize me for not having a son, I take out my anger on my wife."

Moji replied, "You must trust in God. These girls are his amanat *[gift]. They have their own destiny, which will take care of them. If you see them as a burden, they will burden you. If you see them as an asset, they will bring you joy." Ashamed, Shafi lowered his head, and with that, Moji passed a resolution. "Every member of this* kabila *[family] must respect Bashira for being a mother of five children. Shafi must never be disparaged for not having a son." This decree was announced to the extended family, who all fell in line, leading to the rejuvenation of Shafi and Bashira's marriage. Moji concluded the session by praying that God bless them with a son. When the room had emptied out, my sister Gudi, who had been eavesdropping, walked in, and Moji derided the family to her for their ignorance. "Our Prophet never had a son, and his lineage was carried out by his daughters. Why don't people value their daughters?"*

I F MY PARENTS HAD BEEN TOLD THAT THEIR CONTENTIOUS DAUGH-
ter would grow up to marry an imam and step forward to challenge
thousands of years of tradition, they would not have believed it. Still,
my family was an anomaly. My parents placed great value on education, even while most Kashmiris did not. This strong belief in education originated with my grandfather. Dadaji had aspired to be a
teacher. After completing his matriculation, he left the Kashmir Valley to go to Aligarh Muslim University (Sir Syed Khan's AMU) in
Uttar Pradesh to pursue an MA in mathematics. Fortune was on his
side. Kashmir's maharaja, Hari Singh, invited students from Sri
Pratap College to apply for a highly competitive scholarship to study
abroad. Forty students from India were to be chosen to go to the
United States on a fully paid scholarship. My grandfather was the
only one chosen from the state of Jammu and Kashmir. This was a
major accomplishment—for the family and for Kashmir. Dadaji became the first Kashmiri to attend Harvard University and the first
Kashmiri Muslim to receive a master of science degree in civil engineering.

Dadaji spent three years at Harvard, from 1927 to 1930, and he was
inducted into the Tau Beta Pi honor society. One semester, his world
affairs professor, who was impressed with this keen young man from
the other side of the globe, asked if Dadaji could prepare a lecture on
Islam for his class.

Dadaji was hesitant. He had never had any religious training.

The professor added a sweetener. The school was prepared to give Dadaji a stipend of twenty dollars for his preparation time.

Dadaji began reading widely on Islam in Harvard's vast library. Ironically, it was at Harvard University in the United States, rather than in Kashmir, India, that my grandfather's serious study of Islam began.

Harvard opened my grandfather's eyes not only about his religion but also about the world. Dadaji would remind us that although he met no Muslims in America, he did see the tenets of Islam being practiced by most Americans. Islam, he pronounced, could be practiced in its purest form in America.

As an example, Dadaji told a story.

"One day," he told us, "I went for a swim in a lake along with my fellow students. I cut my foot badly and needed medical attention. For seven days, I had to stay off my feet. My landlady and her sixteen-year-old daughter changed my bandages, even insisted on washing my feet regularly so there would be no infection. They brought me food so I would not have to walk, washed and folded my laundry, and tended to me—and in the process, I learned they were Jews. I was in a foreign land, living in an alien setting, and these people showed me such acts of kindness."

This was Dadaji's first experience living in close quarters with—and depending on—people from another religion. The love and affection that his landlady and her daughter showered upon him left a lasting impression.

"After someone is willing to wash your feet," he would say, "it is impossible not to open your heart."

Trying to fit in at Harvard, Dadaji kept one big secret—he didn't tell anybody that, at age twenty, he already had a wife and two children in Kashmir. Frankly, he was embarrassed and worried that people would judge him—or doubt him. "I was so young; even if I had told them I was married with two children, no one would have believed me," he told us. He also kept another secret: that he had been only nine when he was betrothed.

Dadaji's father had had a neighbor who was a very close friend. This neighbor had had a daughter and was concerned that if he died—and in those days, life expectancies were short—there would be no one to care for her. This was not an unusual concern. Men were the breadwinners, and if they didn't have sons or other relatives who could look after their daughters, they needed a contingency plan.

In this spirit, my great-grandfather's friend spoke to his neighbor: "If I die, I know you will take care of my daughter." Implicit in those words was the request that my grandfather marry the man's daughter. My great-grandfather was agreeable—why wouldn't two friends want to have their children wed? My grandparents were betrothed when he was nine and she was twelve—a younger man marrying an older woman! Though they were legally married, there was a customary period, almost like an engagement, when the contract between the two parties had been signed but the girl did not yet leave her parents' care. So, my father's parents grew up together. They played together with the understanding that they were betrothed, and they remained devoted to each other for their entire lives. When Sarah, my grandmother, turned sixteen, she gave birth to her first child, Rashid, a boy. Shortly before Dadaji was accepted to Harvard, she delivered a baby girl, Ruqquiya.

During the three years her husband was studying abroad, my twenty-year-old grandmother Sarah, with her two young children, was supposed to act like a dutiful daughter-in-law and live obediently with her husband's parents. But she had other plans. She left the house every day to do her job as a headmistress, at a time when most girls didn't even finish school.

My grandfather received a terrible shock when he returned to Kashmir with his degree. He had barely set foot back in his family home when his father ordered him to divorce his wife. Dadaji was stunned to discover that his absence abroad had set off a chain reaction that had left his young family in disarray. He learned that his two children had been living apart from their mother, forcibly "hijacked" from her for the past three years, while Sarah was living with her parents, heartbroken and pining for her children. The excuse his father gave him only infuriated him: His wife's character was questionable. She flaunted her teaching job; she wore green, open-toed, sparkling sandals and white *shalwars*—pantaloons. Her exposed white *shalwar* and green sparkly sandals were scandalous for Kashmir in the twenties and thirties.

Dadaji asked exactly what the offense was. He trusted his young wife, but his father was the head of the family. So Dadaji concocted a strategy—he would stall for time to build his case. He asked his father for one month to make a decision.

During that month, Dadaji secretly followed his wife every day to see where she was going, whom she met with, and what she did. He saw her going to school and returning home. He confronted his father. "I have seen with my own eyes that my wife is educating children, and what can be more important than education? You yourself have told me this," Dadaji said.

He sent shock waves by refusing to divorce his wife and broke with the age-old tradition by leaving his father's home.

My grandmother gave birth to five more children and gave up her headmistress job, but she continued to wear open-toed sandals. And peace was restored within the family.

As a young girl, I wondered how something as simple as a pair of sandals could cause so much discord within a family as close as ours.

"What would happen to us if we wore the wrong shoes?" I whispered to my sister Fifi.

She scoffed at my worries, pointing to the closet full of colorful sandals.

My grandparents' story is a good indicator of how societal mores have shifted in the last ninety years. When I was growing up, women and girls were free to wear local attire or dress in Western clothing, even if they sometimes set tongues wagging. Unfortunately, the pen-

dulum has swung back in time in many Muslim societies. The rich
and varied cultural expressions of modest attire have gradually begun
to be replaced by conformity and uniformity—eroding cultural expression and resulting in standardized notions of modesty.

MY IMMEDIATE FAMILY WAS made up of my mother, my father, and
five children, born in a span of eight years. But at home, we never felt
quite complete. When my middle sister, Gudi, was born, less than a
year before me, my maternal grandmother, Moji, aware that her
daughter was overwhelmed with taking care of another child, suggested that Gudi come live with her for a while. Moji's nest had been
empty since Mummy married, and her husband's death had left her
with ample time to care for a baby. Unexpectedly, "a while" became
open-ended, and Gudi was raised by Moji as her own child.

I would still see my sister, of course, and she would join the family
for holidays and vacations, but Gudi never lived at Khan Manzil—
the Khan dwelling—with the rest of us. This was not unusual at the
time in Kashmir, where the nuclear family did not exist as it does in
modern America. Families were very fluid; extended families might
live together, or they might share households, with children traveling
back and forth between them, raised as if by a village. Not much
thought was given to how the children, especially girls, felt about
such situations—or many things—at the time. It was like the mountains above the valley: They remained the way they were for centuries. Along with my parents and siblings—Fifi, the oldest; Abid, the
next after me; and our baby brother, Zahid, who was three years my
junior—I lived together with my uncles and aunts, my dozen cousins,
and my father's parents, all under one roof.

Khan Manzil was a large, Tudor-style, ivy-covered house surrounded by acres of gardens. The household had a pecking order: My
father's mother, Sarah, was the matriarch, the head of the household,
and the house manager. Household help was shared by all the
families—we had a gardener, a driver, and a cook, plus two or three
servants who assisted with serving, cleaning, other day-to-day chores,

and laundry. We grew our own produce, raised our own farm animals, churned our own butter, and made our own bread. The community was self-contained, and there seemed to be no need to reach outside of our private ecosystem or to depend on, or even interact very often with, the rest of the world. The world inside this bell jar ran on an endless loop that had repeated itself for generations.

Besides having milking cows, I had a German shepherd named Rocky who lived outside in a kennel, but strays would also invariably come onto the property. One day, a mad dog wandered onto our lawn. When I tried to chase him out, he snarled, lunged, and bit my leg. I fell, and while I was wrestling him, I felt incensed that he had hurt me, so I bit him back. A crowd watched in horror, with Fifi screaming hysterically and Mummy crying. As for the older cousins, they taunted me. "Stay away from her. She will get rabies and die," they warned one another.

Papaji's youngest brother, Uncle Faroque, whom we called Chacha, which means "uncle," was studying medicine, and he was charged with taking care of the bite. Using the longest needles I had ever seen, over a period of weeks, Faroque Chacha gave me a series of injections in my stomach. As he pumped the medicine from the syringe, he was a little nervous, because he was still a student. But from then on, Chacha always said, "Don't mess with Daisy. She even bit a dog back." Even as a child, facing a mad dog, I wasn't afraid to defend myself.

Early morning, at around 6:00 A.M., was my time to be with Dadaji. Customarily, my grandparents would have a private breakfast after *fajr,* the dawn prayers, before the whole household woke up and there was the predictable pandemonium of getting a jumble of kids off to school. Dadaji and Dadiji breakfasted by themselves in a room with three picture windows looking out on Dadaji's beautiful rose garden and flower beds. The two of them would have their tea in thin glass cups, along with toast and marmalade. But I would always sneak in, disrupting their peace, annoying my grandmother to no end. My grandfather, though, would reach out to me and say, "Come, sit with me," and I was always delighted, because I got to join them in eating the best food in the household and to listen to Dadaji's discourses on the wisdom of the Quran. Dadaji always made me feel special during our mornings together.

WHEN PEOPLE TEASED MY father about his three daughters, Papaji would shrug and boast that he was blessed with a hat trick of daughters. He would go on to explain that in 1955, when his first daughter, Fifi, was born, he received his first promotion, to supervisor in the government transportation department. When Gudi, his second daughter, was born, he was made a manager, and when his third was born, he was promoted again—his daughters had brought him only blessings. From the dark days when a girl child was considered barely worthy of life, Papaji had come to consider his daughters not only assets but also good-luck charms. And of course, my younger brother Abid's birth had taken the pressure off my parents.

A gadget freak, my father was a natural engineer. He was obsessed with cars, so it was no surprise that he became fascinated with the American automobile industry. After he completed his auto-engineering training in Madras, India, Papaji applied for a scholarship to study in the United States, just as his father had. He was selected for a scholarship from USAID, along with ten other lucky candidates, for training in industrial engineering in America. Then, also like his father, Papaji left behind his young family to pursue his education at the University of Pittsburgh. Two years later, before returning to Kashmir, Papaji spent several months in Manhattan working for the New York City transit system, where he was offered a long-term job. He declined. His family needed him at home.

After Papaji's return, Western pop culture gradually seeped into our household.

One day, a large package from the United States arrived, a gift for the entire family from my father's best friend in America. We children were wild with excitement as we opened the parcel. And what was in it? Head & Shoulders shampoo. And bubble bath. And a jar of liquid soap that we could make bubbles from with a little wand—things we had never seen in our lives. All these products for taking baths! Our bath routine had always consisted of rubbing ourselves with washcloths every morning and washing our hair once a week with egg and yogurt.

But even more exciting than bubbles were the records for the turntable Papaji brought back to Kashmir with him. To us, Western culture meant pop culture—which in those days was the Beatles. Beatlemania hit our home, and Fifi and I could be heard constantly singing, "It's been a hard day's night." But I soon realized that something was desperately missing from my rock-and-roll fantasy—a guitar. I told Papaji I wanted one.

At first, he refused. A guitar was a big expense, and he saw no future for me in music. If I had asked him for a badminton racket, there would have been no questions asked: He understood sports, and he knew I was a good athlete. But music was something else. Ironically, we eventually found a guitar in a sporting goods shop.

In Kashmir playing music was relegated to trained musicians who came to your home for weddings to sing Sufiana Kalam (classical devotional music of the mystics), accompanied by a hundred-stringed instrument, the *santoor*. Although music classes were not part of the curriculum in schools, Kashmiris participated in folk songs and dances called *chakri*, where the bride and groom were serenaded, and in *wanwun*, in which women and girls would arrange themselves in two or three rows and then sway and sing with interlocked arms, a cherished tradition passed on from mother to daughter. But becoming a musician was not just impossible—it was unimaginable.

Yet a different door opened to me thanks to my father's younger brother Rafique, who also lived in our house. Rafique Chacha was a dreamer and an artist who was studying architecture. I would stand for hours watching him, immersed in an inner dialogue with himself, and was mesmerized as he turned his ideas into sketches.

Every time my father went on a long business trip, it was his tradition to bring back gifts for each of us, toys or little games. When one time he pulled an artist's paint box out of his bag, equipped with a palette, tubes of oil paints, sable brushes, and turpentine, I was ecstatic. I thought I was all set to begin painting as my uncle did when I realized that I had no canvas, no easel—not even paper. My father, as usual, solved the problem. He pointed to the plain white wall in my room and suggested I use that space.

During my winter holidays, I began painting in earnest, letting my imagination run wild. Eventually I created an eight-by-ten-foot mural-size piece of modernist art that depicted natural elements juxtaposed with distorted human figures. My father was astounded by my work, and proud. A family friend suggested we take pictures and submit it to a children's art contest in New Delhi. I was shocked when I learned that I had won. Papaji recognized that I had an innate talent, but although Kashmir is known for its natural beauty and handicrafts, there was no more a concept there of pursuing a career in contemporary arts than there was of pursuing one in contemporary music.

Schools that fostered the arts were focused on traditional arts that evoked nature—such as woodworking, papier-mâché, carpet weaving, crewel embroidery, and embroidering shawls, none of which I was interested in pursuing. Then one day an acquaintance of one of Papaji's friends came to the house. She was a lovely, stylishly dressed woman—and an architectural designer. I immediately peppered her with questions: Where had she gone to school? When I heard she had graduated from a design school in New York, I asked her what her job was like. How could I become an architect like Rafique Chacha? Or perhaps I could become a designer like her?

My parents smiled indulgently, but at that moment, their daughter's life took shape. In this woman, I saw a path to my future. Of course, I thought this notion would take my family completely by surprise. Only much later did I realize that distant friends very rarely came to our house, and Papaji probably knew exactly what he was doing.

Wʜᴇɴ I ᴡᴀs ꜰɪᴠᴇ ʏᴇᴀʀs ᴏʟᴅ, I ʟᴏᴠᴇᴅ ᴛᴏ ꜰᴏʟʟᴏᴡ ᴍʏ eight-year-old sister, Fifi, into our mother's dressing room. This was an Aladdin's cave, a sacred place for us, sequestered behind an unimposing four-foot door with a heavy padlock. The small room was jam-packed with treasures, and I would swoon from the scents of amber, rose, and musk that wafted up from the intricate glass perfume bottles and mingled with the soft smells of Mummy's face powder and rouge. But the most dazzling things on the dressing table were the lipsticks Mummy would wear on festive occasions, lined up like gems in their elegant gold cases, novel gifts that were even more special because they had been brought back from America by my father. In the corner of the dressing room stood an enormous iron chest about four feet long by three feet high, so heavy that it took a few people to pry it open and prop up the lid. The chest held my mother's trousseau, part of the dowry she brought to her marriage.

We adored the ritual of watching our elegant mother get dressed up. I especially loved touching the beautiful gold brocade fabrics she wore and hoped that she would deem our behavior good enough to allow us to put on her red georgette *dupatta,* a long bridal stole with gold-threaded floral embroidery, or let us wrap ourselves in one of her beautiful shawls. Staring at Mummy's long, shimmering blond hair, pulled into a thick braid that hung below her knees, I would think of my own dark, freckled, prepubescent image and wonder, Why don't I look like her? Fifi had flawless olive skin, but my mother's porcelain skin was light and translucent: She was a paragon of Kashmiri beauty. Only Gudi's and Abid's light complexions and golden locks matched Mummy's.

Sneaking a peek under the massive lid of the trunk, Fifi and I would whisper excitedly about the magnificent things it held: a pair of solid silver shoes, custom-made for my mother's wedding; a pile of silver plates and cups; exquisite enamel and gold jewelry; heavy twenty-two-karat bangles and earrings; necklaces studded with precious gemstones of all colors; a tea service carved from solid jade; and because my mother's family were fabric retailers, silks woven with real gold thread, French brocades, and wondrous shawls.

Mummy's treasures were more than wealth though; they meant her financial independence. My father was a struggling government employee on a fixed salary while Mummy's dowry made her the chief financial officer of the family. Although she had only ten years of formal schooling, the equivalent of a high school education, in those times her traditional family considered even that much education progressive. My mother was convinced that a woman's financial independence allowed her to make her own choices. Her mantra was "Stand on your own feet," a phrase she loved to repeat to us.

A dowry was security. Having her own resources insured that a woman would not be entirely dependent on her husband or his family. My sisters and I were just little girls who could barely do math, but thanks to our mother, we completely understood that equation.

Mummy presented herself as a humble wife, but we all knew of her financial liquidity. One day a local broker informed her that he had a choice almond grove to sell. He described a vision: "You must buy it—when spring comes, the whole orchard is covered with white blossoms and almonds!"

All of us piled into the car to look at the property.

As Mummy paced the perimeter with us children tagging along, she abruptly stopped and pointed out a well. Having its own source of water meant that the irrigated almond grove would flourish and could produce income. Days later, when the deal was closed, my sister and I exchanged glances: None of our friends' mothers went out and purchased almond groves. Back home, we watched as Mummy rummaged through her treasure chest and carefully chose one of her heaviest gold bangles. "Here is our almond grove," she announced. Years later, when our family needed financial liquidity, Mummy sold the almond grove at a hundredfold profit.

We learned our lessons not only from books but also from the world around us. The gold bracelets in the treasure chest told one story, Mummy's shawls another. The shawls connected me to my heritage. My grandfather had told Mummy, and she in turn told us, tales of these shawls, which were unique to Kashmir. The shawls were the organic product of a tight-knit community. Men like my great-grandfather traded the *shahtoosh* yarn, the "king of all wools," but it was the women who spun the delicate thread into fabric. "People come together to make something," my mother would tell us, "and when skilled people work together, cooperating without greed, something magnificent can be created." She wanted us girls to get the best education—to become doctors or teachers—so we could have the freedom to choose our own path in life. "If only they had let me go to college, I could have been a teacher," she would say.

Fifi and I vowed to each other that we would have careers and never be dependent on a man.

But Mummy was also a woman who hedged her bets. She hoped that her daughters would have the careers she dreamed of for us so we could provide for ourselves; at the same time, this was Kashmir in the 1960s. So, Mummy was constantly adding to the treasure trove to make sure that her girls would one day receive an impressive dowry. Her message was confusing: We would be self-sufficient, but we would be wives; we would be well educated, but we would be mothers. Mummy's world was one of conflicting cultures, brought about by traditions whose scaffolding was eroding around her.

As the first son after three girls, my younger brother Abid was the

little prince of the house from the day he was born, when he was carried home with great fanfare. As a baby, he was often dressed in a
long brocade jacket and a matching hat, like a miniature groom,
while I got Fifi's hand-me-downs. I committed myself to obtaining
justice, to revealing my brother for the naughty snake that he really
was. And "snake" was the appropriate word, because he could quickly
and stealthily enter a room and cause trouble—eating my mother's
precious lipsticks, pushing walnuts up his nose, or once even guzzling
a bottle of sleeping pills that sent him to the hospital to have his
stomach pumped, leaving everyone on tenterhooks waiting to see if
he would survive—and somehow, he always managed to slither away
from blame. The household would just reward him with custom-
tailored clothes or fancy birthday cakes from Ahdoos.

OUR HOUSE HAD FOUR STORIES and was built in several tiers, so
we had access to the roof from our windows. Two large windows
opened onto the sloped roof outside the bedroom I shared with Fifi,
and they were often left temptingly open. Fifi and I had very different personalities. I was an extrovert, the one who would entertain
people and make them laugh, whereas Fifi was cautious and intro-
verted, a bit of a dreamer, and very calm. If she'd had her way, she
would hardly ever have left her room, whereas I was always running
around and getting into things and into trouble. Just as I considered
myself something of an artist, so did Fifi. She would look at the J.C.
Penney catalog that Papaji had brought back from America and turn
pieces of fabric into fashionable clothes for us, without ever seeing a
pattern. And unlike with my baby brother, I never fought with Fifi.
She was my closest confidante.

I would often convince Fifi to climb out our bedroom windows
onto the roof with me. There we would survey the entire backyard of
our home. Below, I could see the dog kennels and my dog, Rocky,
pacing the property. Looking out over the beautiful Kashmir Valley
from our vantage point, we'd see the vast orchard of fruit-bearing
trees and the majestic peaks of the Himalayas, rising some sixteen

thousand feet. The region of Kashmir is known by the name "Paradise on Earth," and there is something undeniably life altering about being conscious of living at the foot of such a magnificent backdrop. What others may have perceived as daunting heights were, for me, the yardstick by which I measured all else. I had no idea my understanding of the world was predicated on a more monumental sense of scale than that of most people.

This was never more apparent than when I went out on the roof, especially at night. Sitting there, alone or with Fifi, I would see nothing but infinite stars, galaxies of them in a dark sky. On some nights the moon would shine brightly, and occasionally there were magical shooting stars. Stepping out of my room at night, I would enter another space entirely, a room outside the realm of the physical world. For me, the rooftop and the worlds beyond it were a spiritual place, one that surpassed human understanding.

The most magical holiday we celebrated was Shab-e-Qadr or, in Arabic, Laylat al-Qadr, the Night of Power. On that night, we were told, if we stayed awake until dawn, the *paris* (fairies) or angels would descend to earth. You could ask God for anything, for on that night, angels came to listen to your wishes. Trays of food were prepared for the adults of the household who were observing the night vigil, and we children were encouraged to join in.

One year, while the adults were praying downstairs, I decided that it made much more sense to pray from the roof, and I enlisted Fifi to join me. "We can't see the *paris* from down here," I said, "but we can see them from the roof. Let's put out some sweets for them so we can entice them to come to us first."

We stole some biscuits, macaroons, and toffees from the trays and arranged them on a plate. We went upstairs and carefully placed the plate on the window ledge, then climbed onto the roof. As shooting stars and the Milky Way sparkled above us, we called on the fairies to join us. I prayed that someone would give me a Cadbury chocolate and that I would score goal after goal in hockey. The next morning, Mummy found the window still open and the treats on their tray on the ledge. She discovered us asleep, seated on the floor with our heads resting on the window ledge.

IN THE HOME NEXT door to ours lived a neighbor who had three boys, Nejib, Talat, and Ayub. I loved to show off to them: I would tiptoe in my bare feet along the sizzling-hot tin roof, and then I would straddle each side of the sloping roof and edge my way to the very end, with Fifi panic-stricken. I would then stand and lean out with my arms extended, and from that precarious position, I would call out at the top of my lungs: *"Mummeee!"*

That was the cue for my mother to come running out to the garden from wherever she was, screaming, "Please, I beseech you, go inside!" while all the servants streamed out behind her, staring with frightened faces up at me. They all thought I was surely going to fall off and kill myself. But that was how I was—always pushing the boundaries.

MY ENTIRE FAMILY WERE devout Muslims. The adults generally prayed five times a day; we observed Ramadan, a monthlong fast, and celebrated the two festivals of Eid. Two of the basic principles of Islam are *iman* (faith) and *ihsan* (righteousness), and my family lived and breathed by the verse of the Quran that states that "there is no compulsion in religion." No one's religious adherence was policed; everyone's faith was mandated not by dogma but by his or her own devotion. Yet of everyone in my family, the most spiritually committed was Moji.

While my family lived in the suburbs, Moji lived in the downtown neighborhood of Khanyar, home to Kashmir's most revered shrine. I loved to visit her there. To me, she was the living embodiment of a saintly woman, and sometimes I tried to imagine that I would become not a doctor, as my parents wished me to, or an artist or architect, as I dreamed of becoming, but a religious devotee like Moji, destined for a life of prayer, religious night vigils, and Quran recitation. As I rolled bread dough with my grandmother and put the roti on the kerosene fire, I envisioned living, as she did, on water and one piece of flatbread a day, made by my own hands. At dawn *fajr* prayers, Moji would perform her ablutions with ice-cold water while I froze from the drops of water that would splash on me. Moji was detached from the world, her only concern raising the awareness of God in herself and imparting this awareness to others, especially her progeny. Sometimes, I would close my eyes and imagine myself in Moji's place, surrounded by throngs of people who listened to my words as I helped them to find empowerment in their souls. It was hard to envision what I might say, but I was inspired by the act of helping and supporting others. Whether I could exist on bread and water was another matter, however.

Every time I visited Moji's house, there would be a room full of people sitting in her presence, seeking her guidance. She would dispense prayers, food, clothing, and counsel to countless people at a time. Moji exemplified how Muslim women had for centuries played an important role in religious life and thought without ever being publicly recognized. Sometimes I would watch as she responded to a steady stream of destitute people asking for help. Gudi and I would stand by her side as she dropped coins into the outstretched hands of women and orphans who would beseech her from the street below. Moji taught us to never refuse anyone in need. She kept the beggars' pride intact, treated them with dignity, and they responded with love and respect, always politely thanking her and, when I helped, even me. They would walk away with eyes shining, standing a little taller. As would I after standing beside my Moji.

One visit sticks out in my mind. A poor woman came to ask for help for herself and three children, but Moji's pockets were empty. My sister Gudi, who was ten at the time, noticed Moji desperately searching for coins. My little sister, on her own, placed several pillows on a chair, which she climbed up to reach the top of a shelf that held her Eidee money piggy bank. She handed Moji the entire contents of her bank. When Moji refused to take the child's money, Gudi insisted that Moji give the poor woman all her eleven rupees, "because she needs it more than I do."

MOJI HAD BEEN LUCKY to have a father who valued women, a feminist of his time, in practice if not in name, who fiercely protected his three daughters. Mohammed Shah was a wool merchant by day and a scholar by night who had mastered the Quran in both Arabic and Farsi. Moji's mother had died when she was three years old, leaving him to raise his three girls by himself. He never remarried; instead, he passed on his academic knowledge to Moji, who was of a spiritual bent. Although she became well versed in the Quran, she was married as a teenager. But her husband did not value his studious sixteen-year-old wife. When Moji's father heard that she had been struck by her husband, he was so incensed that he sought a divorce and brought her back to his home. In the 1920s, divorce was practically unheard of, but Moji's father was a devout man who followed in the footsteps of the Prophet Muhammad; he named Moji, his middle daughter, Fatima and his youngest Zainab after the Prophet's daughters, and he named his eldest daughter Khadijah after the Prophet's first wife, and like the Prophet, he had lost an infant son. Moji received her divorce.

MY GREAT-GRANDFATHER BUILT a mosque, Mughal Masjid, and made sure fresh drinking water was brought to the public. Some years after her divorce, Moji bemoaned to her father, "I have become a *bojh* [burden] on you. Why don't you throw me in the river?" He died soon after. Moji's uncle Mohammed Yusuf Shah, a pashmina and *shahtoosh* wholesaler, stepped in to care for his nieces. He began to inquire among his business circles for a suitable man for Moji, asking his acquaintances to "look for a Syed," a descendent of the Prophet with a religious pedigree. The prerequisite was that his niece not be prevented from deepening her religious devotion. Syed Mohammad Shah, a successful businessman, accepted the proposal.

Moji was married at twenty to a handsome sixty-year-old widower with grown children, three sons and two daughters. She inherited a joint family of thirteen people, five house helpers, two horses, one tonga (carriage), a Morris Minor—a British car, and a big house surrounded by smaller houses, all in one compound. After a few years, Moji gave birth to her one and only child, Halima, my mother.

At sixteen, Mummy got married, and two years later her father died, leaving Moji a widow at age thirty-five. The family conferred on her the title of Bodh Moji, Big Mother. As Moji was head of the household, her permission was needed in all family decisions, including marriages, long-term travel, personal dilemmas, religious edicts, educational decisions, and financial disbursements.

HANDMADE GREETING CARDS

. . .

Lena from Brooklyn called me in 2008 to ask if I could speak to her ESL literacy class, in which Arab Muslim women were learning to speak English. She wanted me to talk to them about women's rights in Islam. When I entered the small conference room at the Arab-American Family Support Center and met my audience, I saw that these were not educated women. I learned that many of them had been battered and were seeking to start a new life.

I realized that the speech I had prepared would go over their heads and decided, instead, to speak to their hearts. God had entrusted them with His divine breath, and I said that because their dignity was God-given, it was an act against God for any man to raise a hand against them. An Egyptian woman in her thirties with a baby boy resting his head on her shoulder asked if a Muslim woman could earn her own living. I excitedly told them about my mother's purchase of an orchard and how she had taught her daughters to always stand on their own feet. I told them that they had every right to earn a living and accumulate wealth. They just had to believe in themselves.

A few weeks passed, and I received a note from Lena. "I had no idea just how much our women would be inspired by your presentation!" she wrote. "They talked about the concept of

Islamic human rights and the value of women in Islam all day—in class, and in their support groups."

A month before the holidays, I received a lovely note in the mail written on a handmade, stenciled greeting card, which said: "Your words inspired us so much, we decided to start our own business, so we could become independent. The card sales allow us to buy our own MetroCards."

IFE IN KASHMIR WAS VERY COMPARTMENTALIZED. AT SCHOOL and related activities, which took place in the daytime, we spoke English, and when we came home, we immediately switched into our mother tongue, Kashmiri. Although we hardly ever spoke English at home, Western culture had seeped into our lives there, but it was relegated to cornflakes, pop music, *Archie Comics,* bell-bottoms, and the novels of Enid Blyton and Barbara Cartland.

Fifi and I attended a Catholic girls' school, but there was no formal religious instruction beyond one class called Moral Science. Still, we would pray in the chapel around exam time, and every morning assembly began with the recitation of the Lord's Prayer. It's funny in retrospect to think that there was only a handful of Christians present while most girls were Muslims, Hindus, and Sikhs, but we all prayed and played and learned together and accepted the occasional prayers as part of the daily drill. In fact, it never occurred to any of us that the Lord's Prayer was a Christian prayer; it was simply a reminder to us that God dwelled in our hearts. At home with our families and at school, we were not afraid of other religions, and it was unimaginable that any group would be made to feel unwelcome. But I was never confused about my religious identity. What I understood from school and home was that there was only one God and that God created us in many communities so that we might get to know one another. In later years, I would hear that the Christian missionary schools in India had an alternative agenda—to "neutralize" the non-Christian community. And yet this notion of an agenda did not conform with the high ethics that were imparted to me and my classmates by the Irish nuns who dedicated their lives to educating girls. Sometimes, perhaps, those ethical standards were even too rigid. While at Mallinson Girls School, where Gudi and I were in the same class, I was asked to leave kindergarten because I was accused of cheating when Gudi tried to help me write the ABCs on my slate. When we were separated, she was heartbroken to lose her playmate, and I was delighted to be sent to the convent school along with the rest of my siblings and cousins.

WEEKDAY SCHOOL LUNCHES WERE picnic-style. At twelve o'clock, we all went out to the big athletic field behind the school where we usually played hockey and other sports. Family servants would park their bicycles, then spread out tablecloths on the ground. The field would be crowded with hundreds of them, and we children would hop from tablecloth to tablecloth to find our respective lunches. Abdul Razzaq was our servant, and he would place plates and spoons on our picnic cloth, open the latch of the four-tiered stainless steel tiffin carrier, and remove a hot lunch of steaming rice, chicken, lamb, and kale and serve it to all the children in our family, regardless of age or grade level. Our classmates had the same setups—we all ate regional, home-style dishes, mostly curries and rice, brought to school by our household servants.

There was one exception, and her name was Halima.

Our classmate Halima was a subject of great curiosity. Her mother was an American who had come with a Peace Corps mission to India, where she had met and married Halima's Kashmiri father, a prominent businessman. Halima was the only student in the class with golden hair, and she was also the only Kashmiri whose mother was a foreigner. But most exotic of all was her lunch. The first time I saw a sandwich I was stunned. What kind of lunch was that? And white bread was a breakfast food.

One day, after watching her for a while during lunchtime, my curiosity got the best of me, and I approached and asked her what on earth she was eating.

"I'll share it with you, if you'll share your lunch with me," she answered, and in the timeless tradition of children everywhere, we traded lunches. I watched Halima scrape the plate clean of rice, curried chicken, and kale salad while I devoured her scrambled-egg-with-mayonnaise-and-ketchup sandwich. With that, a lifelong friendship began. Halima and I became inseparable. We climbed mountains, rode horses, and read *Archie* comic books and young-adult novels together. We were known as the school's chief trouble-makers, famous for a prank that involved puncturing the bicycle tires of a group of boys from the nearby Burn Hall School.

One summer, after we had been close friends for many years, Halima's uncle, aunt, and cousins from America came to visit, and I was invited to spend time with them. I was curious to meet my first real American children, and I couldn't help laughing when Halima's cousins Kathy and Peter began speaking in American English, which was so different from the British English we spoke. Peter was especially fun—a blond, all-American boy who loved to laugh and tell jokes. We rode bicycles on the bund, took a shikara boat across the Jhelum River, ate chocolates at Ahdoos Bakery, bought softy ice cream in wafer cones, and went with Halima's uncle Lee to Halima's mom and dad's arts and crafts store, the oddly named Suffering Moses. Peter was this easy, breezy American boy, and later when I moved to the States for high school, remembering my time with Halima's American family allowed me to feel a little more at home in my strange new environment; at school, when I walked the halls, I would catch glimpses of blue-eyed blond boys who reminded me of Peter.

MY FAMILY, AS WELL as our school, strictly limited our exposure to boys, but of course, I could never resist pushing the envelope. One day my classmate Anjum and I were called to the principal's office for the transgression of waving at boys from the window of our school bus. Sister John, the head nun, with her white habit, her polished black patent leather shoes, and a long black-and-silver rosary with a giant cross hanging from her belt, was a formidable figure. I realized that things were not looking good for Anjum and me when I saw Sister Immaculata, the mother superior, sitting in her office waiting for us with Sister John.

Sister John proclaimed her deep disappointment in my behavior, her blue eyes piercing me from beneath her *Flying Nun*–style headdress. Was I not one of the school's star hockey players, one of the school's leaders? She seemed to know that I was the ringleader, that poor Anjum, who hardly ever did anything wrong, had just waved along with me. Sister John announced that she was calling my home. Unfortunately for me, the only adult who was available in the household was my dadaji, who insisted on coming to the school himself.

Dadaji had been the principal of Kashmir Government Polytechnic College and Kashmir's chief engineer, so his being called in by the head nun was ominous indeed. Although he was under five feet, five inches tall, he had a commanding presence—he seemed to take up as much space as his six-foot-four brother. He entered Sister Immaculata's office dressed in a suit and hat, as if he were going to an important business meeting. He greeted Sister John and the mother superior but made no eye contact with me or Anjum whatsoever.

Dadaji treasured education and believed that girls had the same right to it as boys; his motto, "Oh Lord, increase me in knowledge," from a verse in the Quran, was displayed around our house and written in his books. Immediately upon entering the office, Dadaji noticed a framed poster of the Lord's Prayer on the wall. After the nuns gave a brief explanation of my transgressions, he started reading the words aloud: "Our Father who art in heaven, hallowed be Thy name. Thy kingdom come. Thy will be done, on earth as it is in heaven. Give us this day our daily bread, and forgive us our trespasses, as we forgive those who trespass against us." At that point, Dadaji stopped reading, looked meaningfully at the mother superior, and repeated the words "And forgive us our trespasses." Then he was silent.

I froze in my seat. Anjum clutched my hand. Then both nuns simultaneously looked at Dadaji and nodded. Sister John turned to us and announced that we were forgiven. We were free to go home with my grandfather.

To err is human, to forgive divine. The Lord's Prayer, a daily prayer for Christians, embodies an idea that is a common thread in Islam, in which we are instructed that, in addition to seeking God's forgiveness for sins we commit, forgiving others for sins against us helps us achieve God's forgiveness.

Dadaji never said a word to me about what had happened that day. He knew that I understood what he had done. And he knew that I needed no further punishment than the humiliation I had already experienced. I kept my mouth firmly closed on that drive home.

DRYING THE LAUNDRY
AT NIGHT

...

In 1977, the chief minister of Kashmir, Sheikh Abdullah, instructed my father, then head of Kashmir's Youth Services and Sports, to visit Kargil, in the Leh district, to determine why the newly built girls' school had such low attendance. The school was built for two hundred girls, but only twenty-five girls had enrolled in it.

Papaji traveled to the picturesque town known for its glaciers and apricots. There he was joined by a woman who was Kargil's official doctor, who had been assigned to assist with the investigation. All of the students, my father learned, were Buddhists but for a few Sunnis. Papaji was struck by the fact that, while Kargil's population is 90 percent Shia, there was not a single Shia girl enrolled in the school.

On his first night there, Papaji was unexpectedly awakened by hushed voices outside his window. He jumped out of bed and peered through the window. He saw women and young girls carrying buckets of wet laundry to hang on the drying line. He was perplexed: Why on earth would these women dry clothes at night and not during the day when the sun was out?

The next morning, he asked his host, a physical education teacher, to explain what now in the light of day seemed like a strange dream. "Out here, women's and girls' faces cannot be seen during the day," his host told him.

My father was confused. "Why are they applying this ruling to young girls?" he asked.

The teacher shook his head and continued. "Unfortunately, all girls and women of Kargil are required to observe the strictest form of purdah—a religious ruling that secludes them from all of society."

In that moment, Papaji realized why Shia girls were not attending the school. He had to find a solution. He decided to take the matter up with Kargil's highest Shia religious authority, Imam Agha. When my father and the woman doctor arrived at the imam's house, an expressionless girl with a sallow complexion peeked her head through the door. Papaji was visibly shaken by her jaundiced appearance. He recalled when Maryam, his twenty-eight-year-old sister-in-law, had died of tuberculosis, leaving behind four young children. He was sure the girl was suffering from the same disease. He politely asked the imam, "Since the doctor is here, would you like her to examine the ladies and girls of your household?"

Imam Agha was overjoyed, since he had realized that the female members of his family were indeed ill. He agreed on the spot. Papaji's diagnosis was correct; the girl was suffering from TB, and other family members already had signs of it. The doctor immediately prescribed the proper medication.

Days later, Papaji again visited Imam Agha, who was so grateful to my father that he asked him how he could repay him for saving the girl's life. Papaji pointed to the woman doctor. "If your daughters go to school, one day they can become doctors and save other people's lives," he told the imam.

Without hesitation Imam Agha, visibly emotional, said, "We

*must not cut our girls and women off from the rest of the world.
I am issuing a fatwa that all girls shall start receiving an education, and I will start by sending my girls to your school."*

Imam Agha's message spread like wildfire, and the movement for educating girls rapidly spread all over Kargil and the
adjoining villages. Today, Kargil is known for producing women
physicians and nurses.

That one conversation, which took place forty years ago,
eradicated purdah and the seclusion of women in Kargil, and
now, two generations later, I am proud to be following in my
father's footsteps with the work we do at WISE (Women's Islamic Initiative in Spirituality and Equality). WISE has been
using scriptural and legal justification to train and mobilize
imams to champion girls' education in Afghanistan.

ONE DAY I VISITED MOJI TO FIND HER SEATED ON THE floor, deep in her prayers. I loved lying down on her prayer mat, and this time I fell asleep with my head in her lap. I had the following dream:

A magnificent light cascaded like a bright tunnel from the sky to the ground where I was standing. I felt small and insignificant looking at this radiant light as it extended itself toward me, calling to me, inviting me to join it. I felt a gravitational pull and a sense of alignment with the light and began walking toward it, but Moji intervened, grabbing my hand tightly. She pushed me behind her and said to the light: "No, it is not yet her time!"

I woke up with a jolt, filled with wonder, and told Moji that I had seen God in a dream. She asked me to explain everything in detail. I told her that I had wanted to enter a portal where God was present, that it had been unlike anything I had seen on earth, and that I had been transfixed when I gazed upon God's light. I told her that I had been eager to join the light and become one with it.

Moji listened intently, and as she gave me a joyous hug, she whispered to me, "*Mubarak,* this is a true dream, a dream of *nūr,* of God's light," and then she recited to me the verse of God's light in the Quran (24:35):

God is the Light of the heavens and the earth. The example
of His Light is like a niche wherein is a lamp; the lamp is in a
crystal, and the crystal, shining as if a pearl-like radiant star, lit
from the oil of a blessed olive tree that is neither of the East
nor of the West. The oil would almost give light of itself though
no fire touches it. Light upon light! God guides to His Light
whom He wills. God strikes parables for people. God has full
knowledge of all things.

Moji proclaimed that we must make a special offering on my
behalf and ordered the household to immediately start preparing
an offering for the poor. This involved inviting thirty or so poor
people from the neighborhood to the house and serving them
tahri—rice made with turmeric, onions, salt, and ghee. Moji found
a new dress for me to wear and put ribbons in my hair. I was lifted
before an assembled crowd, and an appeal was made to them to
"make a special *dua* prayer supplication for this girl, so she may be
blessed." I looked down at all the people gazing at me, most dressed
in tattered clothing, many toothless—they were smiling at me and
asking God to bless me. I have no doubt that their prayers were
answered. I have stood in front of many crowds since then, but my
audience that day of those who had nothing but smiles and prayers
is etched in my memory. They made me feel so special, so blessed,
so empowered. That experience, of being surrounded by God's light,
brings to my mind the Quran's words "To God belongs the East
and the West, wherever you turn there is the presence of God"
(2:115).

In my tradition, true dreams are those seen by the soul and understood by one's consciousness. They are a gateway, a form of communication that reflects the innermost being, the spiritual state of the
dreamer. From the time of my earliest memories, my life has been
guided by a series of these special dreams, and many of them have
informed my current life and work. It is impossible to know which
came first, the dreams or the direction. Would I have sought to do

certain things had I not had dreams to guide me? Did these dreams really express my truest soul or just my hopes or fears? I cannot know. Dreams themselves hold these secrets. Yet there exist those, like Moji, who seem to understand them.

Other than the examples set by Dadaji and Moji, we children in Khan Manzil didn't have much religious training. So a local mullah was enlisted to teach all the Khan children the recitation of the Quran. When the mullah entered the house, he found a dozen children of all ages obediently assembled. However, unbeknownst to him, one of my teenage cousins, Ghazi, had managed to hide a dead mouse underneath the chair where the mullah was going to sit. Within five minutes, the mullah ran out of the house as if it were on fire. The family had to beg and plead with him to come back. Finally, he agreed to try again, but we were no more appreciative.

Ghazi decided to step up his game and pulled a kitchen knife on the mullah. Ghazi said in a threatening voice, "If you don't get out of here, we are going to do something!"

The mullah shot to his feet and announced, "I swear, I am never coming back to this house again." He glared at Ghazi, who glowered back. It was a standoff. "These are crazy, ill-mannered children!" the mullah announced as he stormed off for the last time.

After that mullah's abrupt departure, our religious education, such as it was, ended. No other teacher in Kashmir would come near our house. Still, we followed religious rituals, celebrated holy days, and received religious instruction from family members.

ONE OF THE FIVE PILLARS of the Muslim faith is the hajj. This is the pilgrimage that Muslims from all over the world undertake during Ramadan, the last month of the Islamic calendar, to Mecca, in Saudi Arabia, where the Quran was first revealed to Muhammad. Hajj is a religious duty for every Muslim who can perform it, to be carried out at least once in his or her lifetime. The pilgrimage culminates at the Kaaba, a cubical black structure that God commanded Abraham and Ishmael to build over four thousand years ago. Abra-

ham was told to summon all of mankind to visit this place and pro-
claim, "At Thy service, O Lord, at Thy service."

One of the other rituals performed in Mecca during the hajj is the
slaughter of a lamb and the distribution of its meat in three portions,
one for ourselves, one for our family, and one for the poor. This offering commemorates the sacrifice that Abraham made to God to spare
his son Ishmael from the death that God had initially commanded.
Muslims all over the world, even those not participating in the hajj,
perform this rite. Our family would raise our own lambs for the
slaughter, and one year, when I was twelve, I went along to visit the
mountain village where we chose the animal. I took one look at one
of the baby lambs and announced that I would raise one myself.

I chose a lamb and named her Dolly, and I took the responsibility
of raising her very seriously. She grew to be a good-size sheep with
beautiful white wool. And then the day came when it was Dolly's
time to be sacrificed. I had become so attached to Dolly that I threw
my arms around her and screamed, "No! You can't take her. I can't let
her go!" But there was no point in arguing. The slaughter team forced
her away from me by her horns while I stood sobbing hysterically.

They butchered Dolly, removed her skin, hung her upside down
from a tree, and let her blood drain. Then they began to make kebabs
out of her. And all this time, my stomach was churning. I knew that
this was a part of life, part of the food chain; I had grown up watching chickens being slaughtered and had never minded. But now I
was in physical pain. And then my grandfather said to me, *"Kya
daleel?"* What's the matter?

I sobbed that Dolly had been my pet, they'd taken her away, and
she was dead now, and I would never see her again.

Dadaji told me not to worry. I would see her again. And he explained to me that any sacrificed animal goes to paradise and becomes part of one's receiving committee. Dolly was going to give me
entry into paradise, and she and all the lambs we had sacrificed would
be with me again in the hereafter. "Dolly will always be with you,"
Dadaji told me.

Sometimes when I am having trouble understanding or articulating my thoughts, it helps for me to draw. After Dolly was sacrificed, I consoled myself by taking out my charcoal, paints, and paper and making a diagram. I drew myself with Dolly inside a big circle. Decades later I sat in a Sufi circle listening to the recitation of a poem by Rumi about the cycle of life and thought back to Dolly:

> *I died as mineral and became a plant,*
> *I died as plant and rose to animal,*
> *I died as animal and I was man. . . .*
> *I shall become what no mind e'er conceived.*
> *Oh, let me not exist! for Non-existence*
> *Proclaims in organ tones, "To Him we shall return."*
>
> —*"I Died as Mineral,"*
> *translation by R. A. Nicholson*

There was great excitement in 1965 when Dadaji and Dadiji prepared to leave for Saudi Arabia to perform the hajj. The journey to Mecca is so long and the pilgrimage so arduous that historically many did not survive it. For that reason, there is a tradition that before Muslims embark on this transformative trip, they go from door to door seeking the forgiveness of everyone they may have wronged. For her traveling clothes, Dadiji dressed in her usual white burqa, a combination of a knee-length overcoat made of thin fabric with an elegant headdress that could be tied like a scarf and could reveal the face when the face flap was flipped over the head. Dadaji wore a peaked cap and dressed in a sherwani, a knee-length tailored coat, buttoned to the neck and worn over pants, and he carried a man's shawl. As we lined up for our grandparents' departure, they approached each of us, including the children, saying, "I seek your forgiveness for anything I may have said knowingly or unknowingly that may have hurt you."

All the family members then replied, "You have not wronged me in any way. May God be with you and return you in good health."

When they returned two months later, my grandparents were given the honorific title *hajji*. They brought back gifts of prayer beads, scarves, moist dates, prayer rugs, and Zam Zam holy water, symbolic of the miracle that occurred when Ishmael's mother, Hagar, was left in the desolate valley by Abraham.

Shortly after returning from the hajj, Dadiji called the women of the family together. She announced that she was removing her burqa forever. "I will no longer need this burqa," she said, "and all other daughters of this family can follow my example as well. Going forward, our women will observe modesty by covering their bodies—especially their bosoms—with a veil or a shawl."

Until then, my grandmother had always worn a white burqa in the summer and a black burqa in the winter. Her action seemed bold and counterintuitive; often people who returned from hajj dressed even more modestly afterward, to signal their increased devotion. Although I understood the brevity of this decision, no explanation was provided at the time. It was years later, when I delved into the Quran, that the reasons became clear to me. Verse 24:60 explains that elderly women who are past marriage age can remove their outer garment without being blamed. It stresses that it is best for them to observe modesty. This had been the rationale for why Dadiji and married women of the house permanently replaced their burqas with modest attire.

GOING BACKWARD,
NOT FORWARD

...

Most Americans cannot fathom a liberated Afghan woman. This point can be illustrated by President Donald Trump's reaction when, in 2017, General H. R. McMaster showed him a photograph of Afghan college students dressed in short skirts, walking in the streets much like young women in Boston or New York. Trump was shocked at this photograph, taken in 1972. He probably wondered how and why Afghan society had gone backward.

Kashmir is a neighbor of Afghanistan, and Papaji would often regale us with stories of Afghanistan in the sixties, telling us how impressive it was to see the progress the country had made. My Afghan friends also tell a different story from the one most Americans imagine. Their mothers, who were educated, enjoyed more freedoms than their daughters, who grew up facing the armed resistance against the Soviet-backed government in Kabul. Suraya is one of these friends. Her mother was so fearful for her daughter's future that she arranged for Suraya to marry at the age of fourteen. At fifteen, Suraya gave birth to her first child, a daughter. Her father and her husband were both educated Muslim men, and neither of them stopped her from studying. But she hid her marriage from classmates and teach-

ers, since school rules prohibited wives from studying alongside unmarried students.

By the time she had earned her literature degree at Kabul University in 1990, Suraya already had three daughters. Understanding the importance of education, she defied the Taliban's oppressive rule that banned girls' education and, in 1998, set up covert schools for girls in her home. She was the first to register a woman-focused NGO, Voices of Women Organization, in the post-Taliban era, and she told me, "Then I never looked back."

As a mother of three daughters, Suraya knew that she had to save the life of a young girl who had been sold to a powerful warlord by her father. To gain the release of the girl, Suraya succeeded in collecting funds to pay off the warlord. Her efforts resulted in the girl's rescue and, eventually, the warlord's arrest and sentencing to eighteen years in prison. Her direct confrontation with the perpetrator has put her in the crosshairs of the warlord's dangerous men. She continues to live with death threats to herself and her family and has received a letter from the intelligence directorate of Afghanistan warning her that, because of her activities, she and her family are being targeted directly. Groups who oppose her work on behalf of Afghan women are pressuring her to give in to their demands by threatening to abduct her children. Even though the personal attacks have taken a toll on Suraya's mental health, she has focused her efforts on meeting the increasing demand for her services by establishing four additional women's protection centers in the provinces of Badghis, Farah, Ghor, and Nimruz.

Through her direct intervention, Suraya has saved at least ten women from death during her tenure at Voices of Women. Her actions and courage have inspired many other women's rights activists to step forward and raise their voices.

Suraya recalls stories of Afghanistan in the sixties, when women like her mother played a vital role in society. She wants Afghanistan to regain its stature among the world's nations, and her work revolves around a singular purpose: to serve humanity and defend human rights.

CHAPTER

6

N 1971, WHEN I WAS THIRTEEN YEARS OLD AND IN SEVENTH GRADE, I was suddenly jolted into the awareness that we lived in a conflict zone. In the halls of my school, I could sense a shift. A more modest form of dress was gradually taking hold. As we girls moved into the upper grades, we were required to wear new uniforms: Instead of the skirts, Oxford shirts, and ties worn by the younger girls, the students in the upper classes now wore *kameez shalwar* with *dupatta*— traditional dresses and pants—along with chiffon veils, which many of the girls wrapped around their necks. Very few girls covered their heads.

At home one evening, there was a sudden blaring siren, and the whole house went pitch-black. We all ran outside and saw what looked like red balls shooting across the sky. Indian MiGs and Pakistani fighter planes dominated the skies with their sorties. It turned out that some incident had triggered a border war between India and Pakistan. The planes were fighting over Kashmir, which had been declared a "disputed territory" in 1948, after the independence of India from the British.

Politics were not discussed in our household, and this new conflict was complicated and hard for me to understand. What was unmistakable, however, was that the men in the family, along with the servants, began digging huge trenches at the back of the house so that the entire family could hide in a bunker. My cousin Ghazi, now sixteen, shook his fists skyward and yelled at the planes as they streaked overhead, but all I could do was stare in terror.

Adult conversations were suddenly afire with debates about India versus Pakistan. At school, we were rushed into underground bunkers whenever an air attack occurred. Before, the girls at school had all seemed alike, and our biggest worry had been running afoul of the sisters. But I began to see that there were differences among us— some people in school were pro-Pakistan, while others were pro-India. Girls who were best friends were now suspicious of each other, whispering behind one another's backs. What was happening at the national level was mirrored in our halls and on our athletic fields. In general, the Hindu girls supported the Indian side, while the Muslim girls supported the Pakistani side, though many of us were neutral or didn't know what to think. I had friends on both sides of the conflict, and I found it impossible to decide whom to agree with.

Nineteen seventy-one was also the year that my cousin Ghazi was jailed for his political activism. Unrest had grown to the point where the authorities would simply sweep a group of people, particularly young men, off the streets and throw them in prison for a month or so to set an example and quell any activism. When Ghazi got out of jail and returned home to Khan Manzil, he looked somber and haggard, as if he had not slept for the entire month. I overheard the servants whispering that poor Ghazi looked hardened after thirty days behind bars.

A few days later, I was running after Rocky along the treelined driveway, wearing my bell-bottoms, my long hair swinging loose behind me. Then I saw Ghazi standing on the side of the drive with his arms folded across his chest, glowering at me.

Suddenly he yelled at me, "Cover your hair!" It was a command.

I stopped in my tracks. Why? And who was *he* to tell me to cover my hair?

He shouted back that he was a man of the house and he was telling me that he didn't want anyone seeing me without a veil. He again ordered me to go cover myself.

"And if I don't, what will you do?" I yelled back, defiant.

Ghazi swore that he would throw acid on my face—before *they* did, he said, referring to other men.

I raced away, yelling over my shoulder that I was going to tell Dadaji and Papaji what he'd said.

I ran into the house and bounded up three flights of stairs, looking for Fifi. I told her, gasping, that Ghazi had threatened to throw acid in my face if I didn't wear a *dupatta* over my hair.

Fifi's advice was to stay away from Ghazi. "We must pity him," she said. He had been jailed, and who knew what they had done to him? The other prisoners must have put ideas in his head.

I told her that I would tell Dadaji what Ghazi had said, but Fifi thought I shouldn't. If I complained about Ghazi, he would get into more trouble. There were things I did not understand, she told me. She again advised me to just avoid our cousin.

I steered clear of Ghazi after that, but I could not shake the feeling that my childhood was over. It was a casualty of the conflict. I never again felt as free.

AS THE HOSTILITIES ESCALATED over the decades, I found I could identify a girl's political beliefs by what she wore. I was shocked to hear that a few of my classmates had become political activists and started wearing burqas to assert their newfound ideologies. And then there were those whose families simply fled the country out of self-preservation. Our family did not flee, but many of our relatives decided to relocate quietly when the time was right.

In the sixties, America needed doctors, so when my uncle Faroque obtained his medical degree, he and his classmate and bride received their blessing from Dadaji to emigrate to the United States. My artist uncle Rafique became an architect and moved to Los Angeles to become a town planner. My young aunt Mumtaz became a pediatrician and moved to New York along with her husband.

I watched my beloved Khan Manzil, once so bustling and full of life, empty out as my brothers, Abid and Zahid, and other family members sought a more secure way of life. I couldn't help feeling that I was on the deck of a boat that the passengers were abandoning one by one.

Ghazi was swiftly sent to America for his own protection.

At the time of my cousin's threat, I was stunned at the audacity of men to believe that they had the right to scar a woman. Ghazi had become a fanatic in prison, and one of the things he had been brainwashed to believe was that it was a man's duty and religious obligation to ensure the purity of women.

The notion of men needing to "protect" women was a foreign concept to me. In Kashmiri society, each person, male or female, was responsible for his or her own actions. Years later, when I had found my voice, I was often asked to explain why veiling is part of the Islamic religion. The Quran certainly does not advocate this kind of "protection"—it is not a religious issue. The Quran does not sanction taking a human life, defacing a woman, or robbing her of her dignity. But by corrupting scriptures, militants find justification for their actions. Sadly, the practice of attacking or defacing women is not uncommon in Islamic societies, just as it is not uncommon in many cultures in which women are oppressed and men find strength as maintainers of women's morality.

THE BEAUTY GURU

...

Although I have met many female leaders in my work, includ-ing politicians, CEOs, and heads of state, one of the women I most admire is Misbah, a Pakistani beautician often called the "beauty guru," who operates a salon in a mall in Lahore. Mis-bah's name surfaced in January 2015 in the aftermath of a spate of acid attacks on women.

For more than a decade, Misbah and her team of beauty experts—many themselves survivors of atrocities—have, for no fee, helped over six hundred survivors of acid attacks receive medical treatment. Misbah goes beyond the medical and cos-metic aspects—she also helps these women to regain their con-fidence and trains them to enter the workforce. The women who come to her know that her staff have experienced what they themselves have been through and will never judge them. So much of a woman's beauty is found not on her face but in her soul.

According to Acid Survivors Trust International, there are roughly fifteen hundred documented acid attacks every year, most of which take place in India, and many more cases go unreported. It's estimated that 70 to 80 percent of acid-attack crimes are perpetrated against women and girls. One woman, who works in the Lahore salon, was attacked by her in-laws for not paying enough dowry money. After 150 operations, she now leads a productive life. In another instance, a respected university lecturer had acid thrown on her ten days before her wedding. "It's not about being educated or not," she said afterward. "It's a mindset."

Legal steps are finally being introduced, but importantly, the image of women as victims is being turned on its head. In 2012 Sharmeen Obaid-Chinoy won an Academy Award for an inspiring documentary, Saving Face, *profiling a British Pakistani surgeon, Dr. Mohammad Jawad, who returns to his native country to perform reconstructive surgery on scarred victims. In addition to breakthroughs like the beauty salon in Lahore, outreach is helping to shift perceptions of acid-attack victims. On International Women's Day in 2015, female survivors who work in a café in Agra, India, called the Sheroes' Hangout launched a calendar in which survivors posed as models, in the hope that these images of strong women would inspire others, deter acid-crime perpetrators, and help broaden the perception of the standard of beauty.*

What in the world could be more beautiful?

ALTHOUGH I DIDN'T GO TO THE UNITED STATES UNTIL I was in high school, Western values played a major role in our household, influencing my upbringing and eventually my thinking as an adult. This was thanks to Dadaji. He had barely set foot back in Kashmir from the United States when he took my father out of a public school in Kashmir and enrolled him in St. Joseph's, a private Catholic school run by missionaries. The Catholic educational system had been established in India by the British colonials, and even today India has more Catholic-school students than any other nation in the world. And so in due course, I attended St. Patrick's Presentation Convent School, a prestigious private girls' school in Kashmir. The ghost of the British colonial influence was still evident in our nicknames—Daisy for Farhat, Fifi for Husnara, and Gudi for Musarat.

From my early childhood on, I seemed to live between two worlds that at times felt compatible but at other times collided. It seems somewhat surreal, when I think back on it, that in the heart of the Kashmir Valley, Muslim, Hindu, and Sikh children sang Christmas carols in a convent school run by Irish nuns and celebrated Saint Patrick's Day with the full regalia of a marching band and bagpipes. Always up for athletic activities, I eagerly donned my knee-length tartan skirt and a green sash with four-leaf clovers printed on it to perform the Highland fling, a Scottish dance. I climbed trees with

Sikh girls, bought freshwater pearls from Buddhists; my teachers were Hindu, and later in life I discovered that Kashmiris were thought to be descended from the lost tenth tribe of Israel. The value of celebrating and honoring all religions was normal, especially during their holidays. I was forbidden to participate in the free-for-all festival of colors, Holi, in which Hindus celebrate the onset of spring. "There is drinking there, and it's no place for a girl," I was told, but that did not deter me from finding a way to join my Sikh neighbor, Gugoo, and watching with utter joy as people young and old smeared and drenched one another with colored powder and burst colored water balloons.

It was the Jews who intrigued me most. I knew nothing about them: The only pictures I had were the ones painted by Dadaji of his landlady and her daughter in Boston. Dadaji's book *The Kashmiri Mussulman*, published in 1973, mentioned that historical evidence indicated that Jews had once inhabited Kashmir, but there was no longer a Jewish community there. Little did I know that I would one day find myself living in a 99 percent Jewish neighborhood in Jericho, Long Island.

MY CHILDHOOD IN KASHMIR was close to idyllic. I had a loving, supportive family that nurtured my lifelong interest in art. It became increasingly clear that I did not want to be a doctor or a teacher—the only two honorable professions for women in Kashmir at that time. The decision to send me to America to pursue my education was serendipitous. My aunt and uncle who lived in New York had come to visit family in Kashmir. My uncle was curious about the fate of Daisy, who had bitten the dog. He inquired about me and the plan for my further education. Mummy told him that with the dispute between Pakistan and India, with Kashmir in the middle, my family was questioning whether I should remain at home. The natural solution was to send me to New Delhi to continue my studies—yet I had no family there. I would be alone and unsupervised. Faroque Chacha, who had saved me once before, had a rescue plan: I could go with him and his wife to New York, scope things out for myself, and if necessary continue my education there.

I was thrilled at the prospect. Although Dadaji was agreeable, he set down certain conditions: My uncle and his wife had to treat me as their own child, along with their two children; give me a good education; and—the aspect that troubled me the most—find me a suitable husband. But these were basically the same as the conditions that I lived under in Kashmir. And so I simply focused on the idea of going to America, the land of bell-bottoms, hippies, and rock and roll.

My mother was delighted that her daughter was going to a land that would enable her to carry out her own dreams of a career. Mummy's dream also pushed my sister Gudi to leave Kashmir to pursue her medical studies in Madras, which at the time was a very controversial move because the culture there was so different from that of Kashmir. Fifi was sent to medical school in Pune.

I had never been allowed even to leave home alone, and now I was going to the United States to live away from my parents—albeit with my aunt and uncle. Despite my excitement, I was torn about being separated from my schoolmates and a bit nervous about leaving home. Kashmir and Khan Manzil maintained a deep hold on all of us who crossed the ocean.

I was accompanied on the trip to New York by my aunt and uncle, and most important, for my protection, Dadaji gave me a copy of the Quran. Inside the cover, in case I might forget, he had written his mantra in his meticulous handwriting—*Rabbi zidni ilma.* Oh Lord, increase me in knowledge.

The trip lasted more than twenty-four hours and was exhausting. Once the plane landed at John F. Kennedy International Airport and I walked through the arrivals terminal, I looked everywhere and at everything, trying to drink in the surroundings, but forty-four years later the most vivid memory I have is looking at a sea of white people. I'd had no idea there were so many in the world! My new home was a brand-new modern split-level with two large windows overlooking a manicured lawn. And what was the odd-shaped thing standing at the entrance of the driveway? A mailbox? I felt disoriented as my little cousins were brought out by the babysitter to greet us. I met Arif, Faroque, and Arfa's naughty eight-year-old son, who stuck his tongue out at me. He immediately reminded me of my brother Abid, the snake. I picked up my tiny cousin, Shireen, and held her, comforted by her baby scent. I missed the busyness and constant noise of the crowded Khan Manzil.

Uncle Faroque, who was my father's younger brother, was a brilliant and successful pulmonologist who did not act the part. He drove a dinky Volkswagen Rabbit and wore horrid polyester suits, as he saw no need to waste money on unnecessary luxuries. Arfa Auntie, a radiologist, had beauty, brains, elegance, and a gift for diplomacy.

Settling in was an adjustment. The second day after my arrival, I ventured out to the front lawn. The concept of a lawn was odd to me—where were all the fences? How did anybody know where their lawn ended and the neighbors' began? Occasionally a car would drive slowly by, but otherwise the street was dead quiet. My real cultural immersion, though, began in a department store dressing room. Even though I had never worn anything to school but a uniform, I knew from watching television that I would need new clothes for my senior year at Jericho High School. When Auntie suggested an expedition to Sears, Roebuck to buy school clothes, I jumped at the chance. I relied on Auntie's judgment, so when she held up a blue polyester pantsuit with red and orange dots and proclaimed that the outfit would look nice on me, I assumed that this must be the height of American fashion.

But when I walked into school the first day, in September of 1974, wearing two long braids, no makeup, and my new pantsuit, I was shocked to see the other girls in T-shirts and overalls or in long, flowery skirts, their hair loose, or in halter tops and tight jeans with big hair, as if they were about to step out to a disco party. The boys wore torn dungarees or overalls. I spent a frantic few moments wondering how I was going to talk Auntie into buying me tight jeans, then realized that it was hopeless. It wouldn't matter what I wore—I could wear a pantsuit or a paper bag. I was different from these kids, and that was going to be that.

There was silence in my first class, Social Studies, as the teacher, Mr. Greene, read aloud the class list. When he announced my name, Farhat, I stood to respond to him, as I had done at Catholic school. Meanwhile, the rest of the class was lounging in their seats—some were blowing bubbles with their chewing gum; others seemed half-asleep or so stoned that they didn't even know they were in class. I recognized their drugged state from the hippies we saw who came to Kashmir seeking nirvana. And there I was, standing up straight and saying, "Yes, sir," as if I were in a military academy.

Everybody started snickering when they heard my name—not to mention what they must have thought of my tight braids and pant-suit.

"Why is she standing?"

"She's some new girl."

"Where did she come from?"

"From India."

"Did she go to school on an elephant?"

"What's her name?"

"Far Hat."

"Oh no, it's Far Out."

"Ha-ha, she *is* really Far Out!"

Mr. Greene jumped in with a threat: He would throw out of his class anyone who made fun of Ms. Khan.

The teasing quickly ended, and I informed everyone that I went by my nickname, Daisy. When at some point Mr. Greene inquired whether I was a Muslim and I replied yes, he asked if I could tell the class about Islam. I thought back to Dadaji, who had also been asked to lecture about this subject he knew little about at Harvard. When I told Mr. Greene that I had no idea what to say, he suggested I study up and come prepared for the next class. My uncle was thrilled when

I complained to him about the assignment, also thinking of his father's experience. He advised me to keep my presentation simple and to use Dadaji's book *The Kashmiri Mussulman* as a resource. This was the first major work to describe the political, spiritual, and social history of the Kashmiri people. It also discussed how Islam came to be embraced by the Hindus and Buddhists of the Kashmir Valley.

Standing in front of the class, talking about the basic tenets of Islam to a group of mostly Jewish kids who knew little about their own religion, much less mine, I felt as if a switch flipped inside me. At first, I was nervous, but as I gave my very basic description of my religion, I began to feel a sense of control and of leadership. And my audience was intrigued—not so much about Islam, it seemed, but about me and my life. I was no longer the odd kid out, the girl people were pointing at—I was a part of the conversation.

Thinking back, even now, to my sixteen-year-old self who was just beginning her journey, I am grateful for the path paved by my grandfather and his cherished books.

ONE OF MY CLASSES was a co-ed sex education class. A male teacher stood in front of the room and lectured us on condoms. I could barely process what he was saying. What was a condom? Inside I clung to my conservative cultural values, but I also sensed that it would take a lot for me to maintain those mores. A part of me wanted to retreat, to pull back into a shell—to go to school, then go right home afterward, and stop at that. That would be safe, and Uncle would approve. But, I thought, why cross the ocean just to stay within my comfort zone? It would be such a waste. I needed to find a way into this new culture. I decided to choose a few activities I could succeed at and throw myself into them.

At school in Kashmir, I had been a superb field hockey player, as well as prefect of the school's four houses. I began to think that field hockey could be my entrée, especially when I saw the dismal performance of Jericho's hockey team. I asked Mrs. Schwartz, our phys ed teacher, if I could join the team, and she asked if I knew how to play.

When I said yes, she agreed to let me try out. I surprised her in my first tryout by scoring goal after goal. At the end of the season, after we had won the championship, the girls lifted me onto their shoulders, and I knew I had arrived.

At the Italian restaurant the team went to for our celebration, the group ordered spaghetti. When the food arrived, I didn't know how to pick up the pasta. Mrs. Schwartz leaned over and quietly said, "You don't know how to eat this stuff, do you?" Picking up a fork, she dipped it into the spaghetti and rotated it around to demonstrate for me. I was both grateful and astonished. And then, I thought of Dadaji's fateful trip to America. Once again, I was following in my grandfather's footsteps. The whole family knew the story. On the boat trip to America, Dadaji had been served a dish of peas. Having no idea how to eat them, he tried to use his knife, but they rolled off and bounced onto the floor. Dadaji might have given up, but he was hungry. So instead he observed his fellow passengers spearing the foreign objects with a fork. He had never seen or used a fork at home, where food was picked up with fingers. After a few tries, Dadaji finally got it right. He could now break bread at the table of his new friends and associates. Without his newfound knife-and-fork skills, would they have listened to his ideas or respected his opinions? And wouldn't not adapting to their customs show disrespect? To be honest, my grandfather never entirely agreed with the efficiency of Western cutlery over good old reliable hands and fingers, which had worked just fine for his ancestors for hundreds of years. But he considered the awkward cultural customs part of his education. As eating spaghetti was now part of mine.

GOD INC.

...

During a lunch overlooking the Hudson River, my friend Ali introduced me to his Jewish wife and his stepdaughter Erica, who was exploring internship ideas. I invited Erica to my office for an interview, and she told me she was interested in doing peace-building work with an NGO, maybe with Arabs and Jews or with Muslims and Jews. I probed further, and she mentioned some unpleasant confrontations she had had with her own family members who stereotyped all Muslims. For Erica, this was personal! Her stepfather was a Muslim, and Erica had no line of defense. She had previously attended Seeds of Peace, a summer camp in America for youths from conflict zones.

I immediately knew I had a small social justice warrior on my hands, and the best weapon I could give her was knowledge! It would have been easy for me to explain Islam 101 to Erica, but I felt it was more important for her to understand the concept of the one God that is central to both Islam and Judaism. I wanted her to comprehend how God had unveiled His divine plan through the world's different religions, that there is only one God, who has many names and is worshipped in different languages and ways.

"You will research every religion that exists in the world, its tenets and beliefs, its founders, its various denominations or

schools of thought," I told her. "Then organize them on a time line from the oldest to the newest, and draw an organizational chart called God Inc." Finally, I tasked Erica with developing a manual of God's plan!

Erica was shocked and delighted at the same time. "I would have been happy to answer the phone, but God's plan will be fine too," she told me.

When Erica, then a seventeen-year-old, began the project, she immediately became intoxicated with it. In her youth, learning about religion had gone hand in hand with Middle East politics, and being a good Jew in her family meant you could not separate the politics of Israel from religion. The God Inc. research and exercise forced her to challenge her narrow views of religion. She learned how God could manifest Himself through so many different religions, how others could relate differently to the same God, and how different people lay equal claim to God.

While reading a book I had assigned her, A World of Prayer, a collection of writing by people of different faiths, Erica was drawn to "Clearing," a poem by Martha Postlethwaite:

> Do not try to save
> the whole world
> or do anything grandiose.
> Instead, create
> a clearing
> in the dense forest
> of your life
> and wait there
> patiently,
> until the song
> that is yours alone to sing
> falls into your open cupped hands

and you recognize and greet it.
Only then will you know
how to give yourself
to this world,
so worthy of rescue.

—*from* A World of Prayer, *edited by*
Rosalind Bradley

Erica was so moved by this poem that she included it as her quote in her yearbook. Equipped with her God Inc. project and her guiding principle, she went back to Seeds of Peace for a second summer so she could actively share and engage in its leadership dialogue program.

Today, Erica is a senior at Yale studying English. She wants to be a playwright and is already writing a play, which was influenced by Jason Alexander, whom she saw at the 92nd Street Y when we were co-panelists on "Time to Lead," a discussion organized by OneVoice. This young woman is coming into her own. She is no longer afraid of difference. And now that she understands the tenets of her faith, she can define her Judaism and bring politics back into it whenever she needs to. She feels no conflict in relating equally to American Judaism and to the state of Israel.

Her roommate and best friend is a hijab-wearing Jordanian whose father is an ambassador. Equipped with facts and figures, she can talk seriously about the Middle East and relate humanly to anyone who seems to be different from her.

As the December holiday season drew near, I began to feel more acclimated to American culture and was looking forward to singing the Christmas carols I'd learned from the nuns in school in Kashmir. But there were no carols sung at my school, and there was not a single hint of the holiday. If Christmas was nearing, why were the houses all dark?

Arfa Auntie explained that in Jericho, Long Island, most of the residents were Jewish and therefore did not celebrate Christmas. In our neighborhood, there was only one house that had a Christmas tree, and it belonged to a Christian couple across our street. It turned out I wasn't the only one trying to figure things out. When Shireen started attending school, she asked her father at the dinner table one evening if we celebrated Hanukkah or Christmas.

Uncle told her that we celebrated neither and that Eid was our holiday.

Of course, nobody else in my school or our neighborhood commemorated Eid al-Fitr, the celebration of the end of Ramadan, the culmination of the sacrifice of a month of fasting and prayer. If I closed my eyes, I could recall Eid in Kashmir: its music, the songs on the radio—*Eid aye rus rus. Eid gah wus vo* . . . Eid is here. Eid is here. Get ready to celebrate Eid. Along with a sumptuous meal, sharing and joy are important aspects of the Eid festival. Some members of our household would attend Eid prayers at mosques, while others would stay at home to pray so they could prepare a lavish meal—with extra lamb and rice to feed any hungry person who came by. Dadaji would emerge in his brocade jacket and take out his stack of rupees, fold the notes with his right hand, and place them into the beggars' left hands. "Charity must be given by the right hand so that the left does not know," he would tell me. "In secret! It's a sign of humility." And he would always peel off one rupee from his stack for each of us children. After the Eid meal, the chase would begin. All the kids would race from house to house to meet relatives—not to see them, but to gobble down macaroons, *jalebis,* and three-layered cakes and to collect our Eidee, an activity that was akin to hunting for Easter eggs.

On Eid, the doorbell would ring nonstop from friends, relatives, and neighbors delivering gift baskets and cakes. Hindus and Muslims alike came to the house to offer greetings; in Kashmir, Eid was honored and shared by those of many faiths. A highlight of the day was always a visit to Moji and Gudi. Moji, usually so Spartan, on this special day would give us a gift of intricately handwoven ribbons for our hair. "May God make you the joy of our eyes," she would say, cupping our faces.

ON LONG ISLAND, THERE were no such festivities for either Eid al-Fitr or Eid al-Adha, which commemorated the end of hajj. There was not even an actual place we could go to celebrate the holiday, no community or cultural center, not even a local mosque. Shireen was a child, but we both sensed the same thing—a feeling of displacement. There was no way for us to meet other Muslim children, no place for our families to gather in faith. I felt I had lost two sets of traditions— the Eid we had celebrated so joyously in Kashmir and the Christmas I had shared in celebrating at my convent school. My aunt and uncle would invite their Kashmiri doctor friends, and we would have a special meal at home, but there was no sense of real celebration. I had to remind myself that celebrations were not the point—that I should focus on the spiritual meaning of the holiday. Back in Kashmir, I had been more interested in the trappings of the celebration than in the message of the holiday. Still, when I went to the window, drew back the curtains, and peered outside, I felt a sadness looking out into the dark and quiet. No lights or candles flickered. No music embellished the night.

I had been expecting a full-blown Christmas in America. Now, living in a nearly all-Jewish neighborhood, I had neither Eid nor Christmas. On the other hand, I was fortunate to become fully immersed in the Jewish experience. I was eating matzo ball soup, pastrami, and challah bread. I participated in Hanukkah, Passover, and the Jewish New Year. My American family felt a kinship with the Jewish families in our community. Like the Jews, we were also members of a minority, and as I began, later in my life, to address issues within the Muslim community, the Jewish experience in America served as a template for me.

THE WORLD IS FLAT AND
MADE OF COOKIES

. . .

Forty years after I first came to the United States, a child asked me why we Muslims don't have a holiday celebration like Christmas or Hanukkah. It was the same question that my little cousin Shireen had asked her parents, the same question that would years later trigger the building of a mosque in Westbury, Long Island. I realized that Muslims who had emigrated to America still had no comparable religious festivities to those celebrated by most Americans and that children growing up in a cross-cultural environment were still asking the same questions. I decided to create an American celebration of Eid al-Fitr.

In 2014, I invited six women to form a committee to design the first uniquely American expression of Eid, a commemoration like no other. The women were an eclectic group: an Afghan, an Indonesian, a Pakistani, a Bangladeshi, a Saudi, and an Egyptian. We would blend the various cultural expressions of these countries and spice them up with activities that were quintessentially American. We decided to make this a party for the children in the community.

My husband liked the idea. "When Islam spread from Arabia to other ancient cultures, it adopted the local cultural practices. Creating a uniquely American Eid will be a positive Islamic experience for the children and their parents," he told me. We booked the grand ballroom of New York University's Rosenthal Pavilion and invited people of Muslim faith and other faiths to experience the atmosphere and meet new friends. There would be prayers and readings of meaningful poetry, but also fun entertainment such as trivia games, balloon animals, face painting, and music.

"Let's introduce an American dessert that children love," said one of the women. "Cupcakes and Eid cookies," she suggested. I envisioned the design: star- and crescent-shaped cookies decorated in royal blue and gold icing. Janice, a young mother and home baker, volunteered to bake them herself. A Bosnian mom suggested we get helium balloons. She searched the Internet and found balloons with EID MUBARAK inscriptions on Amazon. On Eid day, we picked up the balloons, held them up through the sunroof of the car, and drove through the streets of Manhattan. The reaction was exhilarating. Taxi drivers returned the greeting by honking at us, Muslims standing at streetlights held up their thumbs to us, immigrant street vendors shouted their support at us as they paused from working at their halal carts to watch us pass, tourists in Times Square stared in disbelief, and random New Yorkers waved in solidarity.

The first Eid celebration was a huge success. A crowd of two hundred guests came together for an evening of commemoration and festivities. The table settings had Eid motifs on the tablecloths, cups, and napkins. In the center of each table stood a tall filigreed lantern with purple glass. Popular in the Middle East, these lanterns symbolize the act of waking up at dawn for suhur, a meal before the fast. The balloon-crafts lady lived up to her promise by sculpting unique designs such as the crescent, a lamp, a genie, and a camel. A young Pakistani immigrant painted elaborate henna designs on the hands of the kids. A face-painting artist decorated their faces with butterflies and

the flags of their parents' countries—India, Pakistan, and Af-
ghanistan. One mother instructed the face painter to paint the
Israeli flag on one of her son's cheeks and a Palestinian flag on
the other. "He is a future peacemaker," she told the artist. We
placed gifts for the children under a plywood crescent made in
the garage of Nabil, a young graphic designer. We'd chosen the
crescent because the end of Ramadan is marked by the sighting
of the new moon. People had bought Islamic-themed orna-
ments to hang from the crescent. Children with painted faces
raced around with balloons, stuffing themselves with star- and
crescent-shaped cookies. We sang songs and even played musi-
cal chairs; the winner was an eighty-year-old grandfather.

The Quran talks about paradise, under which there are gar-
dens and flowing rivers, and for that reason the color green has
come to symbolize Islam. Many Muslim countries use this
color on their flags in addition to crescents. As sunset ap-
proached, we assembled at the window. "Here is the best gift of
all," I told the crowd over the microphone. "Look who is wish-
ing us Eid Mubarak!" *Just then, green lights lit up the top of*
the Empire State Building, and the room burst into applause.

One mother told her son, "See how much they love us? They
lit up the Empire State Building just for us!" Everyone was tak-
ing selfies and sharing them with their relatives around the
world. I was especially thrilled because since 9/11 the green
lights had ceased to appear to commemorate the Muslim holi-
day, and I had had a hand in reinstating them. With our celebra-
tion, a new tradition was born. And on that night, everyone in
the room was one big family.

SITTING IN MY ROOM IN MY UNCLE'S HOME, I STARED AT THE turntable watching a Beatles record go around and around. I finally had my precious collection of Beatles records, but John, Paul, George, and Ringo could not help me become part of this new environment. Back home in Kashmir, the Beatles had been a novelty, and listening to them had transported us to a faraway, exotic world that I had learned about from my grandfather and father. But now, surrounded by American culture, my main concern was learning how to fit in. I craved acceptance. I did not want to be a misfit. I internalized a lot of things and stressed about them, because I didn't have another person I could talk comfortably with about what I was going through. My uncle and aunt tried to be supportive, but they were from another generation. As far as Uncle Faroque was concerned, my focus was supposed to be 100 percent on my studies. Friends, socializing, and rock-and-roll music were just distractions to be avoided. But they were the things I sought out, the things I needed.

My aunt and uncle felt responsible for me and worried that I might be distracted from my studies by pop culture and influenced by its lax moral standards. And one thing was certain—boys were completely forbidden. There was no word in Kashmir for prom because no such event existed. So, when the time came to tell them about it, I decided I would start with Arfa Auntie. Surely she would understand my need to go. All the girls were going, I told her. *Every-body*. It was *necessary* for me to go to the prom.

Auntie shook her head. It was doubtful that Uncle would allow it.

As predicted, my uncle adamantly refused to allow me to go. It was too risky, he said. He was acting in my father's place. He was responsible for me. In the end, instead of coming around to my way of thinking, Auntie ended up agreeing with Uncle Faroque.

It was the same with movies—I absolutely had to go, but I wasn't allowed.

Auntie finally agreed to allow me to go to a daytime movie with girlfriends. I didn't realize that my friends had invited some boys along. When the car pulled into the driveway, my uncle, who was peering out his study window, saw them and immediately came downstairs to interrogate me. My aunt tried to intervene, arguing that this was just a movie during the day and I would be fine. Uncle came out of the house, shaking his head at the car and muttering that it was insane to let me go out with this bunch of lunatics.

I ran past him and leaped into the car without waiting for him to say no.

Of course, Uncle was waiting for me when I came home. In fact, every single time I went out, I would return to find him pacing the living room in his plaid silk nightgown. Even when I went out while I was in college, he would be there waiting and pacing, no matter what time I came back.

My high school graduation was a low-key event, but I took great pride in being part of the ceremony. I understood that I had come to America for a purpose; I had not come to party. Although my family believed I was here simply to further my education, as my classmates and I threw our tasseled caps into the air, I wondered if Uncle and Auntie were too protective. Surely, learning to be part of a culture—*feeling* a part of it—was just as important as the academics. Was this way of thinking rebellious? Between thinking for myself and rebellion, there seemed to be a very fine line.

———

ART IN ALL ITS FORMS was my passion. At Jericho High School, I had immediately enrolled in a class specializing in drawing and painting. I had wanted to improve my skills, but I had also wanted to test the waters, to see if I really had the necessary artistic talent to pursue a career in the arts. Much to my joy, I came away with a grade of 97 percent in the class. I was hoping to attend the Pratt Institute, in Brooklyn, but my uncle preferred I stay closer to home. He was worried that I was not mature enough to be on my own.

I saw his point and enrolled in college at C.W. Post in Brookville, New York. I had no idea what a liberal-arts education entailed, but I was gung ho because the name of the curriculum contained the word "arts." There I studied the humanities: philosophy, literature, and art history. At Jericho High, I had met mostly Jewish kids, but at C.W. Post, I interacted with a melting pot of students. There were African Americans, Catholics, and South Asians—Indians like me. Within this group were kids who liked to party, but I felt safe with them because we shared similar cultural mores. I was also friendly with a group of athletes on campus, but when one of them, Walter, a tall, elegant black basketball player, asked me out on a date, I had to tell him I was very sorry, but I didn't date. Walter accused me of being "one of those girls who won't date black men." I was shocked because I had no idea what he meant.

Walter didn't give up easily. He insisted that the only way I could prove to him that I wasn't a racist was if I agreed to go to the movies with him.

I desperately wanted to prove that I wasn't a racist, but would going on this date really have any purpose? I was still of the mindset that I had to marry a Muslim.

I explained my dilemma to my aunt and asked her if I could go to the movies with Walter to prove to him that I was not a racist.

Eventually, I wore her down. My aunt said, "Well, if you are going to go, there must be strict ground rules. You must go to the earliest movie, and I'll cover for you. Then you must come back as soon as it's over, because Faroque's going to be very upset."

I nodded hopefully.

Auntie continued, "Your uncle is not going to want you to do this."

I said, "I have to do it to prove to Walter that I am not a racist."

I agreed to be back by four.

Arfa Auntie and I had everything planned with military precision. The key was to work around my uncle's schedule. We knew that he left for tennis at a certain time, so I told Walter to come after he'd left. Faroque Chacha would be gone for three hours, and the plan was that we would be back before he returned.

I was getting dressed when my uncle's tennis partner called to say that he was sick and couldn't play, so my uncle was unexpectedly at home when Walter arrived. My aunt and uncle's study window overlooked the driveway, and my uncle watched as Walter pulled up in a yellow-checkered cab, which was not exactly unobtrusive. My uncle thought that perhaps this tall black man, who had emerged from the car and was walking up to the house with his shirt open to reveal a mint's worth of gold chains and medallions, had gotten lost in the neighborhood.

Suddenly the doorbell rang, and Auntie panicked: "Oh my God, your friend has arrived, and Faroque is still here!" My aunt came up with a plan of the sort that Ethel and Lucy from the sitcom *I Love Lucy* might have concocted. She said, "I will open the door." Then she told me we would go tell him to leave. That plan was foiled when my uncle got to the door before she did. He opened it, peered out suspiciously, and said, "Hello, hello. Yes, can I help you?"

"I am Walter, sir. I am here to pick up Daisy."

With that, my uncle shut the door in Walter's face, turned around, and asked, "Who is this man—and why is he here to pick up Daisy?"

My aunt jumped in. "Faroque, I can explain."

He put his foot down. "No explaining. Tell him to go away." An argument ensued.

I was hoping that Walter couldn't hear all the screaming. Auntie took my uncle into the kitchen while Walter was still waiting outside and said, "You know, Faroque, you have to understand that Daisy is only going to the movies in the daytime, and this is fine."

While they were talking, I quietly ducked out of the house.

Let me tell you, Walter couldn't wait to bring me back home. The minute the movie was over, he said, "You have proven your point. Thank you very much. We can be friends from here on."

Despite everything, we did remain friends.

I KNOW A LOT of young women who say they feel their biological clocks ticking when it comes to marriage and children. In my case, when I was eighteen, it was my uncle who had the added burden of watching over the ticking of my marriage clock. He never forgot his promise to my grandfather. One night, while I was in my room studying, Auntie appeared with a serious look on her face. She and Uncle had received a proposal for me from a Pakistani man. He was an athlete, she said hopefully. What's more, he was an Olympic athlete! He had played hockey for the Pakistani Olympic team. Auntie had his photo—did I want to see it? Auntie chattered on excitedly. This godlike specimen had noticed me at an Eid prayer service held at a rental hall in Queens. She pulled out a five-by-seven glossy head shot, like something from Central Casting. It was true that he was a very handsome man, with olive skin, deep brown eyes, perfectly chiseled features, and wavy, jet-black hair. He was wearing a dark tailored suit, a white shirt, and a tie with stripes. But on close inspection, something about him didn't look right. How old was this man?

Auntie hesitated before she answered.

He was, it turned out, thirty-three. I was eighteen. While it's true that I was not exactly a child bride, by my family's standard I was too young to marry.

Auntie and Faroque wanted me to know about this proposal so I could decide for myself. When I looked at her in silence, she acknowledged that the fifteen-year age gap was too great.

It was a reprieve, but I understood that the process had begun. I was now on a conveyor belt leading only one place—to marriage.

A year later, there was a second marriage proposal. This time, when Auntie informed me that she had sent a photograph of all of us to her sister Abida in Saudi Arabia, and Abida had just happened to call that morning . . . I already knew. An eligible man, in this case a prince, had "just happened" to see my photograph. Not only had this candidate asked to marry me, but he had even sent an engagement gift via Abida. Auntie explained: The prince wanted an educated wife; I would never have to worry about anything ever again; I would have wealth and comfort. . . .

As for work and a career, Auntie had never heard of a princess who worked. Then there was the issue of a second wife. Auntie admitted that, yes, there would probably be additional wives involved.

I tried to remain calm as I asked Auntie if she really wanted me to marry a man who would have another wife.

She immediately responded that she would not want this for herself, so, she said, why should she want it for me? She was sure my papaji would not agree to it either—perhaps it was best to forget the whole thing. She would tell Abida that I must continue my education.

But I could see her mind working: An Olympian, a prince—who will ever be good enough in this girl's mind?

Part of me wanted to do what I knew would make my family happy. But hadn't Papaji raised me to think for myself? Hadn't my mother drilled into me the value of an education and the importance of standing on my own two feet? I thought of the red boxing gloves that Papaji had strapped onto my hands when I was a small girl. Would I always have to fight? Auntie left my room, closing the door softly behind her. But I knew that the door to the marriage question was far from closed.

MATCHMAKER APP

...

In 2005, *when I began to get involved with premarital counsel-*
ing, mothers would corner me at weddings and, in a hushed
voice, make a request: "You know so many eligible bachelors.
Please find Aisha a good husband." I understood their anxiety
but was surprised at how naïve they were when it came to their
children's love interests. I was quite sure that their children
wanted to find their own mates.

However naïve the parents, the religious imperatives remain
the same today as they were when I was a teenager. Muslims
remain bound by religious tradition, which prohibits casual
dating, opposite-sex friendships, or sex before marriage. I was
intent on mentoring the young Muslim women I counseled in
balancing their faith with modernity, but they complained that
they were being stigmatized for being single. "How and where
am I supposed to find a Muslim man?" they'd ask. They pointed
out that of course they could not go to bars, and while Muslim
men dated non-Muslim women, marrying outside of the faith
was not an option for women.

Of course, they had a point. I remembered my own single
days and the pressure I had been under and decided to address
the problem of upwardly mobile Muslims in New York City

who needed to find a spouse but loathed the idea of match-maker aunties.

I planned a singles event on Valentine's Day and positioned it as a social networking opportunity for Muslim men and women to meet in a religiously appropriate context: They could feel free to hand out their business cards without the obligation to share their personal contact information. When the registration was complete, I was in for a shock. We had sixty women and fourteen men signed up to attend. Why was the expected male attendance so low? What had we said or done to discourage men from participating? An intern in my office chuckled, "Four-to-one ratio."

Confused, I turned to a trusted young man in our network, Junaid, for an explanation. He responded dramatically. "This is no surprise to me. Muslim men are raised to behave honorably toward girls: 'Don't look, stare, or touch a Muslim girl; she is your sister!'" he said. "And because men and women in a mosque are segregated, we don't have an opportunity to meet women, and if we do, we feel awkward around them. We don't know how to approach them. We can't casually date without marrying them. Ultimately, because it is so ingrained in us that Muslim women are our 'sisters,' psychologically it is even difficult to develop an attraction toward them. When we dream of a girlfriend, we think of Wonder Woman. When we desire a sexual partner, we hook up with a nice white woman in college or at work. When we are ready for marriage, we either marry our non-Muslim girlfriend, or we go back to our home country and let a professional matchmaker do what he does best: find a nice traditional girl who is not only a doctor but is gorgeous too. It's a win-win. . . ." When Junaid saw the horrified look on my face, he concluded: "Therefore, your male attendees are not *showing up, and so many Muslim women are single, including my own sister."*

The situation was depressing. Professional American Muslim women were waiting patiently for Muslim men, only to discover that they were all taken or looking elsewhere. It seemed unfair to me that these young women should remain single for the rest of their lives. I canceled the event we were planning and instead created a smaller group with fifteen men and women. The results were promising: A good-looking investment banker took a liking to a young woman named Neema and treated her to a fancy dinner. As it turned out, her fiercely independent side did not appreciate the gesture; she wanted him to consult her on where to eat, but instead he was trying to impress her with his wealth. He tried again, with a low-key event, a Saturday drive out of the city. This went against her traditional Muslim sensibilities. "How can he suggest I drive all alone with him? Doesn't he know how to treat a Muslim woman?" she complained to me. I gave up on matchmaking and decided to focus instead on finding a long-term solution for Muslim women so they could find their soulmate and experience love, intimacy, and motherhood.

Fortunately, major Muslim organizations have begun to address this problem by doing away with traditional arranged marriages. They now organize American-style speed dating by promoting matrimonial mixers and matchmaking websites.

The millennials have choices we never had.

The baton of matchmaker is now in the hands of young entrepreneurs like Asad Ansari, who with Rumana Rashid, a matchmaker who pairs clients with one another, has developed a website called Beyond Chai. Parents are relieved and grateful that there is a solution—kids today are texting, chatting, and even doing online dating in a way that is not only pleasing to the parents but halal (permissible) too!

WHEN IT WAS TIME TO CHOOSE A LANGUAGE TO STUDY
in school, I decided to study Farsi, partially because it is
considered a very literary and poetic language and partially because
there were hundreds of Iranians on campus, and I felt a bond with
them. I was comfortable socializing with them, visiting their homes,
and sharing their food, because they had cultural and religious similarities to my own background. My aunt and uncle approved of my
friendships with the Iranian crowd—people like us, they thought.
They had no idea that the Iranians I knew were hard partyers, into
alcohol and lots of dancing—they were wilder than most of the
American girls that I had met. I discovered there were Iranian Jews
and a whole Iranian subculture as I became good friends with a stylish girl named Farah with leather pants, kohled eyes, and long, silky
raven hair.

Then one day, the Ayatollah Khomeini returned to Iran, and my
friends all disappeared, including Farah. Seemingly overnight, entire
families vanished from the area—returning to their native country. It
was as if a spaceship had landed and an entire group of people had
been lifted off the planet. I heard rumors that Farah's parents were
back in Iran arranging her marriage and that she now wore the
chador. Some of the young people left because they wanted to join
the Ayatollah Khomeini's revolution to replace the shah of Iran, a
ruthless monarch who had suppressed any opposition. For others it

was because their families wanted them safe and close to home. There were also financial considerations. The shah had been funding the educations of many of these students, and with the revolution, they had lost their patron. And with their departure, we, the remaining students, lost our community. School, like life, just soldiered on. But having lost so many friends, my heart was emptier.

AFTER TWO YEARS AT C.W. POST, I enrolled at the New York School of Interior Design to complete my education, but certain things had not changed. Every morning, Uncle Faroque would drive me for forty-five minutes in rush hour on the Long Island Expressway to the Sutphin Boulevard–Archer Avenue station in Queens, where I would cram myself into the subway with other New York straphangers bound for Manhattan to make my way to the school, on Fifty-sixth Street on the Upper East Side. At the end of the day, Uncle Faroque would wait at the train station to drive me home.

The thirty-odd design students in my class were an eclectic mix of New York City artist types, exotic foreigners, and a sprinkling of Californians. Among them was a former ballerina in her forties who wore all black, always had her hair tied in a bun, and pranced in and out of class on her toes, as if the classroom were her personal music box. There was a tall, tanned Japanese guy who wore white suits that never wrinkled and a Norwegian girl who nearly quit school after a few months to become a fashion model. Everyone was a bit off-kilter, and I fit right in.

HAVING GROWN UP IN a nonpolitical home, at twenty-one I found myself enthralled by a new intellectual set of New Yorkers who were questioning everything. These friends and acquaintances—about twenty men and women—seemed to me to be quintessential liberals. I was like the younger sister to them, hanging on the fringes, watching, and observing—inexperienced, impressionable. Fiery and independent, they brandished their staunch progressive views.

This group was led by my family friend Muz, a Woody Allen–like cynic who loved to provoke me. We would stand inches from each other in his tiny kitchenette and challenge each other with a barrage of questions and accusations about our faith, demanding to know the problem with "our people."

Muz was a slight man with thinning hair and a wry glance that always preceded his pronouncements. He was long out of school, working as an immigration lawyer. Our families in Kashmir were distantly related; he came from a long line of spiritualists and mystics. Given our backgrounds, we were in many ways natural candidates for an arranged marriage. It was never openly discussed, but we were both aware of it. Our families seemed to do everything they could to throw us together. However, we understood and nurtured the depth of our ties and, perplexing our families, slid out of the marriage noose and became close friends. We had a lot in common and were thrilled that we could talk and joke with each other—in our mother tongue, Kashmiri; Muz, who was far worldlier than I was, adopted the role of intellectual mentor. He had a nonconforming philosophical angle on life, which appealed to my burgeoning independence: He was wary of traditional hierarchy and liked to go against the grain.

With my Iranian friends gone, I was left with only Muz with whom to discuss the politics behind the Iranian Revolution. I felt overwhelmed and ill equipped to deal with the daily barrage of negative commentary about the Muslim faith, both in the media and from fellow students. Disturbing images of Muslims demonstrating were flooding the media. I was particularly struck by the footage of protesting women with clenched fists: I had never seen women in Kashmir express that kind of anger. Suddenly, everyone had an opinion on everything, and I had to justify my point of view to others. I found myself constantly confronting the same questions from my new friends: How could I explain the actions that were being perpetrated in the name of my religion?

Muz and I spent a lot of time having intense conversations and arguments. The news on TV made it seem as if Islam had just returned to Iran—but hadn't it always been there? Why couldn't the media comprehend that Khomeini's version of Islam was being exploited for political gain?

Muz emphasized that this was a revolution against the shah, who had westernized the country at the expense of religion. I tried to sort it out more clearly: Khomeini had returned from exile to lead a regressive revolution and set the clock back. I couldn't understand how any religious cleric could allow hostage taking and justify it in the name of Islam. And why were the women all dressed in chadors? I knew what a burqa was, but a chador? And why did they wear only black? Muz reminded me that black was the color of mourning. Did I not remember Karbala'? Karbala', in Iraq, was where the Prophet Muhammad's grandson Hussein was martyred. On the tenth day of Muharram, the first month of the lunar Islamic calendar, the Shia Muslims commemorate his martyrdom; in Kashmir, this is celebrated as a forty-day mourning period in which no weddings or other joyous celebrations take place. Although most Kashmiris are Sunni, out of respect, we would watch the ritual procession as the Shia reenacted Hussein's martyrdom. The streets were wall-to-wall men and boys wearing black; a replica of Hussein's coffin was carried on their shoulders, while a beautiful white horse draped in bridle gear was ushered through the crowd.

I felt distraught; my religion and even my memories of men beating their chests in mourning were now being distorted for political purposes. I felt that someone had to speak up. What was I waiting for? *Why not me?* Those three words had been burning inside me for some time, but once they had pierced my consciousness, I could no longer remain passive.

My weapon would be a pen. I sat down and began a letter to *Newsday,* a leading Long Island newspaper. I did not ask permission or even tell Faroque Chacha or Auntie that I was writing the letter. I thought there was no need; I never expected it to be published. I simply wanted my opinion to be known. Would editors even pay attention to the words of a young woman? It didn't matter. I was writing as much to clarify my own thoughts as I was for the paper. The letter took me days to write as I labored over the wording.

A few days later, in the library, I was stunned to see my opinion in print.

Newsday, Dec. 3, 1979

ISLAM: A LIVING RELIGION

In Iran, Islam has not "returned." It has always been there. The creation of the current explosive situation in Iran has resulted in stereotyping Islam as unmitigatedly harsh in its code of law, intolerant of other beliefs, repressive of women and incompatible with progress. What [the Ayatollah] Khomeini has done in the name of religion is not within the precepts of Islam but is the deeds of a "personal vendetta."

Islam never curbs freedom of thought or allows "holding of hostages" for whatever purpose, nor does it allow the execution of criminals acting under obligation. On the contrary, Islam teaches us Muslims to propagate freedom of thought, justice, forgiveness, honor and sublimity. It is not obsolete or antiquated, but it is a living and flourishing system of life with a just economic system, a well-balanced social organization, codes of civil, criminal and international law, a philosophical outlook upon life and a system of physical instruction.

Khomeini and his followers are exploiting Islam and the popular emotions of the people against the former shah to meet political ends. This has resulted in a misleading introduction of Islam to the Western world. I, as a non-Iranian Muslim, hope that this letter will clear some of the wrong notions and dispel doubts about a comprehensive religion like Islam.

—*Farhat Daisy Khan, Jericho*

I ran my fingers across the page repeatedly as if I could absorb my own words. Then I raced from the library to a newsstand and bought several copies of the newspaper. At home I carefully cut out the page with my letter. I never showed the letter to anyone except Muz. I knew my uncle and aunt would have been shocked to see my name in print. But hundreds of thousands of people would be reading these words, my words!

The one person who would have most appreciated my action, however, was not there to comment. Silently, I thanked Dadaji, because I knew he would have been proud.

ALTHOUGH MY LETTER TO *Newsday* was the first time I was publicly voicing my opinion, there would be many other opportunities in the future to share my views. Eventually, I came to understand that I needed to encourage younger Muslim women to believe that their opinions would contribute to redressing injustices in the name of Islam.

In June 2014, I was asked to address the Interfaith Leaders Conference at the United Nations. My young intern Maleeha, a Pakistani American, accompanied me to the forum to learn how an international agency worked, and she was mesmerized by the experience.

Naturally, I had thought carefully about my short speech. I wanted to address misperceptions about Muslim women, particularly the idea that they are regarded as passive and subjugated. When I spoke, I pointed out that this image was reinforced by media stories that focus on headlines about schoolgirls being victimized by acid attacks, honor killings, or forced marriages or being captured and enslaved, by Boko Haram in Nigeria, for example. The attitudes behind such actions, I said, made me particularly sad because they were perpetrated by leaders with rigid and outdated attitudes that manipulate my faith to justify these outrages. But, I told the group, the best response is to construct religiously grounded arguments to reclaim women's God-given rights.

Maleeha had also been deeply affected by the story of the Chibok girls who were forcibly taken from school. In 2009, Boko Haram had begun an insurgency against the government of Nigeria, and it used the kidnapping as a weapon of war. By snatching young girls from the comfort of their school dormitories, they announced their vision of their caliphate, in which, they claimed, "everything Western and non-Islamic will be forbidden," including education. And yet their dream in fact revealed their disdain for the Quran, which emphasizes education, and exhibited their disregard for the Prophet Muhammad, who said, "The seeking of knowledge is obligatory for every Muslim, even if you have to go to China." While the mainstream U.S. media treated the kidnapping of the two hundred girls by Boko Haram as something that might have happened on a distant planet, for young Maleeha it was deeply personal. As she agonized over what could be done, I thought back to when I had first expressed my own opinion publicly and encouraged her to share her views on our organization's blog. Here is an excerpt of what she wrote for the American Society for Muslim Advancement (ASMA):

I'm a senior in high school, and I'm getting ready to graduate and go off to college. I was taking final exams a few weeks ago. The girls who attended the Chibok Government Girls Secondary School in Nigeria were taking their finals just two weeks before I was. They were studying to become professionals. We go to college to do the same.

The media did not pay close attention to these girls at first, yet they could be any of us. More than 200 girls were kidnapped in mid-April, and it's almost June. These girls still have not been rescued, and we can't forget about them.

I'm not a foreign policy analyst. I don't know all the strategic ins-and-outs on how to conduct global counter-terrorism efforts. But I do know one thing: how dare anyone take the right to an education away from my sisters.

In 2017, after three painful years, eighty-two Chibok girls were released from their captivity and reunited with their parents in Nigeria's capital, Abuja. I wept and cheered as fathers gripped their daughters in tight hugs, while others picked them up and swung them in the air, and mothers shrieked with joy, wiping streaking tears from their daughters' faces. And I thought of Maleeha and wondered if she was watching this on television too. I hoped she was and that she felt joy at their release, just as she had empathized with their desire to pursue an education. She had used her voice to speak for them, and in identifying with those schoolgirls, she had brought me—and all who had read her words—closer to them too.

CHAPTER

II

O N A COLD FEBRUARY DAY, AUNTIE AGAIN KNOCKED ON my bedroom door. She sat on my bed and motioned for me to join her. I envisioned yet another suitor, but this was about something far worse. Moji had died. I was unable to speak; my life had in a moment changed forever. But through my tears, I knew that Moji would never really leave me. Since my birth, she had been the interpreter of my life, the visionary of my future. She had seen a path for me. Now it was up to me to bring those dreams to reality. And with each step I took, I knew Moji would be by my side. Moji was everywhere.

Not long after Moji's death, I saw myself in a dream, sitting on a winged horse, ascending into the sky with neither saddle nor reins, completely fearless. Not understanding the dream, but sensing its spiritual significance, I immediately wrote to Dadaji in Kashmir, hoping he could interpret its meaning. When the *par avion* envelope arrived, I excitedly ripped it open, but to my deep disappointment, the letter simply said, *It's a good dream*, with no further interpretation.

Without my knowledge, however, Dadaji had summoned my parents to his study to tell them about the contents of my letter. My mother felt dread, anticipating some transgression. "What in the world has Daisy written?" she asked my father. "What has she done now?"

When they entered Dadaji's study, my parents found him in his usual spot behind his desk looking out the garden window. He told my parents that I had experienced a true dream. Dadaji went on to explain that in this dream, I was ascending to the heavens on the white, winged horse Buraq. Buraq, as they well knew, was the horse that miraculously took the Prophet Muhammad from Mecca to Jerusalem and back in one night. One day, my grandfather told them, "Farhat will be a mystic, a seeker of God. She will call others to faith and meet a pious, noble man."

My parents were puzzled. I was studying to be an architectural designer in America. What could this mean? Dadaji simply answered that this dream would also shape my fate.

Because the dream had appeared soon after Moji's death, I thought that perhaps it was a message from her from the heavens. It reminded me of the dream I'd had when I was a child, lying with my head in her lap. Much later, when I learned of my grandfather's interpretation, I came to believe in its power.

AFTER GRADUATING FROM DESIGN SCHOOL, I was surprised at how easy it was to find a job. I worked in Manhattan for an eccentric Indian architect who was always searching for new clients. Along with measuring the subbasement of the entire Queensboro Bridge, my job included buying a baguette from a neighborhood bakery every morning and brewing strong French espresso. Although I acquired some skills, there was one drawback: I never got paid a dime. Each week, for six months, my employer would assure me the check was in the mail. When my aunt and uncle learned that I had not been paid, they insisted that I find a real job with a real salary. Fortunately, one of my neighbors helped me find a job at a prestigious architectural firm called SLS Environetics.

Having a paying job helped resolve another issue. I had begun to realize that I had outgrown my cosseted girlhood in Jericho; now that I had graduated from college and had a job, it was no longer fitting that I continue to impose on my aunt and uncle. It was time for me to shape my own destiny. Within weeks, in the summer of 1982, I found a roommate and moved to Queens.

Looking back at the young woman I was, I see she was restless and agitated. There was a current running through her veins; she was ready to plug into something bigger than herself. She desperately wanted to be part of something, but it had not yet occurred to her that being herself alone might be enough. She had yet to discover who she was. She was educated but inexperienced. She was on a threshold.

When my grandfather learned that I had moved out of my uncle's house, he immediately wrote a letter to Faroque expressing disappointment in me. Dadaji asked why a single girl would live on her own—after all, I was meant to live with my family until I got married. Wasn't that the condition under which I had been sent to America? I don't know how my uncle responded, but miraculously, my aunt and uncle didn't try to interfere with my plans. To most people, my tiny steps to independence would have seemed modest, but I felt like an intrepid explorer, boldly forging across the border, moving from Long Island to Queens for a short stay and later to New York City's Upper West Side.

I spent my time like all the other young women trying to make it in New York City—working hard during the day and then, at night, bouncing from dinners to late nights at trendy clubs—and, now that I was free of Uncle Faroque, going on dates with a string of completely ineligible men. I was in sync with my counterparts in the rat race, but I was discovering that the experience wasn't emotionally rewarding. Though I was embracing an American lifestyle, I did not want to do so at the expense of certain moral values.

Yet I longed to be like the other young women I saw on the subway. Whatever stop life took them to, they could jump off and explore without guilt, repression, or repercussion. My gay designer friend Mario suggested I go into therapy—which was then the "in" thing to do—to help me come to terms with my conflict. Unfortunately, my therapist began planting a seed in me, implying that my parents were the root of my problems. In his westernized view, my parents had sent me off to America for eight years, leading to a sense of abandonment. I rejected his analysis and left him, but I still felt conflicted.

I began to feel a gravitational pull to art events, and I especially found solace in art galleries. One day, I went to an exhibit of Joan Miró's paintings at a gallery on Fifty-seventh Street. The combination of abstract and surreal fantasy enthralled me. One lithograph in particular caught my eye, of a tunnel of light descending from a mountaintop onto a man. In a blink, I was transported from Manhattan to Moji's lap and to my dream of God. Was a message being conveyed to me? Then I recalled how surprised I had been as a girl at my ability to spontaneously express my creativity when I painted the mural on my bedroom wall during my winter vacation in Jammu. I realized that, instead of psychotherapy, I could greatly benefit from art therapy. I felt ready to nurture my creativity, expand my imagination, and maybe progress as an artist. I needed to test the boundaries that felt confining. It was time to live a more self-centered life, without the need for outside approval or oversight. I signed up for what to me sounded like the ultimate expression of art: lessons in *life* drawing!

Although it was inappropriate for me to see naked people, I also knew it was not the gravest of sins. I took comfort in the fact that no one would know my offense besides God, who, like Mummy, was always compassionate. After all, God knew me best and would understand my dilemma. But when I entered the studio at New York School of the Arts, I was not prepared for the cultural shock that confronted me head on. I found myself surrounded by a display of stark-naked models—both male and female—standing on pedestals. For weeks, I was deeply uncomfortable and avoided looking at or drawing their private parts.

Although drawing the human body was challenging at first, gradually I began to see the form rather than the function. My eyes were engrossed in capturing that form; my hands were focused on creating lines and blending in shadows. Over eight weeks I drew the upper torso, limbs with muscle tone, and deeply set, expressive eyes. After completing four detailed sketches, I felt a sense of accomplishment and freed from any mental shackles I might have had. When the semester ended, so did my life drawing experiment. I hung my works of art proudly on the white walls of my Queens apartment, which I shared with a Trinidadian girl named Betty.

As a young designer, I was influenced by the minimalist look, which Mies van der Rohe characterized as "less is more." My make-shift bedroom was sparse. My prized Takashima sound system was placed on glass-and-chrome shelves, and my headless platform bed was pushed against the opposite wall. The only splash of color was the magenta Chinese silk comforter. All the walls were bare except one, where I had hung a charcoal line drawing of a woman's bust that I had purchased at an art event. Hanging this sketch in my private space marked my independence and my ultraliberal outlook on life.

Dadaji was visiting our family in New York and insisted that he visit me in my new home. I was excited and worried at the same time. Would he be disappointed that I was living in a $175-a-month apartment in Queens? Would he be glad to see me as a financially independent career girl? Then a feeling of dread came over me. Should I remove my life drawings and the sketch of the woman's bare chest? I was certain my grandfather would feel offended by the display of nakedness.

I asked Betty for counsel, and she said, "Don't you want him to see you for who you really are?" The truth is, part of me was rebelling against everything I felt constrained by, but another part of me longed for Dadaji's approval. Even more than that, I wanted to test the reaction of the one person whose opinion I valued the most. I needed to know how he would react. So, I let the purchased painting hang on the wall, with the rationalization that Dadaji would not invade my privacy by venturing into my room. As Dadaji and I sat sipping tea at the small dining table in the hallway, he asked what projects I was working on.

When I mentioned a "big international bank," he was impressed. "Any hobbies?" he asked.

I said that I had taken art classes. "I can draw portraits now!" I told him.

Before departing, he said, "Will you not give me a full tour?"

Dadaji was too clever for me. I walked him first into Betty's bedroom, then into our shared bathroom and kitchen, and finally I opened the curtain to enter my makeshift bedroom where the nude drawing was clearly visible.

Dadaji was his usual cool self: He did not blink an eye. He just looked around, smiled wryly, and murmured, "Artist?"

Embarrassed that he might be alluding to the bust on the wall, I said, "It was a gift."

He knew I was bluffing, and I felt embarrassed for being smug. As he was leaving, he put his hand on my head and prayed to God that I be granted special favor. "May you guide her," he prayed, "and keep her on the straight path."

WOMEN ELBOWING THEIR WAY
INTO THE DISCOURSE

. . .

For years, I rarely thought of myself as a "Muslim woman." I was simply a Muslim, born in Kashmir, who lived in the United States. As Americans went to war in Afghanistan, there were daily news reports of atrocities being committed against women. Suddenly, I received a request from the Asia Society, asking me to serve on a panel titled "Muslim Women." I worried that the American public was beginning to perceive Muslim women only through the prism of politics. I prepared well for the panel and conveyed my reality as a Muslim woman to the audience. But afterward, I began to feel unsettled; I had that same feeling I had experienced as a young woman who was rebelling for self-definition. I was ready to rebel again, but whom was I rebelling against? I asked myself. Against the pundits who framed the discourse for 750 million Muslim women? Against the men with outdated attitudes, who demeaned my faith? I felt a sense of urgency and found myself turning in the direction of art, both because I was an artist and because of the ancient and revered link between Muslims and art. Art has great power. It is transformative and can speak on a multitude of levels, gently and with emotion.

I had begun to follow the work of several contemporary women artists and was curious to see how they responded to

the societal challenges that had originated from the hostile en-
vironments they lived in. How were they continuing their artis-
tic and cultural heritages? So in 2003, with the help of an
aspiring curator, Ayse Turgut, I organized an exhibition called
Revealing Truths: Muslim Women Artists *at A Ramona Studio*
in New York City. My aim was to use the artists' voices to am-
plify the hidden talents of Muslim women. I hoped that through
their creative impulses the artists I featured would lift up the
truth of Islam, a truth that has inspired positive social change
for fourteen hundred years. The stated aim of the show was to
increase public awareness about the work of contemporary
Muslim artists while at the same time challenging the stereo-
types of Muslim women perpetuated by the media.

Revealing Truths *was a monthlong exhibition held in New*
York City showcasing three distinguished contemporary Mus-
lim women artists whose works were innovative yet traditional:
Egyptian artist Heba Amin; Salma Arastu, an Indian artist who
had converted to Islam from Hinduism; and Moroccan artist
Salima Raoui. Each of them blended Islamic ideals of art and
expressed them within a contemporary vision.

Putting together the exhibition, I realized how heavily influ-
enced I had been as an artist by the modalities of Western art. I
had not been creating; instead, I recognized, I had been copying.
The contemporary women artists deeply impressed me. They
spoke eloquently through their original works—they suggested
their Islamic purpose, their values, and their identities. Most
important, they were developing a culture that would be cre-
ative and dynamic.

On November 13, 2017, my friend Atiya circulated a Rutgers Today *article about her daughter, and my former intern*
Zahra Bukhari. Zahra and Usra Attalla, both Rutgers students,
had co-founded the Muslim Feminist Artists collective. In a

photograph that accompanies the article, they are standing proudly in front of their first exhibition, Hello My Name Is, which showcased their works Beyond East and West *and* Where the Lines Shift.

Just as I had felt the need to tackle stereotypes of Muslim women, Zahra had much the same motivation fourteen years later. When I read her words "My image speaks louder because it already defies the stereotypes of what a Muslim woman looks and acts like" and "We have a responsibility to do something," I felt sad that not much had changed. But I was proud and felt confident that millennials like Zahra had taken the reigns and not allowed others to define them.

CHAPTER

12

AN ELABORATE CARD WITH GOLD LETTERING AND RAISED borders arrived in the mail one day: an invitation to the wedding of my sister Gudi. Gudi had been introduced to her husband, Baba, by extended family. He was the only son among four daughters in a shipping magnate's family. When Baba first saw Gudi, he immediately knew he wanted to marry her. She felt the same way. But when I first heard the news, I was incredulous. I had not even known she was serious about a man. Of course, I was completely out of the loop. This was 1981, and in Kashmir, international calls were complicated to arrange as well as costly. People were still relying on mail as a main source of communication. Having not seen my family for eight years, I was determined not to miss the joyous occasion.

I immediately bought my plane ticket to Kashmir, intending to use my vacation time to stay two weeks. I needed to secure a reentry visa, which most H-1 visa holders obtained from Canada. However, since my plane was stopping over in London, I expected to obtain my reentry visa there. To my shock and dismay, the American embassy in London refused to issue the necessary visa. Instead, they instructed me to return to my country of origin and secure my reentry visa from the U.S. embassy there. The endless red tape of appeals dragged on for a month, leaving me heartbroken about missing my sister's wedding.

When I finally walked into my ancestral home, Khan Manzil, proudly wearing my stylish American dungarees that were patched and torn at the knees, I expected a rousing welcome. Instead, one of my aunts commented, "Oh my God, we thought America was rich—why are her trousers in shreds?" In retrospect, I realized that they expected to see me transformed into a sophisticated New Yorker, and instead I resembled the American hippies who frequented Kashmir.

My new American style and attitude did not resonate well with my family. For the first time in my life, I felt uncomfortable in my own home. I didn't realize how much, in their eyes, I had changed. But even Dadaji had changed when he went to America—how could they have expected that I would not? I felt like I was on a dock with one foot on the planks and another in a wobbly boat that was drifting slowly away from shore. The slightest breeze, I feared, would tip me into the waves.

At the first opportunity, I confronted my mother and asked why she had let me leave home. It was as if I had absorbed my therapist's analysis and was blaming her for the fact that I no longer fit in.

My mother immediately reassured me that not a single day had passed that she had not thought of me. She had endorsed my leaving for my own good, she said, as she and Papaji had both known I would never be happy staying in Kashmir. Her beautiful, sad eyes begged me to understand. Had I forgotten how I had longed to go to America? How I had needed to be in a place where I could pursue my love of art? Mummy held me close, and for a moment, it felt so good to be back in that familiar place, to be a child again.

Of course I knew that there was no way I could have realized my potential as an independent, artistic woman in the Kashmir Valley. Rationally, I understood that my mother had selflessly pushed me out of the nest when I had begged to go. But I still felt torn between my old self and my new one, between my Kashmiri identity and my American one. I returned to New York a confused and conflicted woman. Then, just a short time after my return to America, I learned that my sister Fifi was getting married. There had been no mention of a man in Fifi's life when I was visiting Kashmir. What had happened in my absence?

It turned out that a "nice man from Pune, India" had sent my parents a proposal for Fifi, and surprisingly she had accepted.

Did my sister know this man? No, as it turned out. But he was a very good match for her, my mother assured me. He was a self-made man, a chartered accountant, and was taking care of his entire family.

I was stunned. My own sister—my independent, smart sister Fifi—was now a doctor and was willing to have an arranged marriage! And my mother seemed pleased! How could this be considered "standing on your own two feet"? I remembered the whispered talks Fifi and I had had out on the rooftop under the stars when she and I had shared dreams of falling in love. My values had shifted to the point where I could no longer understand my own sister.

I called Fifi to talk some sense into her. But she explained that, though she'd hesitated for a while, she had decided it was a "good proposal." She was twenty-eight, well past the marriageable age. She knew she needed stability, and he was the right man.

Frankly, I was also worried that Fifi was setting a precedent for me. The parade of potential husbands that had been presented to me appeared like a movie in my mind, each holding out a wedding ring as he walked by. Their faces were a blur. It didn't matter—they all seemed the same.

And then my sister told me that Moji had appeared to her in a dream and said, "He is the man for you. No one else!" Fifi felt that it was a sign that validated her decision. I didn't have an answer to the power of a dream—or to Moji. I too trusted Moji.

Fifi believed in her decision, and so I accepted it and was happy for her. Although I was heartbroken not to be able to participate in Fifi's wedding, I was overjoyed when my two nieces were born. As an aunt, I discharged my responsibilty very seriously. When Fifi's older daughter, Sana, wanted to pursue her higher education in America, I immediately followed in Faroque Chacha's and Auntie's footsteps. I welcomed Sana into my home, supported her intellectual growth, and played the roles of strict guardian and nurturing mother.

MY BIG FAT
INDIAN WEDDING

...

It never fails; every time there is a big wedding my husband, Feisal, asks the same question: "Why do you Indians and Pakistanis cross oceans, rivers, and mountains to attend a wedding?"

I always give the same reply: "Because our weddings are four days of fun and feast." Having missed both my sisters' weddings, I wanted to make up for lost time and involve myself in every aspect of Gudi's daughter Insha's elaborate summer wedding.

The invitations that arrived from India were embossed with gold motifs on a hot-pink and orange card stock. Four hundred guests were expected at the wedding, with fifty of them from overseas and the rest from the United States. Day one of the June 2016 wedding began with a dinner hosted by my brother Abid at his home in Long Island, in honor of the bride's and groom's families. The real festivities began with sangeet, *an event at which women serenade the bride with music and dance—this was hosted by the groom's cousin in her Manhattan apartment. On the night of* mehndi, *on the third day of festivities, two hundred guests stood wall to wall in a two-story New York restaurant to watch the bride's henna ceremony, in which her hands and feet are painted in intricate paisley designs. Henna is meant to calm the jitters and stress associated with marriage. Women and girls crowded around trays to select colored Hyderabadi bangles with ethnic patterns studded with glittering crystals and cut glass. These had been flown in by an aunt from Hyderabad in India. For the final day, the groom and bride decided to combine the wedding ceremony with the* walima, *which is a reception that the groom's family usually holds.*

In India, white is a color worn by families at the funeral pyre, including for Muslims. But in my studies, I had learned that Arab brides wear white dresses and that it is permissible for a Muslim woman to wear white at her wedding. Although my niece Insha looked like a typical Indian princess in her ivory-colored bridal wear, she also carried out a long-standing American bridal tradition. She wore something old, a seven-strand pearl necklace, which was a family heirloom; she wore something new, a chiffon lehenga, *made by a haute-couture Pakistani designer and gifted to her by her future mother-in-law; she wore something blue, a bangle with sapphires; and finally, she borrowed something from me, a* kundan, *a twenty-two-karat gold and uncut diamond choker that I had worn on my wedding day.*

The marriage ceremony was conducted by my husband outdoors in the lush gardens of a country club. The groom, an elegant American-born man of Pakistani background, was even prepared to ride in on a horse. He was deterred only by the club's rule against horses on the grounds on Saturday.

At the reception, Insha wore a new outfit, a heavily embroidered long gold, red, and beige lehenga *and fitted blouse. Her husband wore a black tuxedo. Together they danced the first dance to Frank Sinatra's "Nothing but the Best."*

When we were deciding on who would make what remarks, we were all struck by a strange coincidence. Insha was getting married on the same date as her parents had, which was also the same date as Mummy and Papaji's wedding. The first person to take the stage was Insha's brother, who said he was looking forward to having another brother and finally being left alone by his domineering sister. Then Gudi took the stage and spoke from the heart. Because she was a widow, she said, Insha was not just a daughter; she was her best confidante, whom she consulted before every decision.

Insha insisted that I give the formal toast at the wedding. I thought about it carefully and decided that I would combine a gracious toast with a roast. First, I began by thanking everyone who had made a long journey, some flying for twenty-four hours, among them friends of Insha's deceased dad who had known her at age eleven, when he had died. Then I reminded Insha of all the long conversations we had had over the years and how every assertion she had made in the past was being reversed. I said to her, "When I told you it was time for you to get married, you said, 'Marriage is not for me.' When I convinced you to look for a mate and you were unable to find the right person, I told you to 'look for a Pakistani.' You laughed and said, 'No way, over my dead body!' Finally, when you got engaged to a handsome Pakistani, you said, 'I want a small wedding.'

"Then we discussed plans for mehndi—*you said, 'No* mehndi *for me. I can't stand henna!'*

"Then we discussed your wedding outfit—you said, 'No red and gold. I don't do bling!'

"I asked you what jewelry you wanted to wear—you said, 'None—I hate jewelry.'

"Then I advised you to learn how to cook, and you said, 'I don't cook. We will eat out!'

"So Insha dear, I just want you to know that you did finally marry, and to a man of Pakistani origin. By American standards your four-hundred-guest list is a big fat wedding; your hands and feet are painted in henna; your embroidered red-and-gold dress is blingy; you are bedecked in jewels; and rumor has it that you are learning how to cook!

"Welcome to married life!"

P.S. Insha has become a great cook, and she prefers to eat at home.

THE CONFLICT IN KASHMIR BEGAN ANEW IN 1987 AND BECAME
relentless and never ending. Even today I am always on edge
waiting for what will come next. In 2012, Papaji was shot in the leg
while attending Friday congregational prayers at the mosque my
grandfather had built. Militants were targeting the chief of police,
whom they shot execution-style, and my father was caught in the
crossfire. The doctor said that the bullet had only just missed his
artery—one millimeter more, and he could have bled to death. Still,
my parents refused to leave Kashmir despite the danger. Papaji stated
firmly that he and Mummy belonged there. It was their home.

I feared for my parents' safety, of course, but there was something
more. I mourned the fact that "our" Kashmir was slipping away. At
the same time, I had known even before I left that it had begun to
disappear.

In the Kashmir Valley, we were always aware of the shifting tectonic plates beneath the fertile land. The Himalayas were deceptively
solid. Under them, though, the earth was always moving, realigning
itself imperceptibly, and when the pressure could no longer be contained, it ripped through our valley in the form of devastating earthquakes. In 1555, during the reign of King Shamsha Shah, a powerful
earthquake struck Srinagar, our very town. It is said that the river
Vitasta changed course at that moment and houses fell into the massive holes that opened in the earth, altering the topography of the

region. Periodically, over the centuries, other massive earthquakes would annihilate the region. But in between, for long stretches of time, often centuries, the land would be quiet, a masquerade of inactivity.

In the late eighties, the environment in New York reminded me of my homeland—a calm awaiting a storm. I carried that feeling with me—I wore a veneer of normalcy while things were shifting within me, awaiting the tectonic eruption that would force the conflicts to come to the fore. Work provided a purposeful distraction as I focused on my career: moving from my first real job as a junior designer at SLS Environetics up the ladder to Warner-Amex and then to a job with Mishra Associates, a firm run by an Indian architect, which allowed me to finally secure a green card. One of my first assignments for Mishra was to help design the first Hindu temple in Flushing, Queens. The hours were long, the work intense, and I liked it that way. As I bent over my drafting table, measuring out the floor plans, choosing motifs for the carvings of the deities for the walls and the *pooja*—the prayer location—and detailing the meticulous drawings for the temple, a wonderland of religious imagery was right in front of me, inches from my face, but my own spirituality remained at arm's length.

Still, I made friends, dated, and took part in Indian cultural activities. But I was only going through the motions. Part of me knew that I was waiting, though at the time, I could not have expressed what for.

Then, in 1989, *The Satanic Verses* exploded onto the scene. Salman Rushdie, a noted writer whose earlier novel *Midnight's Children* had put him on the world map, traced his heritage to Kashmir. But this new book was so inflammatory that he was immediately accused of blasphemy, because of his suggestion that the Prophet Muhammad had been unable to distinguish between revelations sent through the angel Gabriel and the devil's inspiration. This cast doubt on the Quran's authenticity, leaving the reader with the impression that the Quran was the work of the devil, not God's word.

Muslims around the world blamed Rushdie for insulting the Prophet and his family—Rushdie named the Prophet "Mahound" in *The Satanic Verses* and alluded to his wives being prostitutes. Most literary folks felt the book was simply being provocative. Still others scoffed at the whole controversy. I poked and prodded Muz about the novel, calling it "your favorite author's book," but Muz only shrugged. To him, the real shame was that *The Satanic Verses* was not one of Rushdie's best books.

The global conversation polarized Muslims even further when the Iranian cleric, the Ayatollah Khomeini, issued an edict—a fatwa calling for Rushdie's death and those of his publishers. The fatwa came as a shock wave to Americans, as it was outside the realm of normative Western behavior. In Muslim-majority countries and India, where Hindus are a majority, the book was banned and burned, and it ignited fires among some people I knew as well. No one was neutral about it. There were two contradictory forces at work: the West's cherished value of "freedom of expression" and the East's deeply held reverence for all religious icons. And everyone seemed to have an opinion.

Culture clashes of this kind are not new. This one raised many issues—the sensitivity of host cultures to religious sensibilities, what sacrilege is, religious intolerance, and freedom of speech. Those Muslims who opposed Rushdie knew Americans would not tolerate urinating on the American flag, so they wondered why Americans would give a pass to Rushdie for defiantly defecating on something Muslims consider to be sacred. At the same time, they knew that no fatwa calling for death would ever be issued by America. Rushdie went into state-sponsored hiding in London. There were bomb threats to his publishers and to bookstores that carried the book, and attempts on the lives of his translators—his Japanese translator was stabbed to death, and his Italian translator and the head of his Norwegian publisher were seriously injured.

The book left me bewildered, but on principle, I defended it. I could not condone the burning of books. They had been considered almost sacred in our house—after all, the first revelation to the Prophet Muhammad began, "Read [*iqrā*] in the name of thy Lord, who created man and taught him with the pen that which he did not know" (Quran 96:1). The first commandment to Muhammad was to acquire knowledge, to learn from God, to gain an understanding through reading. To me, these lines were an indication of God's great respect for the written word.

My Muslim friends all rallied in support of Rushdie, and we all lobbied to fundraise for the cause. The whole ordeal left me deeply conflicted as it challenged the core of my beliefs. My faith required both critical questioning and reverence for the Prophet, divinity's mouthpiece. On the other hand, for the first time, I got involved in American-style activism and campaigning.

Muz thought that as American Muslims it was our responsibility to clarify the issue. We had to make a clear statement to other Muslims that there was no place for banning books in our religion, and we had to defend our American values. He decided to do this in a full-page ad in *The New York Times*. We would raise the money to get our message out.

Muz and I wrote the statement, and then we circulated it among friends. We tried our best, but we never succeeded in raising enough money for the ad; in fact, as we'd feared, an alternative Muslim narrative never got any traction. For the media, the fatwa against Rushdie and the controversy around it were far more intriguing than explaining that such a fatwa was a fundamental use of censorship to keep people in line.

The experience made me begin to question my own faith. When the Ayatollah Khomeini issued his fatwa against Rushdie, I, like most Americans, reacted to the violence and manipulation of the Islamic faith for political gain. But for me, there was a larger concern. My identity as a Muslim could no longer remain neutral. Islam was being used by extremists to terrorize, hurt, and kill. This madness was not the faith that my family lived by. As I grew more aware of Islamic issues, both in America and around the world, I did not know where to turn. My childhood friend Halima, who had emigrated to the United States at the same time I did, had joined the U.S. military and ended up fighting in the Gulf against fellow Muslims in Desert Storm. Nothing was making sense to me. There were very few Muslims I engaged with socially, and there were few people aside from Muz with whom I could share or discuss my feelings and fears.

On many nights, I would take out the Quran that Dadaji had given me when I left for America and try to understand this ancient text's relevance in the modern world. I had been taught that the Quran is the word of God and must be accepted as such. However, there were many things in the Quran that conflicted with my lifestyle. The question I kept asking myself was how I could accommodate the dictates of the Quran and still have a modern life. These contradictory concerns would ultimately precipitate my spiritual search.

Books and learning had been the foundation of my world, and now two books separated by centuries were pulling that world apart. Each represented a pole of my values. And so I found myself facing a wrenching choice. Was I going to stand with Islam, which seemed so remote and violent, or break away and affiliate with the doubters who now surrounded me, people who scoffed at the seventh-century religion? In some ways, it would have been easier to abandon my religion, but I found that impossible to do. It was part of who I was. I was at a spiritual impasse.

At work, I managed to appear confident and competent, but within me, I felt a roiling turmoil. I knew, of course, that it wasn't just a book that made me feel this way. The images surrounding my religion were so negative that I could no longer defend them or integrate them into my westernized view. Instead I found comfort in my American values.

Internally, I walked away from Islam.

The Rushdie conflict precipitated a full-blown identity crisis for me. When I returned home to Kashmir in 1990, the controversy over *The Satanic Verses* was waiting for me. Not only was I met with criticism, but, worst of all, my own relatives were mocking me. The scandal had influenced them. Acquaintances would shake their heads accusingly and say that only Muslims living in America would read the kind of rubbish Rushdie had published. When I told them that Rushdie was from England, their retort was that America had given him haven; therefore, Rushdie was America's problem. They would look at me suspiciously, as if I were personally harboring Salman Rushdie in my apartment. It pained me to admit that I no longer felt comfortable in either of my countries.

As soon as I returned to Khan Manzil, I rushed directly to my mother's bedroom, my former sanctuary, stood before her, and stated that I hated organized religion and did not want to be part of one anymore. I no longer believed in God, I said. I realized I was acting like a petulant child, but in the presence of my mother, my shell crumbled.

In retrospect, I realized that I had turned to my mother, whom I could unequivocally trust. To my mind my mother was totally non-judgmental and compassionate; I must have known that she would help me through this spiritual malaise. She calmly reminded me that just because I had forgotten God did not mean that He had forgotten me. Tearfully, she vowed to start praying for the day when I would find Him. I proclaimed again that there was no such thing as God, that God was a figment of everyone's imagination. When I was a child, I had not infrequently felt the need to test limits by seeing how far I could push Mummy. I could remember succeeding at upsetting her only one time, when I had misbehaved until she chased me, and while running she fell in the driveway. That was the first time I had felt intense guilt for something my behavior had caused. Now, as an adult, I found I still felt the need to push limits. It wasn't enough for me to have her love—she had to prove it.

My mother's default strategy in response to any outburst was to turn to God. Now she told me she would take me to visit the most important shrines of spiritual healers so that I might have a change of heart and reconnect with my faith. Kashmir is dotted with shrines of saints; in fact, it is called the Valley of Saints. Mummy's theory was that after the storm one needs a balm. Perhaps visiting sacred places could lead to some enlightenment, help her daughter reignite her spiritual commitment or, at least, make sense of things. She mapped out a spiritual excursion for just the two of us.

Early the next day, Mummy enlisted a driver to take us first to the five-hundred-year-old shrine that was dedicated to Baba Reshi. Baba Reshi had been living a life of luxury at the court of the king of Kashmir when, walking in the woods, he saw a colony of forest ants. He noticed the precision with which they functioned and realized this must be God's handiwork. He renounced his worldly existence to serve the common man. A renowned Muslim scholar, he promoted meditation to become close to God. Baba Reshi's shrine and burial place was situated near one of my favorite childhood places, Gulmarg, the "meadow of flowers." More than eight thousand feet above sea level, it was where, on school excursions, we had ridden on horses and glided to the top of the mountain on the world's highest gondola. The shrine was at the center of a huge green lawn that could accommodate thousands of devotees.

As we approached the massive edifice, its three-storied spire came into sight first. People of all religions, especially childless couples, came here to make wishes, joined by tourists entranced by the beauty and history of the region. Baba Reshi had built a mud stove with his own hands to feed the poor, and years later visitors would maintain the stove by plastering it. They believed that when they performed this practice their wish would be fulfilled. Mummy urged me to join the line of people and ask God to grant me my wish, but I was too skeptical. I could not see how rubbing a stove would wipe away my inner conflicts. I wished I had the spirituality to emulate the great saint who rested there, to go through a process of cleansing my heart and purifying my lower self of its reprehensible traits, but the pilgrimage brought me no closer to my faith.

The winding road to the location of our next stop on our pilgrimage route, the Charar-e-Sharif Shrine, felt like the pathway to heaven.

Up and up we drove, winding through lush valleys, fields, and meadows—it was such a dramatic contrast to the concrete jungle of Manhattan. Nestled in this perfection of nature, with the Pir Panjal Mountains as the backdrop, was the five-and-a-half-century-old shrine, a mausoleum of Kashmir's greatest mystic saint, Sheikh Noor ud-Din Wali. Known as the "light of faith," he preached a message of unification that resonated with both Muslims and Hindus:

> We belong to the same parents. Then why this difference? Let Hindus and Muslims together worship God alone. We came to this world like partners. We should have shared our joys and sorrows together.

Mummy reminded me that Sheikh Noor ud-Din believed in the transcendence of God and, like Moji, he preached against indulgence and promoted sharing. Mummy reinforced the ideal taught by Kashmir's mystics—to strive for unity rather than divisions.

A minaret rose from among the multistory buildings, and I heard a muezzin do the call to prayer. I saw people praying, but I felt like an outsider looking through frosted glass. I was still perplexed as to how the religion I was taught, based on ethics and morality and on building harmonious relations—a practice faithfully honored and revered at these shrines—could have been distorted and even smeared so badly. In my mind, if my core identity was shaped by Islam, and if Islam's stature was damaged in the social and religious firmament, then my inner self was likewise damaged, and my relationship with the religion of my childhood was destroyed.

But Mummy wasn't giving up yet. She asked if I would like to visit Moji's grave. She instinctively knew that my love and respect for Moji would transcend my spiritual crisis. When Moji died, I had been in America. I had been devastated, but somehow I had missed—or perhaps I had shut out—the details of her interment. Now my mother told me that Moji had asked to be buried in a place where she would be able to "hear people praying." And so, her wishes were honored when she was laid to rest in the most revered place in Kashmir—on the footsteps of the Makhdoom shrine.

Saint Hazrat Makhdoomi, the patron saint of Kashmir, was called the "lover of knowledge." He had died in Srinagar, not far from our home. To visit this 430-year-old shrine, we had to climb 113 steps, each two feet tall. As Mummy and I ascended, all types of people climbed alongside us—one young man was carrying his old mother on his back; a young mother sobbed at the recent loss of a baby, while a middle-aged man in a suit was strolling crisply up the stairs, as if he were heading to a business meeting. All of them were coming here to seek a safe place to share their pain. Everywhere I looked, supplicants were praying or imploring God. Some wishes were simple: "*Medad, medah,* help, help, so I can pass my exam," prayed one young man. "Please let my husband heal from the accident," sobbed a woman. "Don't take him from us!"

Did these people believe in miracles? Did they really think that once they reached the top of the shrine, they would be miraculously freed from their pain?

No, Mummy said—but they had *iman,* faith, that they *would* heal. She was confident that I too would heal.

But I wasn't sick—just confused about the way my religion was being hijacked by fanatics. Wasn't there a difference? If God could not discern between the two, how could He be of help?

Finally, we reached the threshold of the shrine. Hundreds of pigeons swooped and circled around us. Flowers laced the arabesque lattice windows of the wooden structure while intoxicating rose incense burned my nostrils. Quranic chanting brought back childhood memories of Moji. I had never missed her so much as in this place. In America, there seemed to be no place for me to seek solace and renewal with the souls of those I had held close and lost. Here, each step was like a remembrance of a moment or a prayer. But still Moji remained out of reach.

My mother, who knew me so well, squeezed my arm and suggested we get some *Tabarrok,* blessed holy water and rose petals mixed with sugar pellets, dates, and dried fruits—edibles that devotees had prayed over all night so that the supplicants would receive divine blessings.

As we peeked through the lattice openings at the tomb of a true saint, I felt myself teetering from the East to the West and back again. It all felt so extreme. I was standing in this spot communing with a saint while ayatollahs were thrusting a rigid dogmatic Islam at me, books were being burned, and throngs of Iranians were chanting, "Death to America"—all in the name of their Islamic revolution. Was I to be a righteous woman driven by piety, as my grandmother had expected—or was I a woman who prioritized personal independence and freedom, the New York version of myself? Would I revere, or would I mock? Or could I be both women? Would rejecting my New York self bring me any closer to Moji? Or to my faith? Were any more answers to be had here, at the top of these sacred steps, than in my office at the top of the World Trade towers?

Before we left, Mummy asked me to join her in *sajdah*—which meant prostrating ourselves on the earth as the ultimate sign of humility.

How easy it would have been to play a role, to fall on my knees, to prostrate myself, to do whatever it took to make Mummy happy. But that seemed duplicitous and unworthy of any religion or morality. I just couldn't do it.

What I wanted to say to Mummy was "I can't feel what you feel." But if I had lost something in America, I had gained something else—the ability to discern for myself my own path. I did not want to follow blindly.

As we walked to Moji's burial place, memories of sitting with her on her prayer mat, counting on her prayer beads as I faded into sleep on her lap, enveloped me. I realized that my faith might have deserted me, but Moji never had. I stood in front of her grave and prayed for her soul. At that moment, I forgot that I was faithless. I wished Moji were alive to guide me, but all I could do was whisper a plea, begging her to keep an eye on me and my lost soul. Prayers from the loudspeaker, chanted day and night, floated through the air. Moji's wish to be able to hear prayers for eternity had been granted.

Moji seemed so rested and I, so conflicted. My identity was still in formation. I was no longer just a Kashmiri. I was also an Indian and an American, a New Yorker and a Muslim. As a designer, I understood that colors individually are crystalline and clear, but when you mix them, their essence can be enhanced, diluted, or lost, depending on the proportions. Mix yellow and blue together, and you can have a myriad of greens. Red and yellow can produce a sherbet orange or a fiery coral. But if you blend shade upon shade upon shade, the color wheel fails you, and you end up with shades of gray or black.

As we ended our pilgrimage and headed home, we drove by the famed Dal Lake, a jewel of the Kashmir Valley with a backdrop of snowcapped mountains, a vast sheet of water reflecting the carved wooden balconies of the houseboats and the hand-painted gondola-like *shikharas* that ferried travelers to and from the houseboats. Our family had often visited the lake while I was growing up. My mother asked if I remembered when Papaji had taught me to swim there.

Yes, I remembered. In Muslim society, girls are generally restricted from learning how to swim because of modesty issues. But my father did not agree with this. While Papaji did believe in observing modesty, this was secondary to his strong feelings that his daughters should be enabled to master anything, especially survival skills. He believed that we needed to learn to swim so that we would not drown.

My father had given me a fat, inflated tire tube to help me float, but I had stubbornly slipped out of the inner tube to see how far I could make it on my own. Doing the doggie paddle, somehow I managed to swim out farther than I'd meant to. As I lay on my back and drifted, gazing upward at the blue sky, I suddenly realized that I could no longer see the houseboat. It would have made sense to panic, but instead I just lolled on my back in the water, ignorant of danger, defiant even, until I felt a jerk on my arm. Papaji had suddenly appeared at my side. What was I doing, he demanded, trying to drown? He grabbed my hand and pulled me safely back to the boat.

In many ways, this experience could serve as a metaphor for the state of my mind at the time. I was drifting defiantly from the familiar shore, the safe place, the ties that had connected me to it for so long slipping from my grasp. This time, my mother had reached out to grab me and bring me back to the shores of my faith, but I had refused to take her hand.

I left Kashmir still unsettled. It would be five years before I saw my family again.

A NIGHTINGALE POETESS AND
THE REBEL SAINT

. . .

As we huddled together in the snowy winter months of Kash-
mir, we were regaled with tales of the legacy of the historical
women poets of Kashmir. Two of these, Habba Khatoon and
Lalla Ded, broke down barriers in their time, challenging cen-
turies of ingrained beliefs with words of gossamer and thoughts
of steel that built bridges between cultures and religions.

Habba Khatoon, born in 1554, also known as Zoon, is
called the Nightingale of Kashmir, as well as the Poet Queen of
Kashmir, since at the age of sixteen, after an early brutal and
nomadic life, she married the crown prince of Kashmir, Yusuf
Shah Chak. When her beloved prince was held prisoner, Zoon
wrote poems of sorrow, longing, and separation that live on to
this day. "Love has consumed me from within," she wrote. "He
has cast me into a hot oven / And is burning me to cinder."

Lalla Ded truly captured my imagination and, in many
ways, inspired me to be the person I am today. Born in the four-
teenth century, she is one of the great thinkers and spiritualists
of Kashmir's medieval period and is known as the rebel saint of
fourteenth-century Kashmir. Her writings connect two critical
periods in Kashmiri thought and history—the pre-Islamic lore
of early spiritualists and the later Islamic academic saints.

Lalla had no personal possessions but plenty of revolution-

ary ideas. She wrote more than two hundred poems expressing her soul's desire to experience the divine. A true agent for change, Lalla was a master spiritual strategist at finding the common ground between various creeds and religions. As a bridge-builder, she defined religious humanism in Kashmir by blending core values of Hinduism and Islam and de-emphasizing their conflicts and differences.

This skill, in particular, had resonance for me: The idea of a woman leading the way to a spiritual and cultural bridge was revolutionary in Lalla's time, but it is also disruptive in our own! In many ways, I have a Kashmiri countrywoman from the fourteenth century to thank for the direction of my life's work.

Lalla brilliantly orchestrated a remarkable balancing act. In the mid-fourteenth century, Islam and Brahmanism (the religion of the highest caste of Hindus) conflicted with each other, and most people found it difficult to decide what was true and what was false. A mastermind was desperately needed to guide people. In A.D. 1335, Lalla stepped forward. She knew that the ideological struggle had to be resolved in order for the spiritual crisis to end, so she fused the two spiritual traditions, exotic Islam and indigenous Brahmanism. She intrinsically understood the micronegotiations necessary in the face of changing social dynamics—the wisdom of emphasizing the finest commonalities and diplomatically discarding aspects that would confront and challenge impenetrable cultural traditions and frustrate the spirit of advancement. The outcome was the enrichment of Kashmiris' own multiple identities and their fusion into one cohesive national identity. From unity, Lalla promised, came strength and power. Such a message would resonate as well today as it did almost seven hundred years ago.

Lalla preached her principles in the idiom of the masses, weaving lyrical words with relevance. There were messages that touched universal nerves in ways that still resonate today. She questioned women's relegation to secondary positions and subjugation in ritual and shone a light on the marginalization and objectification of women. And she introduced a creed that stressed the fundamental unity of religions, the nonduality of God, and religious humanism—including the equality of all human beings. Her creed was then adopted by King Zainul Abidin, the most revered king in Kashmiri history, extolled for his religious tolerance, who ushered Kashmir into a decades-long golden era.

For me, Lalla creates another bridge—the link between the fading past of my beloved motherland and the rising future of my adopted country. The vision and practical application of religious humanism combined with personal responsibility that she proposed over six hundred years ago can be embraced today by both nations and individuals. I often remind myself of her words "The person who has no ideal and cherishes no purpose in life, the one who is engrossed in self-love and blinded by selfishness, does not exist in reality; he is dead, though living."

The doctrine of religious humanism as envisioned by Kashmir's poetesses can serve to heal the divisions created in the name of religions. I hope people today will rediscover their words and take them to heart.

CHAPTER
14

I N A WAY, I HAD SPENT MY LIFE IN THE CLOUDS. I HAD TRAVELED
from the world's tallest mountain range to the top of the world's
tallest office complex—one forged from nature, the other by industry. My office at Shearson Lehman Brothers was on the 106th floor
of Two World Trade Center. Approaching the urban canyon surrounding these buildings was not entirely unlike being at the base of
the Himalayas; both the buildings and the mountains shared phenomenal height and majesty, and both in their own way provided
anchors for the communities sprawled out below. When I was at my
sky-high desk, I could look out and see the molten steel blue of the
Hudson River, the Statue of Liberty, and Ellis Island, where Dadaji
had arrived in America so long ago. In a thunderstorm, it could feel
like being at the epicenter of the lightning. Often, we would see little
planes gliding by and cruise ships docking in the Hudson. Every
time there was some big event such as fireworks on the Hudson, we
didn't mind working late to enjoy the very best view. It was like walking on air every single day because you were literally in the clouds.

Working at Shearson advanced my professional career as well as
my personal growth. My boss, Anne, a six-foot-tall redheaded Texan,
was brilliant and served as my mentor. I hung out with my Italian
co-worker Susan, who became my best single buddy. We would shop
together. When I told my Irish secretary, Mary, what it was like
growing up in a Muslim household in Kashmir and being sent to the

Presentation Convent run by Irish nuns, she screamed in sympathy and gave me a big hug. There was Orlando from the Dominican Republic, an immigrant like myself in a land of immigrants struggling to define our identities. I remember Bob, a flamboyant gay man who died of AIDS. There was Jackie, now deceased, an accomplished African American woman, a Princeton grad, who tried to help me understand what it was like to be black in America. There was the department head, Sheryl, a staunch feminist in her fifties. She gave bonuses and raises to young women like me to compensate for pay inequities. "You work just as hard as the men around here, and you deserve the same compensation," she'd say.

There was no Internet in those days. There was no email. We didn't even have computers. There were fax machines and telephones and regular mail. We had very efficient, old-fashioned secretaries who took care of our work. It was an ancient era, the 1980s, only thirty years ago.

MY JOB AT SHEARSON LEHMAN BROTHERS at last afforded me the budget to move into my own alcove studio apartment on the Upper West Side. I took pains to create a décor that blended Indian and American sensibilities, and I invited Arfa Auntie and Uncle Faroque to see the results. I could hardly wait to show off my new, independent life, as well as my decorating skills, and to introduce them to my pet parakeet. But when they walked in, my uncle had barely looked around before he announced, "First they get a bird, then a cat, and then there is no marriage!" I realized that I could frame my college diploma; put on a so-called power suit with a skirt, jacket, and smart accessories; and blend in with the hordes of young, hopeful women trying to make their way in the New York jungle, but to my family—and perhaps even myself—I would never be one of them. Though my family applauded my career path, I needed to be "settled"—married—to be considered a real success.

All my life I had imagined a kind of peaceful coexistence between marriage and career. Didn't my aunt and sisters work while they raised their families? Marriage was surely in the cards for me some-day, but I had apparently reversed what was considered the natural order of things. Traditional dictates were colliding with my fierce sense of independence. I wanted to experience life, to get to know myself first and spend time with me, and then later I could share my life with someone else. I was confident I could have it all.

Was my belief a matter of faith or simply a force of habit, similar to the way that Faroque Chacha had worn the same style of plaid silk nightgown every single night for as long as I could remember? It was confusing. Did my family see me as a success, a rebel, or just a pa-thetic spinster on her way to a lonely life with a parakeet? I knew that there was a risk in delaying marriage. In my culture, single, accom-plished women carried a liability; they were considered unattractive to traditional families and intimidating to eligible single men. I wanted to believe in who I thought I was, but wherever I turned, there seemed to be different expectations.

As a young architectural apprentice, I had become fascinated by the concept of space. Space, often more so than walls, helps us to define our relationship to our environment. How space is used and allocated really tells a story about the people who inhabit it. By changing the spatial dynamics, you can change the story. Since I was working as an architectural designer, I was asked to review the final floor plans for the new mosque that Uncle Faroque was spearheading on Long Island, which was to be the first mosque in the area. Some-thing about the floor plan was immediately disconcerting, and I called a meeting with the architect. I pointed out that the main prayer hall showed a capacity for five hundred men. But where would the women pray?

The architect informed me that the women would be praying in the basement. I knew it was important to be courteous to this man, but I could barely contain my distress. I pointed out to him that women would not be happy praying in the basement.

The architect shrugged. That was how all mosques were designed, he said. The women were not in the same room as the men. In Kashmir, however, women were in the same room. They simply prayed in a different section of the room.

The architect, who was not a Muslim, was working from his idea of a community. But he had made a big assumption. Clearly, he didn't understand this template for a mosque design or its goals. The fact was, most of the women who would be members of this mosque were modern and independent, including successful doctors, lawyers, and other professionals. Most of them had their own bank accounts, and in fact, their contributions were helping to fund the construction of the mosque. Yet this unequal division of the sexes had apparently been considered and, by this point, approved—or, at best, ignored—by the congregation, including perhaps my own uncle. It seemed anti-thetical to me that a new modern suburban mosque would reflect antiquated attitudes toward the position of women. For centuries, the sexes had been segregated in mosques—I knew that. I had even accepted it. But separate didn't have to be unequal, as I knew from my experience growing up in Kashmir. Relegating women to the basement was another thing entirely. In terms of pure square footage, the basement did have space, but it had no windows. Whoever wor-shipped there would be invisible to those aboveground; they would be in a secondary space, apart from the lifeblood—they would be the feet, not the head. The message this setup sent was clear: Women were second-class citizens. But this mosque was led by my family. I had a say, and I intended to exercise it.

Since Uncle Faroque had led the initiative to found the new mosque, I reported to Auntie that the architect's plan showed the women praying in the basement. Did she know that?

She frowned. No, of course the women wanted to be in the same hall as the men. She agreed that the architect's assumption needed to be corrected immediately.

"So how many rows should we allocate to the women, then?" the architect asked.

"*Rows?*" I repeated back to him. I explained that he needed to al-locate a full half of the seating space for women! Husbands and wives would be coming together to this mosque, and the women needed to have the same amount of space, not less.

The next time I saw the floor plans, I was delighted to see equal spaces assigned to both sexes in the main prayer hall. The men would be sitting in front and the women in the back with no visible barrier between them. As tradition dictated, the men and the women would continue praying separately and with a full view of the prayer leader. Had I been involved at the initial stages, I would have recommended men on the left and women on the right with no visible barrier, but this seemed to be the best compromise I could reach.

Some men in the community were irritated by this change, but they were quickly overwhelmed by most of the women, who now spoke with amplified voices. The women expressed pride, for who they were and for the stature granted them with the rearranged space. A few decades later, I was proud that the Westbury mosque was named one of the top ten spiritual spaces in America in an article in the *Huffington Post*.

On the coldest day of December 1988, the mosque broke ground. When the building was completed, I was doubly proud—of the carpet, a deep teal green with a woven motif of arched windows and arabesque filigree, which I had designed, and of the fact that there was equal space on the main floor for men and women. This design set the tone and raised the bar for how women were treated in the community and helped to erase vestiges of inequality. Though I didn't know it at the time, this dedication to the equality of women in the Muslim faith would become my life's work.

BIRTHING A
WOMEN'S MOSQUE

...

Sherin Khankan, a young Danish woman whom I met at our 2006 WISE conference, told me she could not identify with traditional Islamic values that have been normalized through patriarchy over centuries. She was interested in women's rights and in promoting Islam's progressive values. She was especially interested in female interpretation of scripture. She was looking forward to the work of the Global Muslim Women's Shura Council—a consensus body—which we were creating and which would enable women to issue egalitarian responses to women's issues.

People have different reactions to exclusion. At times, I have felt outside the circle; at other times, I have tried to abandon the circle. Another choice involves redrawing the circle altogether. In 2001, when she was twenty-five, this woman, Sherin, who had been born in Denmark to a Syrian Muslim father and a Danish Christian mother, experienced gender exclusion from mosques in Copenhagen. She attended a class on imam education, where the room was full of male imams, and although she finished the course, she was not allowed to apply for an imam position. But she learned that women's mosques in China, led by imamas, women prayer leaders, have existed since the end of the Ming dynasty, emerging from communities that stressed re-

ligious education for women. There, female imams play the same roles as their male counterparts, and women of faith have equal status.

Following her return to Denmark, Khankan wrote two books on Islam and became a well-known author and academic in Europe. In 2014, she announced that she was planning Denmark's first women's mosque, which would focus on families. Her hope was to bring together traditionalistic Muslims and younger, more progressive ones such as herself who had not felt at home in Islam. Sherin immediately was accused by traditionalists of "diluting Islam." She countered by stating that the goal of this mosque was to bring those people whom these traditionalists had pushed away back to faith.

In 2016, ten years after she attended the WISE conference in New York, Sherin's dream came true. She founded the Maryam Mosque in Copenhagen, named for the Arabic form of Mary. An imama who was fluent in Arabic delivered the first sermon. Sherin has a sense of humor about her journey. "We still have no money for a carpet," she says, "but we have an imama and four walls."

Today, women continue to create a path for spiritual renewal by establishing their own sacred spaces in cities like Los Angeles and Bradford, England. They are setting a new trend, along with male scholars like Jasser Auda, who are supporting women's desire to return to the status they enjoyed in the mosque during the time of the Prophet, in seventh-century Arabia. Auda argues in his book Reclaiming the Mosque *that women at that time, along with men, prayed in the mosque, listened to the sermons, made queries, swept the mosque, and even established their own clinic on the premises.*

CHAPTER

15

Although this small victory of redesigning a women's prayer space was fulfilling, in 1992 I was confronted with the harsh reality of millions of women who had no voices and no advocates. The Bosnian War was in full swing, and I had heard about a Bosnian Muslim girl who had told caseworkers that she and other women had been gang-raped. The girl had shut her eyes but couldn't block out the laughter of the Bosnian Serb soldiers.

The girl said that afterward she escaped through a window and ran more than four miles through the woods to the Bosnian government line. I read that the Sarajevo-based Corridor counseling group had compiled a dossier of dozens of cases of rape victims as young as twelve and as old as sixty-two, including those of women who became pregnant and either gave birth or opted for abortions—often crude kitchen-table procedures at home.

The fact that the Bosnian victims were speaking up was remarkable, since in countries where women have few rights, they rarely talk about how abusively they are treated. To speak up can mean a death sentence, even at the hands of a woman's own family.

Why was the world silent about these horrors? It was impossible for me to stay silent. I turned to my friend Zeyba to discuss how we could respond as Muslim women. I had been introduced to Zeyba by my aunt years before in Jericho at an Eid celebration—Zeyba was very elegant, with long, silky hair, and for a petite girl, she had an unusually husky voice. We liked each other immediately, but we were not able to see much of each other because she lived in Manhattan. That changed when I moved to the Upper West Side. Although Zeyba was a career woman, she shared my passion for world music and was extremely passionate about social causes.

Zeyba, as usual, was a step ahead of me. She had already contacted the International Rescue Committee to ask how we could become involved. They needed money to provide food, shelter, clothing, and supplies to the victims. Perhaps we could raise funds. Since we instinctively knew that music is always a wonderful way to unite people to support a cause, we decided to organize a *qawwali* benefit concert. Approximately seven hundred years ago, in Delhi, Amir Khosrow, a revered scholar and a royal poet, developed a new genre of music with a higher purpose: to unite Hindus and Muslims and spread the message of divine love and purpose. Khosrow wanted his people to lead an ethical life free of greed and envy, so he encouraged daily prayers where men, women, and even young children gathered together to pray in a communal setting. At these spiritual gatherings, *qawwali* was enthusiastically embraced by Hindus, Muslims, and Sikhs alike. Over the years, I had become a *qawwali* enthusiast. During my dark days, *qawwali* had lifted my spirits and deepened my spirituality. Nusrat Fateh Ali Khan's ensemble, a *qawwali* musical group from Pakistan, already had plans to tour the United States, so Zeyba contacted them to ask if they would be willing to donate their time. Neither of us had ever organized a concert, but within two weeks, we succeeded in arranging a benefit at Carnegie Hall.

On the big night, Zeyba and I walked onto the red carpet of Carnegie Hall to see the great auditorium filled. Two thousand people had arrived from faraway states not only to listen to Pakistan's great *qawwali* group but also to lend support to the cause of Bosnian women who were suffering. We knew that no matter how much money we raised, we could not end the genocide and would never even know how many women or girls we helped. But we knew for certain that our response had, at least, shone a small light on a very dark corner of the world for women.

IN THE EARLY NINETIES, my employer merged with a major financial institution and moved from the World Trade Center to Greenwich Street in Tribeca. I tried to convince myself that my commitment to work was my priority, but somehow I could not escape the empty feeling I had inside. My anger ignited by the Iranian Revolution and the politicization of Islam was by then dulled. Perhaps it had been tempered by maturity or professional experience, but instead of looking outward, I was looking within. Instead of passively being swept along by events and emotions, I was actively seeking answers and challenging my beliefs. The very notion that I had rejected God had begun to gnaw at me, creating what seemed like a black hole inside of me. I felt a compulsion to discover the meaning of my existence and redefine my relationship with my creator.

I usually didn't discuss religion at work, remembering the advice a former colleague had given me when I first started working. She had told me that there were three subjects I must never discuss in the workplace: sex, politics, and religion. The safe topics: sports and the weather. But one of my co-workers, a man named Bill, took enough coffee breaks with me that I was comfortable sharing my inner thoughts with him. Bill saw in me a kindred spirit. He had recently come out to his church as gay. I told Bill that my struggle was not with God; it was with man—with the misogynist men in my religion whose outdated attitudes were defining women's place in society. Bill became a sounding board not only for my opinions but also for my complaints about my relationship disasters, all the dead-end dates I was going on. Somehow, I found it easier to talk to someone who came from a completely different background. Bill was sympathetic. He wondered if my spiritual quest had anything to do with these dead ends.

His words struck a nerve. I admitted to him that it sometimes felt as if an invisible hand pushed all contenders aside. My dates were all good men, but one by one, they fell away, as if God had something else in store for me. Maybe it was best to just surrender, I thought, and let Him take charge of my affairs, since whatever I was doing to get my private life together was not working.

Bill listened and advised, but there was only so much he or any friend could do. Thinking back to when I came to America, I remembered how I had found it impossible to connect until I got up the courage to introduce myself to my classmates or they made the effort to introduce themselves to me. Perhaps the same was true with God. Perhaps we could reintroduce ourselves to each other. I resolved to find a place where I could worship and focus on my spirituality without being made to feel like a second-class citizen.

ON FEBRUARY 26, 1993, a little after 12:17 P.M., everyone in the Tribeca office rushed to the window when we heard a convoy of NYPD cars with sirens blaring and saw thick black smoke billowing in the air. We later learned that the terrorist Ramzi Yousef had driven a truck filled with fifteen hundred pounds of explosives into the underground garage of the North Tower of the World Trade Center and detonated them.

They were saying that a bomb must have hit the WTC.

They were saying that Muslims did it.

They were saying that "your people" did it.

Suddenly, my faith was under attack again.

I felt every bit as American as my co-workers, but all eyes were on me because of what one man had done. Six people had been killed, and if the attack had occurred when I was still working in the towers, I would have been among those who'd had to evacuate the premises and watch their fellow New Yorkers gasp for air. I wanted to scream: These are not *my* people! These are the *enemies* of my people!

I had only recently been so proud to become a naturalized citizen and was, in fact, still reveling in the glory of that day. Becoming an American citizen had not been easy—neither the process nor the decision itself. It had taken me ten years to secure permanent residency in the United States, and it had taken another five years after I'd received my green card for me to be eligible to become a naturalized citizen.

And yet as much as I loved America, I had been sad to forego my Indian citizenship. Muz and I had discussed this dilemma. Did giving up Indian citizenship mean we were severing our ties to our home, our family? Muz pointed out that America valued free exercise of choice and allowed immigrants who chose not to become U.S. citizens to continue living as permanent residents in the United States. But talking to him led me to realize that I no longer felt ambivalent about the decision. I wanted to participate fully in America, not only to pay taxes but also to vote my conscience, to have my voice heard. I would always have Kashmir in my soul, but I was no longer satisfied to remain on the sidelines in my adopted home.

But now, when all I wished to do was to fight the perpetrators of this horrendous crime, I found myself relegated to outsider status once again. I decided that the only way to fight back was through knowledge; the first step was to find out more about my religion. I organized a Quran study group made up of my immediate friends and their friends. Ultimately, we were a group of twenty. We would pick a particular topic pertaining to hot-button issues in the news. Some of us would take the lead in researching all the various translations, the scholarly commentaries, any fatwas issued, and how the issue had been legislated in different countries. One person would present his or her findings, and then a group discussion would ensue.

There was no scholar present, and often tempers would rise, but most of the time people left with a deeper and more nuanced understanding. They also felt equipped with the knowledge they needed to speak authoritatively with their fellow Americans. Part of our mission was to explore our relationships with God, searching for eternal truths and looking for ways to incorporate these teachings into our daily lives. Importantly, we were not afraid to think critically about what was written in the Quran, for God himself implores people, "Why do you not use your mind to think for yourself?" (29:20).

SPIRALING UPWARD

. . .

In 2015, an invitation landed in my email with the heading "Qawwali performance at the Brotherhood Synagogue." The event's sponsor was none other than the Cordoba Initiative, my husband's organization. I immediately thought of the concert Zeyba and I had organized to benefit Bosnian victims of war.

Since our Bosnian concert, qawwali had become popular in Manhattan's tightly knit world-music community. In those circles, Nusrat Fateh Ali Khan had become as popular as Pavarotti, and when he was still touring in the mid-nineties, Khan's concerts would sell out immediately. One summer, Muz, Zeyba, and I sat among throngs of New Yorkers on blankets in Central Park to hear him, and when the qawwals began chanting and playing instruments, the tempo put the crowd into an ecstatic state. The devotional quality of the highly rhythmic music had us clapping and dancing along with thousands of New Yorkers. No one cared that the qawwals were saying, "Allah hu," chanting, "God is presence" in Arabic. We were all experiencing something deeper, a stirring feast for the soul.

The event at the synagogue was being coordinated by my friend Dr. Asma Jamil Sadiq, a pediatrician whose father had hosted many great qawwals in his home in Karachi, Pakistan. She'd introduced qawwali to our spiritual group. As a physician *who worked with children with developmental challenges like autism and faced the heartaches of the families daily, she had found* qawwali *to be like a nourishing experiential tonic that helped her to deal with their pain. She told us how* qawwali *had added to her joy and deepened her understanding of the mystical concepts of divine love* (ishq-e-haqīqi) *and the manifest love of God's creation* (ishq-e-majāzi).

Asma had found the idea of moving qawwali *from a concert hall into a spiritual space meaningful. But then it had occurred to her that she had never heard of* qawwali *being performed in a synagogue, and she wondered if the* qawwali *group she had chosen to invite would agree. Then she asked herself, Why did Amir Khosrow create* qawwali? *And the answer she reached was that it had been to unite people of different religions. Convinced by her own argument, she invited the* qawwals *and told them they would be performing in front of a gathering of spiritual listeners at Manhattan's Brotherhood Synagogue.*

Asma worked in tandem with my husband and the executive director of the Cordoba Initiative, Naz Ahmed Georgas. On the day of the event, when I walked into the synagogue's sanctuary and saw the qawwals *seated on the floor, I looked around the room at the mixed audience of Jews, Christians, Muslims, and Sikhs, and I wondered how they would react. Would the Jews and Christians be able to experience the spiritual and social aspects of the music as Muslims and Sikhs did? Sensing my trepidation, Asma leaned over and said, "Don't worry. They will love it. It's a bit like jazz, gospel, and rock and roll all in one." Then she stepped up to the microphone and read from Regula Burckhardt Qureshi's book* Sufi Music of India and Pakistan: *"*Qawwali *remains a living spiritual practice and a musical art form that has been spread across cultures and people, as it addresses the core spiritual needs of man in this time. By pro-*

*viding a powerful rhythm with the ceaseless repetition of God's
names, the music of* qawwali *has a religious function: to arouse
remembrance of the divine and to intensify the seeking of intimacy with the Divine Beloved."*

My husband had wanted to create a unique experience by
fusing two musical traditions, and so Cordoba had invited
Basya Schechter, the lead singer of the Jewish group Pharaoh's
Daughter, to be a co-performer. We were looking forward to
hearing the music these two diverse musicians would create.

As planned, the qawwals started singing, "Allahu hu, Allah
hu, Allah hu," and Basya started singing with them, energizing
them. Then she started singing in Hebrew, "Adonai echad, Adonai echad"—*God is one, God is one.* When qawwals and Basya
jointly began singing "Allah Hu" and "Adonai echad," the room
erupted in applause, both sides recognizing the shared language
of "God is one" and the spiritual alchemy that was capable of
breaking all boundaries.

Taking the audience by surprise, the Pakistanis and Indians
in the crowd started dancing in the aisles, pulling dollar bills
out of their pockets and throwing them at the musicians as a
gesture of blessing. Then more members of the audience got
out of their seats and joined the dancers in the aisles.

When the concert ended, I saw strangers hugging. I heard a
young woman say, "I felt it in my heart, not in my understanding." A businessman reacted by calling the evening "the best
joint venture I have ever seen."

When Asma experienced the sheer joy of the audience and
saw the imam and rabbi embrace, she formed a circle with her
fingers and held it up toward the sky. "This synagogue has spi-
raled upward!" she cried.

COULD FEEL THE MATCHMAKER BREATHING DOWN MY NECK ALL
the way from Kashmir. After all, I was in my thirties—the very far
end of the matchmaking continuum, also known as the desperation
zone. Predating computer matchmaking services by centuries, Kashmiri matchmakers were an integral part of the community, brought
in by families to determine suitable marriages for their offspring beginning in a child's infancy. These men—they were always bisexual
eunuchs—were very highly respected, well paid, and a fixture of everyday life. Not only were arranged marriages the norm; they also
succeeded far more often than love matches. Arranged marriages
were based on matching aligned family values, economics, and other
factors—and the theory was that love would then follow, built on a
solid foundation. The rare "love match" in Kashmir generally seemed
to involve a lot of drama, an elopement or banishment, and occasionally a divorce.

Every year without fail while I was growing up, our family's
matchmaker had dropped by to gauge our progress so he could give
accurate reports to the families of potential mates—height, weight,
appearance, intelligence, manners, economic status.

But I was determined to find my own husband, thank you very
much.

Muz would ask me with a smirk how the search was going.

My response would be a silent glare and to remind him of his own reputation as the most sought-after man by the most accomplished women, who glided in and out of his life. And why not? Muslim men can marry whomever they want. I understood that a Muslim woman could marry only a Muslim man. However, the urge to marry was so strong that I dated respectable non-Muslim bankers and lawyers, with the hope that they might consider converting to Islam. Imagine my shock, then, when the matchmaker reached across the ocean from Kashmir and set me up with a preapproved prospect.

This man was a successful businessman, and the matchmaker was probably gleeful with his global coup, locating a Muslim man with an important job in New York City for this professional near spinster. But over appetizers on our first date, Mr. Pinstripes announced that his wife was not going to work because, in his family business, women did not work. I responded that in my family of professionals, all the women worked. After that, we had nothing more to say to each other. To show he was in control, on his way out he pocketed my doggie bag of leftover lamb chops.

After many such unsuccessful attempts at matchmaking, my family finally gave up. The consensus was: There must be something wrong with Daisy. Miss Picky and Choosy. And they were right. The fact was, I would soon realize my soul was starved. Before I needed a man, I needed God.

One night, after yet another single girlfriend dinner, I confessed to Zeyba that I was missing something in my life, that I felt empty inside. She told me she too had sensed an urgent need in me; she felt that I had been looking for a spiritual home for some time, but she had been reluctant to bring this up. She told me she knew of a magical place where she thought I could find spiritual guidance. "Before you go anywhere else, go there," she insisted, nervous that I might get mixed up with "Fundis," our term for zealots. She explained that this place of "chanting" was in Tribeca, just a few blocks from my office. After she mentioned it, I halfheartedly looked out for it a few times as I walked in the neighborhood, but I didn't seriously think about going there for a while.

Then one day, after working late, I was headed to the subway when I saw a bright green neon sign on the building across the street that read SUFI BOOKS. Sufism is the mystical branch of Islam practiced by both Shia and Sunni Muslims. How was it possible that I had walked past this place for the last two years and had never noticed it? The neon was a bit disconcerting, but it's funny what God must do to get our attention.

Approaching the display window of the bookstore, I saw titles such as *The Illuminated Heart* by Jock McKeen and Bennet Wong, books of Rumi poems, music and dhikr (devotional remembrance) CDs, wooden prayer beads, and a dark green leather-embossed Quran displayed on a stand. I opened the door, walked in, and discovered a store that looked more like a library, with a large table where people sat reading while others browsed through the bookshelves. A man wearing a tall cone-shaped white hat greeted me with the words "*As-salaamu alykum!* Welcome, welcome!"

I wondered where I had landed—could this place really exist in Tribeca? I browsed through the books and fell upon one by Rumi. I opened it and read:

> *Cross and Christians, from end to end*
> *I surveyed; He was not on the Cross.*
> *I went to the idol-temple, to the ancient pagoda;*
> *No trace was visible there.*
> *I went to the mountains of Herat and Candahar;*
> *I looked: He was not in that hill-and-dale.*
> *With set purpose I fared to the summit of Mount Qaf;*
> *In that place was only the 'Anqa's habitation.*
> *I bent the reins of search to the Ka'ba;*
> *He was not in that resort of old and young.*
> *I questioned Ibn Sina of his state;*
> *He was not in Ibn Sina's range.*
> *I fared towards the scene of "two bow-lengths' distance";*
> *He was not in that exalted court.*

And I gazed into my own heart;
There I saw Him; He was nowhere else.

—*Translation by R. A. Nicholson*

Reading these words, I felt the light of certainty flood my being, and I realized that God had always been there, but in my own heart. I remembered how as a child I had loved to garden with Dadaji in the early morning hours. This had often been a time for bonding, and once, almost in the same breath as I asked him how to plant a seedling, I had asked him about who God was.

He said, "God is our creator."

"Where is He?" I asked.

"Everywhere."

"How come I don't see Him?"

"Because He is in everything."

"Is He in my dog, Rocky?"

"Yes, in everything! God is in the leaves and trees. In the animals. In flowers. And He is also in your heart," he said, pointing his finger to my chest. Then he moved his finger up toward my throat and said, "He is also in your jugular vein." That day in the garden so many years before, my grandfather had been right. All along, He had been within me. Or maybe my journey and all its jagged paths, across a mountain range and an ocean, was what finally enabled me to open my heart to Him.

That evening I learned that this bookstore was affiliated with the mosque down the block, Masjid al-Farah. That Thursday night after work, I headed there. Inside, people wore white flowing outfits, the women in tall caps belonging to the Halveti-Jerrahi order of Turkey. Men and women of all ethnicities and of different sects of Shia and Sunni prayed together, and the place was filled with a loving, peaceful presence. There was a minbar (pulpit) made from intricately carved cherrywood. The mihrab (niche) indicating the direction of prayer stood in the corner of the room, slats of cherrywood carved around its arch. A ballroom-size Persian rug with a red-and-blue rose motif covered the wood floor. The walls were whitewashed brick decorated with framed calligraphy panels displaying the names of Allah, Muhammad, and the four rightly guided caliphs, Abu-Bakr, Omar, Othman, and Ali.

A woman approached me and said, "Welcome to our *tekka.*"

I stared blankly. What on earth was a *"tekka"*?

She explained that it was a Sufi lodge. This place was an abode for lovers of the divine. They drank from the fountain of love, she said. She promised I would learn many things there, become a new person. We decided that since the meeting in progress was going to run very late and I had to be at work early the next morning, I would return the following week to meet the spiritual leader.

The next week when I returned, the first thing I noticed was that there was none of the tension, rigidity, or judgment I had experienced at other mosques. No one was policing women with orders of "Sisters, to the basement" or criticism like "Your hair is showing!" On the contrary, I learned that the sustainer of the mosque was a woman, from a Texan Catholic family. Born Philippa de Menil, she had assumed the name Fariha when she was initiated into this order along with the Shaykh Nur. I found the atmosphere jubilant, full of spiritual love, with rituals and interactions centered on *adab*, an Islamic etiquette of refinement and good manners. This was consistent with what my family and fellow Kashmiris had practiced for centuries. Immediately I felt as if I had come home.

Weeks later, I was introduced to Shaykh Nur—Lex Hixon, a white American convert who was a spiritual powerhouse. When he saw me, he said, "*Salaam alykum* and welcome. Come, sit next to me on the white sheepskin rug." Fingering his prayer beads, he closed his eyes and began his Thursday discourse in English. "Through the repetition of the names of God, the attention of the seeker is turned toward God, and the whole being of the seeker becomes permeated with the joy of remembering the beloved, making the seeker increasingly intimate with God," he explained.

Did I want to be among the intimate ones? Yes, I think so, I said to myself. I am not sure!

Shaykh Nur explained that belief in God begins with the *shahada*, the declaration of the faith, which means acknowledging God as the sole creator of the universe, followed by accepting Muhammad as a messenger of God.

I decided to test the waters. Gradually and as if by osmosis, I soaked up what Shaykh Nur was teaching. "Sufism generates not ideas but luminous waves in the ocean of human consciousness," he told us. I was grappling with existential questions that were meaningful and essential to my soul: Who is God? How do I access Him? What is my relationship to God? What is the essence of a human being? Is God a He, or is God beyond gender? I learned that when God created the first human being, He blew His spirit into Adam, and that spark of the divine was contained in all six billion people on the planet. Human equality, I understood, is God-given, not a contemporary idea invented by the modern world. And as a human container of the divine breath, I had an obligation to carry the spark in me with dignity. This realization connected me to a greater power than my own. I felt secure knowing that the "I"—my "essential self"—could not be affected by outside conditions and that therefore there was no possibility of someone undermining my core identity— the spark within me. I learned that when we swell with false pride, we throw the world out of balance: Our bodies and minds, our relationships, and our whole ecology suffer when our fragile being is fragmentated from its source.

I was surprised to learn that God had appointed humankind as His *Khalifa* (his vicegerent or representative) in this world. He vested us with authority, responsibilities, and obligations, which meant my journey toward self-discovery had a purpose: to trust in God's infinite power, be a steward of God's creation, determine the purpose for which I was sent to this earth, act on my convictions, and shoulder responsibility for all my actions.

With this new knowledge and clarity, I began to redirect my life.

The first step was to invite God into my life, but to do that, I had to make sure I eliminated anything that was reigning over it, including veils and filters that blocked me from seeing with clarity.

I gained many of my spiritual insights in the company of fellow spiritualists as we sat in a crowded van traveling from the mosque to our respective homes. A person with a thick Spanish accent tossed out a question: "So, where do we come from? And where are we going?" Someone replied from the back of the car, "We got thrown out from our home—got separated from our heavenly origin and became estranged from our own hearts. We have to make room for God in our hearts." An African American man sang in a soft baritone voice, "It is not the eyes that are blind, but the hearts," words of a Sufi prophet. I asked a blond Turkish woman, "How do you let God into your heart?" She promptly replied, "Housecleaning! Get rid of all your preoccupation with things you cannot change. Just let go, and accept yourself so you can love yourself as you are and become whole again, so you are not divided within. Once you are whole, God will rush over!"

Once again, I found wisdom in the words of Rumi:

> *If the heart is restored to health,*
> *And purged of sensuality,*
> *Then the Merciful God is seated upon it (the Throne.)*
> *After this, the heart is guided directly*
> *Since the heart is with God.*

> —from Mathnawi, *1, 3665–66,*
> *translation by Kabir Helminski*

Months later I read about human fragmentation in a Sufi book. I learned that a human being is a threshold between two worlds: the material realm, where our ego dwells, and the reality of spiritual being, in which our soul is nurtured. Only after our true self is awakened can we become purified. Then we establish a connection with our spirit. The energy we begin to feel at the core of our nature is the power of divinity, the light ignited with us, which the heart experiences as divine love. This force heals us of our existential guilt and lifts us to a new level of beauty and meaning.

This path to self-discovery excited me. As I began to feel the evolution in my own consciousness, I focused less on dogma and more on doing the right thing. This was not just theory; I was my own laboratory, experimenting on the unification of the spiritual with the human. I read books on the levels of consciousness and observed myself carefully. Luckily, I was not beginning at the lowest level, at the domineering self, where one is not able to distinguish between right and wrong. My childhood had prepared me for making the right ethical choices. As I experienced a sense of guilt for sins I was committing, such as not praying or gossiping about others, I knew I was at the "self-accusing" level of consciousness. I adopted a discipline to rid myself of vices like pride, greed, envy, and malice and focused on prayer, fasting, and a daily meditation, dhikr, which literally means "remembrance of God."

When I accepted that God is in control of everything and submitted to His will, I knew I was at the "satisfied self" level of consciousness. Here I had to be perfectly accepting of being governed by the heart and could forgive others easily. I could attain this level, and yet to sustain it required work!

The fourth level is beyond my reach. In the "tranquil self-divine," attributes begin to manifest directly from God. God calls people at this level His "friends." These friends are detached from everything other than God, and anyone who seeks their counsel benefits from their wisdom. One day, I shared my understanding of my states of consciousness with Shaykh Nur, who replied, "This is a dynamic process. It is not static. There is always a danger of slipping back. Make sure you always love God, be righteous, and keep good company."

I loved looking at the Quran that Dadaji had given me, wrapped in a green silk brocade, but I had been afraid to approach it. Now at last, I felt ready to delve deeper into the study of Islam, its morals and ethics, its sacred literature, philosophies, rituals, beauty, and aesthetics.

The Quran was one vehicle that allowed me to get closer to God; it was a direct communication to me from God. It delved into divinity's plan and showed me how to lead a successful life—the Quranic revelations had been transmitted to the Prophet over a period of twenty-three years and enabled him to continue on his mission despite the resistance he was facing. One of my goals became to study the life of the Prophet.

I questioned Shaykh Nur about the Prophet. He advised me that "to love God, you must love the Prophet, and if you want to perfect your faith, then you must follow the tradition of the Prophet."

"Walk his walk, Daisy Fatima!" he told me, addressing me by the spiritual name he and Fariha had given me.

The Prophet Muhammad had been just a historical figure for me; I knew nothing about him except that we were supposed to revere him. How do you love someone you do not know? How do you bear witness to someone who lived more than fourteen hundred years ago? And, most important, how does a woman follow the tradition of the Prophet, a male? These were questions that I could answer only by following in his footsteps and living by his teachings.

As my family in America learned of my new commitment, they were skeptical. They thought I was going through a phase. So did Muz. In fact, he stated that he feared for my soul—not that I would lose it, but that I would go off and become ultra-religious. "Just don't become a Fundi!" he would tease, referring to fundamentalists.

Among Sufis, the Prophet is called *al-Insan al-Kamil,* "the perfected man," because he embodied all aspects of a human being. He was a spiritual teacher, a commander in chief, a judge, a businessman, a husband, and a father. As a spiritual teacher, he was a conduit who received revelation and taught and transformed people by example. As a commander in chief, he taught his community how to fight wars intelligently; he strategized and made peace treaties to create a haven for his followers even against the wishes of his companions. As a businessman, he was known for his honesty to the point that he would tell people about the faults of his own goods, and people called

him *al-Amin,* the trustworthy one. As a husband, he was very devoted to his first wife, Khadijah, and to be supportive would mend
his own clothes, sweep the floor, and milk the goats. As a father, he
loved and respected his children, and when one of his daughters entered a room, he would rise. These things I could relate to—these
were the kinds of values that were timeless.

To me, the Prophet was a protector of women. After he received
a revelation instructing him to warn his followers about the crime of
female infanticide, the Prophet abolished the practice, overturning a
prevalent cultural practice in Arabia in which baby girls were buried
alive after their birth. During his lifetime, women received rights to
inheritance, property, and divorce. As a human being, he embodied
the values I sought. However, even though he was recorded as one of
the most influential men who had changed the course of history, I
still could not consciously bear witness to the Prophet. Bearing witness means not only believing in the Prophet but also following his
teachings. Before I could do that, I needed to experience and assimi-
late his reality in my being.

Now that we had been reintroduced and the foundation of my
faith grounded, I felt confident appealing to God for help and guidance to strengthen my commitment to my faith. It was 1995, and after
four years of attending Thursday-evening spiritual gatherings at the
Masjid al-Farah mosque in Tribeca, I queried Shaykh Nur about the
need to pray five times a day. With a smile he provided a clarification:
"It is more a union with God than an offering," he told me. In his
book *Atom from the Sun of Knowledge,* he elaborates its significance.
"Muhammad, the beloved of Allah, could have brought back from
his ascension any gift from the infinite Divine Treasury. Since he
returned with Salat, we can infer that it is the most precious," he
writes. I knew that attending Friday prayers was not only an obligation but also essential to my spiritual growth. Prayers (*salat*) are one
of the five pillars of Islam. With my soul propelled forward, I made a
conscious effort to attend congregational Friday noon prayers even
though I knew it would prove to be difficult. It would involve dash-

ing in at lunchtime, then rushing back to work. I micromanaged my lunch hour; I commuted to the mosque in five minutes, attended the Friday congregational prayer service (called *Jumma*) for forty minutes, grabbed a sandwich in five minutes, rushed back in five minutes, and devoured my lunch at my desk, all within one hour.

Imam Feisal Abdul Rauf, the prayer leader who had been preaching sermons at Friday congregational prayer at the mosque for fifteen years, was preaching on my first day of attendance. I had heard that he was a gifted and prolific writer and an erudite speaker with a reputation as a formidable intellect. On that first Friday I heard him speak, Imam Rauf's sermon affected me powerfully. I found myself mesmerized by his resonant voice, which had a touch of a British accent, and his openness and tenderness toward his followers. The very first sermon I heard spoke to my quest:

> Dear brothers and sisters, how does one become an embracer of truth or an *insan kamil,* a completed human being, like our Prophet? Following the prophetic norm has two aspects to it: outer and inner. The outer aspect is given by the rituals and their formality. The inner aspect requires that you become a friend of the Prophet. This places upon us a more challenging yet more exciting path. It means trying to be like the Prophet in the value of one's actions. This can be attained not only by an act of the mind but by divine love. God's love helps you change the quality of your actions; it changes the nature of your thinking; it makes you want to seek union with God as your friend. This was the inner path of our Prophet and the quality with which he lit up the souls of his companions.
>
> Brothers and Sisters, love God and befriend the Prophet. The rest will follow!

I was so accustomed to fire-and-brimstone sermons, but this sermon was not only eye-opening but also instructive. I found it both deeply spiritual and practical. It described a way of practicing Islam that I could embrace, one that fit my view of a magnanimous God and a worldview that was universal and loving.

I had gone to bed quite late after one of the Sufi gatherings. Suddenly, I was jolted from my sleep as if an emergency alarm had gone off. I sat up and found myself staring at a man who stood at the footboard of my mahogany sleigh bed. I knew I should have been petrified, but I did not sense any danger. I felt unable to speak—my throat was dry—but even if I could have spoken, I have no idea what I would have said. Thoughts raced through my mind: Who was this man, and why was he in my bedroom? Was I dreaming or hallucinating? Why did I not feel afraid? But the man was smiling at me; he was gentle-looking, surrounded by radiance. He said nothing, but I intuitively knew that he was the Prophet Muhammad. He gave me a nod of approval—and then disappeared.

I felt then that I was on the right path and, most important, that I had finally borne witness to the Prophet. Seeing the Prophet in a night dream such as this is an affirmation of the truth, as confirmed in the hadith—the recorded reports and sayings of the Prophet that provide spiritual and religious guidance, second in this purpose to only the Quran. A dream in which one sees the Prophet is considered a great blessing.

I had to admit, gradually, that my main questions had been answered, key hurdles removed, and all doubts replaced with certainty. I felt prepared to make God my destination and the Prophet my compass.

WINGED HORSE

...

At the time of my dream about ascending into the sky on a winged horse, my parents did not share Dadaji's interpretation with me. Many years later, in 1994, when I had already embarked on my spiritual journey, Papaji and Mummy visited me in New York. Mummy was sick throughout the trip—she was suffering from anxiety attacks and digestive problems.

"I am going to take you to someplace where you will heal," I told her.

I had decided to take Mummy to my spiritual home, Masjid al-Farah. When I introduced her to the spiritual leader, Shaykh Nur, he immediately insisted that she honor the gathering by sitting inside the dhikr (divine remembrance) circle, where transformation and healing would take place. Even though Shaykh Nur spoke in English, Mummy sensed his spirituality, which had neither form nor language. She closed her eyes to facilitate direct communication with God. As she experienced the rhythmic chanting praising the attributes of God, her soul felt nourished.

She told me afterward that the depth of spirituality she felt in that crammed Tribeca mosque reminded her of the powerful spirituality she would experience standing before Kashmir's five-hundred-year-old shrines. Papaji, on the other hand, was *busy with other matters, as some things never change. As we were preparing to depart, Papaji whispered to Shaykh Nur, "I am very concerned about my daughter. She is not married yet! Can you please take care of her?"*

Shaykh Nur replied, "On the contrary, we should put ourselves in Fatima's care."

"Who is Fatima?" Papaji asked.

"Your daughter. We named her Fatima," Shaykh Nur replied.

Mummy's face lit up. She said, "You know what your Moji's name was?"

"No," I replied.

"Fatima!"

Then my parents remembered the dream of the winged horse that I had described to my grandfather. With all that they had experienced, they chose that evening to share the dream's interpretation with me, the prediction that I would become a mystic and a caller to the faith. Perhaps this day was approaching, they thought, and now their daughter would be in the service of God. Perhaps one day I would walk in the footsteps of Moji and guide others on the spiritual path.

Muz had an exciting announcement. His friend Dennis, who taught comparative politics and political philosophy at Iona College, a Catholic college outside of the city, wanted to organize a lecture on Islam. Muz had put forth my name as a potential speaker. Muz had long been my behind-the-scenes guide and goad; now he wanted me to step forward. He felt I was ready—even if I did not.

This made me uncomfortable. I had been attending spiritual gatherings for over four years and was a practicing Muslim. But I barely knew anything about Islamic theology, its jurisprudence or its law.

Muz could not understand how I could have been going to the mosque for four years and still assumed I knew so little. He insisted I was "the most knowledgeable among us all"—more so than I cared to admit. Muz was not one to let a detail like the fact that I had never spoken publicly stand in the way. He brushed off my questions about the audience—this would be just Iona's Catholic faculty and students. No one would question my authority. But I was not about to make a fool of myself in front of a group of clergy and academics. I felt I did not have the breadth of knowledge to be any kind of spokesperson for my faith.

Muz was prepared with an option. Dennis had met Imam Rauf, the imam of my mosque, at a conference hosted by an organization called Gnosis, and the imam had impressed him a great deal. Did I think I could persuade this imam to speak instead?

"Gnosis," which is the Greek word for "knowledge," is an organization that studies the science of religions and attempts to understand the religions of ancient cultures in a deep spiritual way. I realized that if the imam had spoken at the Gnosis conference, he had to be a deeply spiritual person. Although I had heard his Friday sermons, I had never met him, because I always dashed out immediately afterward to rush back to work. I told Muz I would try to make contact.

The next week, the imam, dressed in flowing robes and a skullcap, gave another mesmerizing sermon during Friday prayers. Despite his deep, resonant voice, he had a gentle, almost ethereal quality about him. This time, I observed him closely. Imam Feisal Rauf was around five feet, nine inches tall with regal Egyptian features. He had an unusually large head, a perfectly straight nose, and a deep forehead with receding wavy salt-and-pepper hair. His eyes were shadowed as if naturally lined with kohl. Most notably, he had a certain air about him, a mystique that came from an aura of heightened spirituality. After prayers, I approached him and introduced myself. I asked him if he would consider giving the lecture at Iona.

He refused; a woman should deliver this lecture, he told me. I responded that I was not qualified to speak on Islam to a college faculty. As we spoke, a long line was forming behind me, so he hurriedly explained that women like me needed to take a more active role in community outreach. As we still had not resolved the issue of his speaking at Iona, to keep the line moving, we agreed to continue the discussion over a meal, with the caveat that he would choose the restaurant and I would pay the bill.

This was an interesting development. What a strange proposal, I thought. One thing was certain—I would end up at a New York diner, because everyone knew that while imams were authorities on spiritual matters, they usually were a bit lacking in gourmet tastes.

The evening of the dinner, Imam Rauf pulled up to my apartment building in a Lexus, sunroof open, with Sade's "Smooth Operator" playing from the tape deck. Gone were the flowing robes—the imam was wearing a smartly tailored suit. And he had in mind not the local diner but Café des Artistes—at the time, one of the most elegant restaurants in New York. I was totally shocked, especially when, at the restaurant, it quickly became clear that the imam was not only a man of God; he was also a man of food. Over risotto, osso buco, and raspberry tart, we discussed the lecture, and he finally agreed to give it.

When the bill arrived, the imam was true to his word and made me pay for dinner. A Muslim man making a woman pay? I had to rethink my image of an imam on the spot—which, I later realized, was exactly his intention.

At this dinner, I felt comfortable enough to ask whether he knew of any suitable men for me, since I could not see making a connection with any of the eligible bachelors I knew from the mosque. The imam responded with what all imams say: "Pray to God."

I prayed to God and swore that whomever He selected for me I would accept, including a person from my mosque. I thought I had nothing to lose: I could always say no, break my own oath, and lose face with God.

When the imam and I went to Iona College for his talk, I was vastly relieved that I wasn't the one on the podium. During the Q&A that followed, the audience, filled with theologians, asked very complex questions. One person asked, "What is redemption in Islam?" That alone would have stopped me cold.

I was taping the lecture because the imam had asked me to transcribe it so that I and other women could prepare ourselves to give lectures going forward. It was especially inspiring to me that he felt it was a good thing for women to speak about Islam. It was an idea I had not heard coming from any other religious leader. And I was happy that Imam Rauf clearly had faith in me to take on this kind of responsibility.

That night at home, I tackled my duties as a transcriber. I had never transcribed before, and I was a two-finger typist, but I turned on my big Sony tape recorder, put on headphones, listened to the imam's beautiful baritone voice, and started typing—two words at a time. As I worked, I could sense Feisal Rauf's spirituality, but the typing was a slow, difficult effort. Hours passed. At around 2 A.M., exhausted, I stopped working and went to bed. I drifted into a deep sleep and was transported into an immersive dream.

In this dream, I was sitting alone in a classroom, surrounded by empty desks, taking a multiple-choice test. Through the window streamed a bright light, a light of the same quality as the light in the significant dream I'd had in my grandmother's lap all those years ago back in Kashmir. As the light streamed in, it morphed into a pen. The light pen then magically started writing in the name Feisal as the answers to all the questions in my test. It wrote *Feisal, Feisal,* and *Feisal.*

When I awoke, I immediately recognized that I had experienced a significant dream, but it was disconcerting. I had prayed to God for a husband, but now all I could see was a vision of Imam Feisal. How could this be? I clearly could not marry an imam! I was supposed to marry a banker, a lawyer, an accountant—a professional, someone like me. I forced myself to ignore the dream.

Two days later, I had another true dream, one that would change my life. I was standing alone in the middle of the garage at Uncle Faroque's house, and the imam was standing next to the door. For some reason, he did not see me and pressed the button to close the garage door. I shouted at him to stop him, but he disappeared. Instead of the garage door closing, the entire ceiling of the garage collapsed on top of me. My spirit, however, emerged very much alive. I could feel no pain as I looked down at my lifeless body. Then the imam reappeared and panicked at the sight of my still body. He looked at my astral self, and both of us knew I was alive.

In the Muslim tradition, when a person sees him- or herself dying in a dream, it signifies the onset of a spiritual rebirth. This dream was too significant for me to ignore. Shaykh Nur had talked about the concept of "dying before you die," referring not to physical death but to the idea that our old inner self dies and revives into a new self, and we experience a metamorphosis. I now realized that this was the meaning of my dream—through the hands of the imam, I would be reborn.

Was God granting my wish by finding me a man from the mosque—this specific man? I couldn't miss the irony—*I had asked God for a* man, *not an* imam. *Maybe He had misunderstood me!* Although I was risking great embarrassment, I felt compelled to talk to Imam Rauf.

SOME MUSLIM SPIRITUAL LEADERS are accustomed to interpreting dreams, and yet I felt awkward approaching Imam Rauf. I sat at my desk in my apartment and tried to decide how to proceed. I barely knew the imam. Still, as the dream centered on him, whom better to discuss it with? I nervously picked up the phone and called him. When the phone started ringing, I contemplated hanging up, but I didn't. When he answered the phone, I diffidently told him that I'd had some dreams.

He immediately responded that he had also had a dream.

He had?

I told him about the test, the pen, the whole crazy dream. And then I told him my second, even more compelling dream. He just listened. Then he surprised me by saying, "This means we will get married, and your old self is going to die in my hands, and you will have a spiritual rebirth. God is the ultimate planner, and He is planning our lives."

If someone had told me before this that I would one day marry an imam, I would probably have either laughed or fainted from shock. *Nobody* I knew married an imam—imams usually came from religious families and married within their own circles, far removed from the social scene I was a part of. How imams even managed to ever get married was a mystery to me.

None of this made sense. All else aside, I had expected to marry someone of my own age group—Feisal was ten years older. And, of course, I wasn't expected to marry someone who had been married before; I had learned that he had been divorced twice and had four children.

But I was convinced that God had answered my prayers. I felt myself floating, as if the hand of God was guiding me. Then I looked beyond the imam as an icon, at the man himself, and I thought: He exudes a spiritual aura. He is sensitive and intelligent, a graduate of Columbia University—he holds engineering degrees in plasma physics. He is a linguist, a brilliant orator. He's committed to connecting people of various beliefs, to creating dialogue. He's a charming man, has a beautiful baritone voice, wears nice clothes. None of that hurts. Oh, yes—and he's a Sean Connery lookalike. Was I going to reject this gift that God had sent me?

One thing overrode all else in my mind: I wanted, needed, to marry somebody spiritual. I had gone off the path, and now I was near someone who was very God-centric, and the deepest part of me yearned to be in that same spiritual space. The stage in my life when I had severed myself from God had been such a painful time for me; I had felt empty, and my days had seemed rudderless. They were dark and draining, without a purpose. Being married to the imam would surely channel my energies in a positive way—and yet being married to Feisal would be not just a marriage but also, by extension, a career. I hoped his work would mobilize and motivate me in my own calling. More than anything, I knew I had to trust my dreams.

Feisal and I met a few times, but our meetings were initially awkward because, despite my dreams, I still had trouble believing he could be a potential mate. He was a religious leader, a prayer leader, a published author of works about Islam. But the more I got to know him, the more appealing he became to me, and eventually I felt drawn to him. I felt I had finally found my soulmate.

Feisal had been born in Kuwait to an Egyptian imam and Sunni scholar and his Egyptian wife. In the 1960s his father, Muhammad Abdul Rauf, was appointed imam and director of New York's Islamic Foundation, which later became the Islamic Cultural Center of New

York, now the largest mosque in New York City. As Feisal told me, "I arrived on a steamboat in New York City on the coldest day in December." He had spent his teenage and college years on the Upper West Side.

I was surprised to learn that he had spent so much time in what was now my own neighborhood. He had shopped for delicacies at Zabar's—my Zabar's!—and had had brunch in the neighborhood, as I loved to do. We had walked the same paths in Riverside Park. I had always thought of Imam Rauf as a religious person with little interest in the outside world. Now I realized that our worlds were not so different.

Still, I knew that my family would be concerned about his two previous marriages, as well as the age gap. Feisal was forty-eight; I was in my mid-thirties. I wondered about his four children—his eighteen-year-old twin girls, Zahra and Fatima, from his marriage to his Irish American ex-wife, and his other two children, Omar, his son, and Zaynab, his younger daughter, who had remained in Malaysia with their mother. Feisal saw the younger children when he traveled to Malaysia, but they never visited the United States as children and would come to America only later to pursue their higher education. The twins were going to be a part of my life. What would they think of me? How would I relate to them? What would we have in common? While I was confident in other areas, the role of stepmother was a complete wild card.

Then one day, shortly after our decision to marry, Feisal called me and said, "I am having brunch with my girls this Saturday and would like to introduce them to you."

When I arrived at the restaurant, I instantly noticed the girls' resemblance to their father; they had his Egyptian features combined with their mother's light complexion. Outgoing Zahra, older by a minute, was athletic looking, with velvety, dark eyes, porcelain skin, long, glossy black hair, and a swanlike neck—an Americanized Nefertiti. Fatima, on the other hand, with inquisitive, light brown eyes and curly brown hair, was soft-spoken and contemplative. The girls reminded me of my younger cousins, and I took to them immediately. I asked them what they wanted to do after college and learned that Zahra hoped to be a social worker, while Fatima, who played guitar, dreamed of being a musician.

That day, over French toast, bagels, and scrambled eggs, I saw Feisal through the prism of his daughters, and I got a deeper glimpse of him as a person. I began to feel comfortable with him—and with my new role and new life. I looked at it this way: I was having an arranged marriage, after all—arranged by God. Who could be a better matchmaker?

GOD WORKS IN NEON

...

I had a friend at work who desperately wanted not a husband but a new apartment that was close to nature. After attending endless open houses, each more disappointing than the last, she decided to pray. In her prayers, she listed all the features she wanted in the apartment. "And please, God," she added, "make it close to nature. I want so much to look out my window and see nature." She had all but given up on finding a place when she received a call from a Realtor who told her she had found the perfect apartment.

Arriving for the showing, my friend was disappointed to see that the building was located at a busy intersection without a tree or leaf in sight. Still, she'd come this far . . . She went in to find a very well-maintained building, and four floors up was, indeed, her ideal apartment, right down to the closet space. Being a pragmatist, she was about to write a check for the deposit when she remembered to go to the window and look at the view, which she realized would be of another building. She pulled back the shutters to see a neon sign for a produce shop. It read, NATURE'S BOUNTY. As it turned out, the market sold organic fruits and vegetables along with freshly squeezed green drinks. She was finally close to nature.

Who would have guessed God was working in neon!

Although we knew we were going to marry, according to protocol we had to first meet with my parents. Even though we were mature adults, their consent was important to me, so I quickly arranged a trip to Kashmir to introduce Feisal to my family. We weren't sure what their reaction would be. In some ways, I was conforming to their wishes: I was certainly marrying a Muslim man. Yet I knew they had the power to say no. I did not know how I would respond to such a pronouncement, but I knew I was more fortunate than many women, because my parents were thoughtful and progressive—to a point.

Although I had told my parents a bit about Feisal, I hadn't worked up the nerve to mention his age or profession. They were expecting a much younger professional man and certainly not an imam! My father picked us up at the airport and was shocked when he met Feisal. My parents were gracious but were eager to speak to me alone.

After we settled in, Mummy and Papaji were waiting for me when I burst into their bedroom, my old routine from childhood. At the sight of the crewel-embroidered curtains, the decorative wood panels, and the intricately carved ceiling, I was suddenly flooded with the sensations of my childhood, a Proustian reminder of the feelings I'd had when I trailed my mother into her room, absorbing her warmth and perfumed scent.

Papaji posed the questions in our native language while Mummy sat pensively. Who was this man?

I looked at the situation from my parents' perspective: Their daughter, previously so confused, was calmly stating that she had met the man she wanted to marry—someone so different from the image they had drawn in their minds that they were now the ones who were confused. I told them I knew that Feisal was my soulmate but that their blessings were important to both of us.

My father protested that such a marriage was a risk. He curtly pointed out that Feisal had already been divorced—twice!

But wasn't all marriage a risk? An arranged marriage, such as my parents', seemed far riskier to me. Fortunately theirs had worked out. In taking a risk, in being bold and entering this marriage, I was sure of at least one thing—I was going to be placed in a relationship that would enable me to continue on my spiritual path. What opportunity in life could be worthier?

Clearly, my parents' opposition was going to be a problem, but in Feisal's mind, our visit was a mere formality, and there was no cause for concern.

Instead, it was the start of a standoff.

We adjourned to the living room, where Feisal was waiting. My mother stared at her prospective son-in-law. She didn't sugarcoat her thoughts and spoke in plain Kashmiri: He was so old! He had gray hair!

I reminded myself to put the situation into a cultural perspective: When my grandparents had become betrothed, my grandfather had been nine years old, and my grandmother had been twelve. When my parents had married, my mother had been only sixteen, and my father had been eighteen. Feisal probably seemed like a dinosaur in comparison. For that matter, I probably did too.

Feisal immediately noticed that I was becoming flustered and realized something was amiss. He was an imam, but he was also a man, and every man on the planet is a human being with a self-image. I could sense that beneath his stoic, mature façade, he was confused. After all, by most standards he would have been considered quite a catch!

Then my mother proposed a solution—Feisal could dye his hair.

Feisal sat there stone-faced. Fortunately, he didn't understand Kashmiri. Regardless, I knew he wasn't going to rush out and purchase a box of Clairol, even for me.

I realized that my parents and I needed to continue this conversation in private, and we adjourned to a different room.

During this discussion, my father explained his concern. He had sent his daughter all the way to America for an education, but by marrying an imam, I might lose my independence. Would I be able to have my own career living in the shadow of an imam? Who had ever heard of a career woman as an imam's wife? And, again, both my parents were very worried about Feisal's previous marriages.

My father commented that he had been praying to God that his daughter would marry a good Muslim, but he had never expected that the man I would marry would be *too* Muslim and, on top of that, a "mullah."

The word "mullah" connotes a religious leader and teacher, but it also implies the stereotype of a long beard and unkempt hair. To refer to my prospective husband as a "mullah" was an insult to a man with such distinguished accomplishments. My father's words infuriated me, but I tried to remain calm. I reiterated that Feisal was an *imam*, a scholar, an author, and a businessman who worked in real estate. I realized that my parents simply didn't know how to behave around Feisal. They had to treat him with formality—he was of Egyptian background, a foreigner, and an imam, not to mention my prospective husband.

My parents were relentless. They begged me to find somebody else.

I had never given my parents an ultimatum before, but I now did. I knew my mother was the safest one to turn to and that I had to explain to her that I knew what was right for me. The fact that she was unyielding crushed me. I understood that it was important to my parents that I marry. I cornered my mother and whispered in her ear that I was thirty-six years old and she needed to accept that if I didn't marry Feisal, I would never marry anyone else. I knew it was true. With that, I left the room. All my bravado was on the surface—inside, I felt terrible. Why should anyone be forced to choose between loving parents and the man you have chosen as your life partner? This was an issue beyond faith. It was personal!

I told Feisal they were not coming around.

Feisal reacted professionally. He put on his clergy hat, as he would for any couple, and asked for their specific objections; then he addressed them one by one. Always the rational one, Feisal was confident that he knew how to win an argument. But this was not an intellectual debate or, strictly, even about religion. This was about us. And the fact that, as I was quickly learning, no marriage is, in the end, just about two people. I had been naïve to think it was that simple. Especially when a couple is older, there are always going to be complex issues. Even when you think you have the answers, you don't.

Feisal had to understand—my parents had hoped I would marry someone they could relate to. But he was a foreigner, an imam, and divorced with children.

Feisal was confused: Hadn't they wanted me to marry a Muslim? Did he not fit that most critical qualification?

I told Feisal that there were still too many unknowns for my parents to be comfortable. For one, we had not yet discussed the financial considerations. My parents had inquired about a dowry, for instance. Feisal informed me that in Islam a woman is not required to give a dowry—in fact, it was the groom who was required to offer it.

I was stunned and wondered who in Kashmir had reversed the dowry system. All those years, my mother had collected a treasure box that wasn't even necessary. Feisal asked me what I wanted, but I really couldn't answer. I didn't want a house or a car. I wanted a soulmate with whom I could grow spiritually.

But to me, and to my family, a woman having financial independence was very important. My mother had always maintained her own finances, and I had always intended to manage my own money. In Islam, when a woman comes to the marriage with her own wealth, she has the right to dispose of it in the way she wishes, which gives her financial freedom and allows her not to be dependent on her husband. What could Feisal assure them—and even me—about my future status? they asked.

Feisal insisted that my money would be my money; I could maintain my own bank account. He would manage the household, and my income would be mine to keep. And we agreed that I would continue to work after our marriage. The Prophet's first wife, Khadijah, he asked me to remind my parents, had been a workingwoman—a merchant whose income had been important to the household.

I could have gone over my parents' heads, but since they had sacrificed so much for me, I was reluctant to do so. I turned to Dadaji. All he knew was that I was interested in marrying someone and that we were in Kashmir. I went and paid my respects to him and gave him a book. So, as the tumultuous marriage conversations continued, Dadaji was sitting quietly and reading Feisal's first scholarly book, *Islam: A Search for Meaning*. In it, Feisal defines Islam as a universal religion that transcends the cultural settings of the Prophet Muhammad's seventh-century Arabia. When Dadaji finished reading it, he told my parents that this book was the work of a true scholar. My grandfather admired scholars, and while my husband would go on to author many significant books, this one will always hold a special place in my heart because of its role in our marriage.

Then Dadaji reminded my parents about my dream, the one in which I was flying through the sky on the Prophet's winged white horse, Buraq—which my grandfather had interpreted to mean that I would one day bring people to faith and meet a pious and noble man. Would not my marriage to an imam fulfill this prophetic dream? My parents had to agree.

It took the intervention of the family patriarch to finally allow my parents to see the wisdom of the choice made by their educated, adult daughter—and suddenly, the obstacles to the marriage seemed far less insurmountable. As with when I was born, Dadaji had only to give his approval, and the rest fell in place. My parents gave their blessing.

THE IMAM'S DAUGHTER

...

In 2000, Dana, an Uzbek artist, was thirty-five and wanted to marry an artist she was dating from New York's edgy Tribeca neighborhood. When she told her father, an imam of an Uzbek mosque, he and her mother refused to accept her choice, insisting she maintain their cultural tradition and find an Uzbek Muslim man.

Dana came to me nervously, seeking my counsel. I immediately identified with her dilemma and reassured her that since her future husband was willing to embrace Islam, her father had no religious grounds not to accept him.

This was welcome news, but I could hear the exasperation in her voice. "No, he will only accept an Uzbek man! Where, where am I going to find an eligible Uzbek bachelor in Manhattan?"

I understood from my own experiences that Dana's father's opinion and blessing mattered to her. Her father was a leader in the Uzbek community, and he and his people married Uzbeks. By allowing his daughter to marry an outsider, no matter whether the prospective husband converted or not, he would be setting a bad precedent for his entire community.

I told Dana to set her marriage date and leave the rest to me, convinced of my ability to persuade her father.

I offered to host the marriage ceremony in my apartment. A few weeks before the event, I called Dana's father to appeal to him. I explained that his daughter's wedding day would be incomplete without his presence and blessing and I hoped he would join us. He listened while I built a strong religious case for Dana. I told him what I had told my mother, "If Dana does not marry now, she will probably never marry," and I expected him to leave the door open and say, Inshallah, God willing. Instead, his response was a resounding silence.

The day of the wedding, there was still no word from her father, so Dana resolutely prepared for the disappointment of being married without him at her side. She realized that, in the end, although her father's support was very important to her, she was determined to marry the man she loved. Then, minutes before the ceremony, the intercom rang, and the most significant guest walked in. When Dana's father saw his daughter in her wedding gown, the imam was overcome with emotion and welcomed his future son-in-law with an embrace. The marriage ceremony commenced, as did many tears of joy. Everyone realized what it must have taken for this resolute man of ironclad will, a religious leader, to take the walk that led down the aisle to the altar. It was not dogma; it was love. Sadly, her mother was unable to breach the chasm and did not attend.

I F DEALING WITH MY PARENTS HAD BEEN A DIFFICULT HURDLE, dealing with my friend Muz was like trying to get over a concrete wall. When Feisal and I returned to New York and announced our engagement, Muz was astonished. When I reminded him that it was he who had pressed me to meet with Feisal in the first place, a vein started throbbing in Muz's forehead. I thought he was going to have a stroke as he wagged his finger in my direction. Did I not realize that this marriage could compromise my life? There were traditional expectations of an imam's wife. It was a very restricting existence. He went on to list a litany of issues—the wife must stay home, cook all day, make babies. . . .

I could only shake my head and smile. Muz had known me for decades: He had been my mentor since I had moved to Manhattan. Perhaps he could not grasp that I was an adult now and that I had never been so sure of anything in my life as I was of this marriage— and this man.

Zeyba, on the other hand, was perplexed. "*You* are marrying an *imam*?" she exclaimed. Then she freaked out. "Have you gone crazy?" While she was trying to bring me to my senses, I was busy planning my trousseau. I knew that Zeyba had just begun designing jewelry and asked if she would design my engagement ring.

Zeyba finally met Feisal after I cajoled her, and he of course charmed her. "This ring is the main gift I am giving to Daisy, so please make a ring that is pleasing to her," he requested of her.

I added that she had to remember my family. "Make it *big*, so they will be impressed," I told her.

Zeyba crafted a ring shaped like a daisy, with diamond studs encased in yellow gold, and assured me, "This will impress everyone—an American version of a classic *kundan* ring," referring to an Indian equivalent of an estate ring. Months later, Zeyba called me and said, "Did you see the ring on Nicole Kidman? She was spotted wearing a *kundan* just like yours."

Like most brides of any age or religion, I had fantasized about having the perfect wedding. I wanted it to be a deeply spiritual event, of course, but I also wanted it to reflect who we were. The intricate white marble Taj Mahal resembled, in my opinion, the world's most beautiful wedding cake—it made sense to use it as a model for my actual wedding cake. One of the wonders of the world, the Taj Mahal is not only a masterpiece of architecture, but also it has a legendary romance behind it.

It took twenty-two years in the 1600s for the emperor Shah Jahan to complete this wondrous monument dedicated to love and beauty and to immortalizing his wife, who was his trusted adviser. India's Nobel laureate in literature, Rabindranath Tagore, called it a "teardrop . . . on the cheek of time." It was a perfect symbol for the beginning of our marriage.

The bakery I went to had never used a building as a model, but they created a miniature Taj Mahal and delivered a magnificent white cake.

My choice of a wedding dress also caused a bit of discussion. Instead of the customary red-and-gold dress, I wore a white gown, designed like a traditional Indian *lehenga*, beautifully handcrafted in white silk with silver-pearl sequins. I carried a bouquet of red roses. My family was not happy about this in the beginning, because in their minds, every bride wore red or gold, while a woman wearing

white was wearing the wardrobe for her coffin. I was trying my best
to bridge Feisal's and my cultures but at the same time have our wedding be American, including my being walked down the aisle. I also
wanted to have garlands of flowers to honor Kashmir's ancient ritual,
so in addition to corsages, garlands of orchids were draped around
the necks of all our family members. We decided that when I made
my entry, instead of an orchestra playing "Here Comes the Bride,"
the women in my family would stand in rows with their arms interlocked and sing *wanwun,* Kashmiri wedding songs, to serenade the
bridal couple. I invited an imam to conduct our wedding, and I told
him that I didn't want a joyless, somber ceremony; I asked him to
please make it a little light, while honoring our cherished traditions.

The makeup artist was applying the finishing touches to my face,
and the hairstylist was arranging the beautiful *tikka* headpiece my
mother had worn at her wedding, when Fifi arrived from India, took
one look at me, stood back aghast, and asked, "So what are you wearing for your jewelry?" I showed her my gorgeous kundun choker
studded with uncut diamonds. She frowned when she saw I was
wearing only one necklace. That was not what brides wore, she ad-
monished. Brides were supposed to bedeck themselves with gold!
With that, Fifi pulled out my mother's treasure box of glittering jewelry that she just happened to have with her—thinking she was doing
me a favor. In her mind, her sister was completely underdressed for
her own wedding, and she was saving the family from disgrace.

I knew that it is customary for brides in our culture to cover
themselves in precious jewels—that wearing a multitude of necklaces, bracelets, and rings is a matter of pride to the families involved.
But that seemed excessive to me. I had thought long and hard about
what I was wearing, I had a flair for design, and I resented my sister's
last-minute interference. I had no intention of looking like a walking
jewelry shop, so I refused her offerings.

Fifi saw it differently. Waving a seven-strand pearl necklace, she
accused me of going against tradition. "What will people think?" she
asked.

By then I was near tears, and the makeup artist was trying to touch up my runny mascara as my determined sister continued to force the jewelry on me. Finally, the hairstylist stood between us like a referee and announced, "Daisy is the bride, and it's her day, and she makes all the decisions!"

In the end, I did not wear the jewelry. I felt I had already made enough bows to tradition. I was wearing an embroidered Indian outfit, I had even covered my head in a traditional way, and my hairstyle was befitting an Indian bride.

I thought we'd dealt with all possible issues when the time came to walk down the aisle to the canopy where my husband-to-be awaited me. But as I made my grand entrance in my gorgeous white *lehenga* outfit, holding my bouquet, I was in for a seismic shock: Tradition had stepped in to take a bigger role at our wedding. Unbeknownst to us, the imam conducting the ceremony was a former student of my future father-in-law and had convinced him to conduct our marriage via proxy. This meant that the bride and groom would passively watch our two fathers perform the marriage on our behalf rather than our proposing and accepting each other in marriage.

There I was, a modern, empowered woman, my husband-to-be in his elegant brocade tunic, being told at the altar that two *men*—my father and my father-in-law-to-be—were going to stand in front of the guests instead of me and my groom and marry their children off. I realized that this ritual had been injected by the imam out of reverence to my future father-in-law, a man of religious eminence whom the imam wished to honor. I was shocked that I had not been consulted, and it was even more incredible to me that my papaji, who had raised me so liberally, would have agreed to it. I could see that my father was not comfortable with the situation either, but he had so much respect for my future father-in-law and his future son-in-law, who were more religious, that nobody, including my fiancé, felt they could say anything to contradict this marriage rite.

The practice of using proxies had come about in cultures in which women and men were not allowed in the same space and for situations like my grandparents' marriage, in which the couple were underage children. In those circumstances, a proxy marriage might even make sense. But it didn't make sense in modern America, at a wedding at which there was no gender segregation, between an adult woman and a middle-aged man who was, additionally, a religious leader. There was absolutely no reason for either of us to be represented by our fathers, as if we were helpless children. No reason—except tradition.

I now saw that my gown, the cake, the guest list, the music, were all superficial tokens. How could I enter marriage without expressing my own rights? I had to make an instant decision. Yet to object was to show disrespect to my future father-in-law in front of a room full of guests. I felt I had no choice but to let the marriage go forward. My husband knew—and everyone at the ceremony knew—that I was an independent woman. I tried to comfort myself by thinking of a traditional Christian ceremony, in which the minister asks, "Who gives this woman to wed this man?" In today's Western world, women are "given away" as if they are property on the market, but the words are simply tradition.

Then it was my turn to shock. At the celebration, my husband and I decided to do a public dance together—something that was almost unacceptable in our culture, in which the bride was supposed to sit in a chair and watch the festivities. But as an American bride, I had dreamed of my first dance as a married woman. Of course, my new husband didn't know how to dance, but he was a good sport about it. And so the imam and his new bride danced together to Louis Armstrong singing "What a Wonderful World." We even danced the Macarena. At that moment, it was tradition that sat on the sidelines.

Zeyba was the master of ceremonies. She was elegantly dressed in a baby-blue silk and chiffon Indian Muslim dress, a *gharara* with a tunic blouse worn over wide, flowing pantaloons. She stepped up to the mic and, in her soft, husky voice, said, "Dear guests, I am Zeyba

Rehman, the human embodiment of the dinner gong—dinner is served!"

Feisal, amused, leaned over to whisper to me, "Very impressive friends, Daisy."

At the close of the festivities, we honored the ancient Indian custom of throwing flower petals. And despite the merging of cultures, traditions, dress, and food, as we ducked out through a shower of petals, I had the same thought as brides the world over have: I'm married!

WHEN I WAS IN my late twenties, an Indian astrologer who worked in my architectural office at Mishra Associates wanted to read my astrological chart so he could convince me to stop my perpetual search for a husband. He said I was wasting my time. "It is all written. You will be married at age thirty-seven," he told me. "Then you will have three children. Until that time, Saturn is blocking everything!" I did not believe a word he said.

But exactly as he had predicted, I was married at thirty-seven. I imagined that I would soon be a working mother, shuttling from a job to the soccer field, with a suburban home and a sedate life working behind the scenes as an imam's supportive wife.

Unbeknownst to me, God was clearing the path for me to do something else.

MY DAUGHTER IS NOT
FOR SALE

. . .

Years later, when I had already assumed a prominent role in aspects of my husband's work, I became a liaison between engaged couples and the imam. On one occasion, a young Pakistani bride stood in tears in her beautiful wedding gown—not because she was feeling sentimental, but because her father and her prospective husband were arguing fiercely, unable to agree on a dollar amount that the husband would provide for her dowry. Originally, a dowry was like a prenuptial agreement that included a gift to the bride, as an expression of commitment and to provide security to the wife in the case of the dissolution of the marriage.

It wasn't unusual for me to encounter families, especially those who came from more traditional countries such as Pakistan, Egypt, Iran, and Afghanistan, to name just a few, who assumed that the old tradition of the dowry was still in place. When I was called in to explain culture and customs, I would at times need to correct or clarify these impressions.

Feisal was to officiate at this particular wedding, and we arrived to find that the ceremony had been delayed. The guests were waiting in confusion. Feisal and I waited and waited until finally my husband announced, "I'm not waiting here any longer. Why don't you intervene?"

It was trial by fire as I inserted myself between the two raging men. The father, an educated man, was offended that the groom was insisting on giving three hundred thousand dollars as a dowry. The father declared that his daughter was not for sale. He was suspicious of the groom's motives. He felt that the insistence on the large dowry was possibly a sign that the groom, who was a young investment banker, would undermine his daughter's future by using money to exert his power in the relationship.

The father told his daughter's fiancé to just give him a dollar or ninety-nine cents—a symbolic amount. The groom responded, "I'm giving her three hundred thousand dollars, and she's mine."

"As if he were buying a Ferrari!" the father huffed.

I told the father flat out that he and his prospective son-in-law should have negotiated this before the moment of the ceremony and that if they couldn't come to an agreement, the imam and I were leaving. With a glance toward the expensively decorated ballroom, the father looked visibly shaken.

My husband then came forward and explained that the custom of the dowry did not mean that the man's daughter was being purchased. If the groom wanted to give his bride something, then why deny him the right to be generous? He was expressing his intentions in a different way than the father understood to show that he loved her.

After Feisal explained the custom in this way, I asked the men to consider a compromise—perhaps a gift of fifty thousand dollars.

All parties finally agreed to that amount, and the wedding ceremony commenced.

CHAPTER
20

MMEDIATELY FOLLOWING MY WEDDING, MY RELATIVES THREW a flurry of parties in our honor. Feisal decided to reciprocate by inviting my extended family to his house, which was now *our* house. My beloved one-bedroom apartment remained our base in the city, but the house had a fully equipped kitchen and a real dining room, as befitted Feisal's love of all things having to do with food. He insisted that I did not have to worry about anything—he would prepare the entire meal.

But I did worry. What if my new husband embarrassed himself in front of my whole family? I knew Feisal was adept at ordering at a restaurant and claimed to be proficient in the kitchen—but, frankly, we were usually so busy that we ate out, and I had no idea how well he could cook for a large group, especially under pressure. My family would have high expectations, and our Kashmiri traditions were not the same as his Egyptian ones. Besides, I had still not completely recovered from the shock of the proxy marriage at our wedding. Would our cultures collide again?

This time, I was determined to manage expectations in advance. I informed Feisal that in Kashmir, when you host a dinner for in-laws, the tradition involves no less than a twelve-course meal. In Kashmir, when the in-laws arrived, the household would turn upside down. We would hire special cooks, *wazas,* to prepare a formal and ceremonial twelve-course *wazwan* meal, which was served on a *trammi,* a large copper tray shared by four guests. By sharing food, we created a sense of community and deepened our connections and identification with one another. The fact that this was our first gesture of hospitality to my family as a married couple added another level of stress.

Feisal nodded confidently and proceeded to do things his own way. He planned to roast a lamb—a whole lamb.

I could see that things were heading in a shaky direction. My family was used to spicy food; if he roasted the lamb the Egyptian way, it would probably be too bland for their taste.

Feisal was unmoved. I had to trust him, he said. Everything would be fine.

A disturbing image flashed into my mind, that of a whole lamb on the table with its head and feet sticking out. It was true that my culinary skills were not at the level of my husband's, but I did know how my family would react to such a sight. Our lamb was stewed or served in bite-size pieces. You are married to an Arab, I told myself. Get used to it. But I told Feisal that by not adhering to the norms of formality he risked embarrassing me in front of my family. If that happened, I would never forgive him. I knew this was just a meal, but I had staked so much on this marriage. Although I was in my late thirties, I found myself acting like a nervous young bride.

The meal was prepared and served entirely by Feisal while I merely set the table. The roasted baby lamb—minus head and hooves—was duly placed in the middle of the table, accompanied by rice, salad, grape leaves, and *mulkhiya,* a staple Egyptian soup made with a green-leaf vegetable called Jew's mallow. My aesthetic sense told me the lamb looked rather plain, so I suggested garnishing it with some parsley. I was reaching for the greenery when Feisal intervened. There was no need to garnish the lamb!

I thought perhaps we could at least slice the meat so the guests could easily serve themselves. This triggered a near argument. Finally, Feisal told me to just relax and leave things alone.

The crux of it was not really the food. I was worried that my family would not like or approve of my husband. I was still not at all sure that my family had accepted the fact that I had married an imam. What was more, nobody could quite comprehend the protocols involved in being an in-law to an imam. Imams were respected religious men and thought leaders in our community, but their role in the family dynamic was a total unknown to any of us, including me. One thing we knew for sure, however, was that no one had ever heard of an imam at the stove cooking dinner. And as for an imam who was a gourmand—well, this phenomenon was about as common as stumbling across an igloo in the Mojave Desert. Feisal, however, took everything in stride. Nothing seemed to faze him. This was his party, he reminded me.

When the family arrived and saw a whole lamb sitting on the table, Auntie was curious as to how they would eat it. I was sure my fears had been validated. Feisal ignored my concerns, reached into the shoulder of the meat with his fingers, extracted a piece, and announced that this was the filet mignon.

Auntie took a bite and said that she had never tasted lamb so sweet. She called over my uncle to taste it. How had Feisal cooked this lamb to such perfection? The whole family hovered around to discuss this novel way of serving lamb. They could not stop raving.

Feisal looked at me and shook his head as if to say, Woman of little faith!

I smiled sweetly. As with politics, marriage, I could see, would have its moments in which diplomacy was required on both sides.

WE HAD ANOTHER GROUP to feed as well. Every Friday for the next ten years, my West Side apartment became the focal point of our mosque's community of young, aspiring spiritualists who loved dhikr—meditation and chanting. It was open to any seeker.

Every Friday when I arrived home after a hectic workday, I switched from my business suit into comfortable, loose clothing appropriate for prayer and meditation. At any given time, thirty or so people would be sitting on the living room floor engrossed in prayers, meditations, or spiritual discussions. The room was transformed, with couches pushed against the walls. A wooden desk displayed spiritual books, cassette tapes, prayer beads, and music CDs. The walls were covered in framed gold-leaf calligraphy, and in the northeast corner of the room hung an oblong orange glass lamp which marked the qibla, the prayer direction.

When the call to prayer was recited, prayer rugs were rolled out, transforming the room into a prayer space. "Can I borrow a scarf to pray?" was a common refrain. Shoulder to shoulder, around thirty men and women crammed into the room to perform their evening prayers.

The gathering was composed of people from all ethnicities: Pakistanis, Egyptians, white Americans, African Americans, Russians, Uzbeks, Indonesians, Bosnians, and others. In age, the participants ranged from college kids to grandmothers. A navy veteran, Tariq, who walked with a cane, would smile at everyone and say, "Thank God it's Friday. You could be in so many other places, but you choose to be here."

Next a twelve-meter-long cloth covering called a *dastarkhān* would be unfurled on the floor, and on top of it, we would place steaming plates of biryani rice, bowls of curries, kebabs, hummus, pitas, naan, *ghormeh sabzi*, French baguettes with sharp cheddar cheese, olives of all varieties, and sparkling grape juice.

I remember when Shahzad, an aspiring actor, leaned over to Tariq and asked, "What brings you here, brother?"

Tariq, a jazz musician, looked up at the ceiling, rolled his eyes back, and circled his finger around. "Spiritual vibration. I've never been to a place that was as peaceful as this. I feel, when I'm here, that I am transported to an intangible, indescribable place."

Then Asma, my pediatrician friend, chimed in. "I feel this spiritual intensity here," she said, and then began reciting some of Rumi's poetry out loud. "Listen to this reed, how it makes complaint, telling a tale of separation: 'Ever since I was cut off from my reed-bed, men and women all have lamented my bewailing.'" Rumi was referring to the human longing to find union with life's source, the one creator.

An Iranian day trader came religiously with his twelve-year-old brother, Ali. We nicknamed the boy Sheikh Ali, since he never missed a night, and when he began reciting the Quran for us, he brought tears to our eyes.

Samina, my longtime friend, a floral designer, admitted to a Turkish man, "My son brought me here. He is a born-again and blames me for not teaching him Islam, and now we are both learning together."

After we had enjoyed the meal and a variety of desserts prepared by Manhattan's best bakeries, my husband would instruct everyone: "Leave your worries behind, focus on yourself, and enter a sacred space. You are here to precipitate positive and uplifting transformation in yourself by granting your soul direct experience and access to the divine realities and truths." With that, we each retreated inward and began chanting God's names rhythmically until we felt a sense of *sakina,* a calm or stillness of being. Everyone looked forward to the spiritual discourse that followed, which might involve a story, a parable, or a commentary imparting spiritual wisdom, such as: "The spiritual challenge is to realize our sacred humanness. To realize that there need not be a conflict between the natural and the supernatural, between the finite and the infinite, between time and eternity, between practicality and mysticism, between social justice and contemplation, between sexuality and spirituality, between our human fulfillment and our spiritual realization, between what is most human and what is most sacred."

Diana, a Hispanic woman, told another person, "I am not even a Muslim, and I come here because hanging out in the company of fellow spiritualists makes me a better Christian."

Once, as I squeezed through the hallway, where a long line had formed for the bathroom, I overheard Shahzad ask Bradley, who made a living as a Calvin Klein model and was doing research on Rumi, "Do you believe in God?"

"Yeah," he answered.

"Really?" Shahzad asked. "How do you know?"

Bradley shrugged. "It's a hunch!" he replied, then disappeared into the bathroom.

For my husband, these Friday-night gatherings were business as usual. For me, they were an apprenticeship. Shaykh Nur had died suddenly a year before we had married, making my husband my de facto teacher. Although I considered myself his student and the equal of the others who were present, they saw me as the imam's wife, who was active in community building. I had no authority personally, but by being by his side, I absorbed a bit of my husband's spiritual aura. At the time, I thought being a mediator would be my primary role. I would serve as a mentor and be a surrogate for him in a clearly defined way. But destiny intervened, and in the coming years, I would play a much larger role in the Muslim community.

BREAKING THE BREAD

. . .

YOUR BREAD IS SEEKING YOU

Listen, put trust in God,
don't let your hands and feet tremble with fear:
your daily bread is more in love with you, than you
    with it.

It is in love with you and is holding back
only because it knows of your lack of self-denial.

If you had any self-denial, the daily bread
would throw itself upon you as lovers do.
What is this feverish trembling for fear of hunger?
With trust in God one can live full-fed.

> —Rumi,
> *translation by Kabir Helminski*
> *and Camille Helminski*

In May 2005, to build bridges, ASMA, along with sixteen other
interfaith organizations including the Cordoba Initiative pro-
duced a theatrical event called Córdoba Bread Fest: Children of
Abraham Break Bread Together. *Through Christians, Jews, and*

Muslims breaking bread together, we hoped to experience interfaith dialogue on both spiritual and earthly planes. By sharing food, we deepened our connections with one another. Essentially, we all survive on bread and by the grace of God.

Bread doesn't care about politics; it doesn't worry about race or religion. Bread is common to all cultures and all peoples, a warm, embracing reminder of our shared humanity. In my faith, bread is equated with life itself, and Muslims are taught to place their trust in God for their daily bread. Bread is so precious in our household that my husband taught me to never throw any away; we save dry bread for croutons.

Over three hundred Christians, Jews, and Muslims gathered at New York City's beautiful St. Bartholomew's Church to celebrate one thing common to the daily life and communities of the three Abrahamic faiths: bread. Guests arrived at a tableau of a court scene from Córdoba, Spain. Córdoba had been the historical site of a great flowering of culture, art, philosophical inquiry, and religious tolerance in the mid-700s, when Muslims, Christians, and Jews all lived in harmony. Likewise, our performers were volunteers from all three faiths. Our audience sat at long communal tables decorated with stalks of golden wheat, baskets of apples, and scattered quotes that mentioned milk, honey, olives, and dates from the Christian Bible, the Torah, and the Quran. The scent of fresh-baking bread wafted from a tandoor oven.

Christian performers told stories about the importance of bread as a necessary ingredient of faith, such as that of Jesus feeding the hungry with loaves and fishes; Jews shared their experience of preparing challah bread for the Sabbath; a Muslim storyteller told of the ninety-nine names of God, one of them al-Razzaq, the Provider. They discussed how bread is a metaphor for food and is sacred because it sustains and protects life.

It is God who has made the earth a resting-place for you
and the sky a canopy,
and has formed you—and formed you so well—
and provided for you sustenance out of the good things
     of life.
Such is God, your Sustainer:
hallowed, then, is God, the Sustainer of all the worlds!

     —*Quran 40:64*

The actors regaled us with the step-by-step preparation of bread—a reflection of the human life cycle, from which we can learn something about our own existence.

The mounting of this production found me dealing with the challenges of disparate cultures and traditions—drawing the fine line between theatrical and liturgical dancing, deciding between kosher and non-kosher wine and nonalcoholic drinks, leavened and unleavened bread. Somehow, a compromise was always reached. At the end, I walked onstage and told the crowd that we had decided to celebrate bread because it is a living metaphor for what unites us as human beings. From the humble breaking of bread can come great things.

M ANY YOUNG PEOPLE BEGAN TO ASK ME QUESTIONS OF A personal nature as well as about their spiritual paths. One Friday evening at a spiritual gathering held in my apartment, a young, newlywed Afghan woman approached me. She had to speak to me right away, she told me urgently, and in private.

We squeezed down the crowded hallway to the only private space—the bedroom.

As soon as I closed the door, the woman sobbed that she had suffered a miscarriage. She was fearful. What would happen now?

I held her hand and said the only thing I could—that I had also had a miscarriage. Together, we shared a moment of sadness that only women who have experienced this emptiness can understand.

What I did not share was the fact that I had had three miscarriages. Three months after my wedding, I had been delighted to discover that I was pregnant. Due to my age, I decided not to share the news with friends and family until medical examinations confirmed a healthy pregnancy. My husband accompanied me to my first sonogram appointment, where the obstetrician pointed to a pulsating dot on the screen. As he moved the wand around, the doctor amazed me with the observation that I was carrying twins. Feisal squeezed my arm and said, "*Mabrook!* Congratulations! Twins again. They run in my family!" I ecstatically imagined holding twin babies in my arms.

At home, I began to picture a nursery, buying two of everything.

Feisal, an experienced father of twins, posed a practical question—how would I manage to breastfeed two babies while I was still working?

To me, the answer seemed simple. I'd heard of women pumping their milk at the office.

His eyebrows lifted in disbelief—I would pump milk for two years?

"Why two years?" I asked him.

"The Quran says that a mother should breastfeed her child for two years," he responded. The infant has the right to receive the best nutrients, and a mother's milk is sterile, its temperature is perfect, and it transfers the mother's immunities to the child. Of course, I wanted to be true to my faith—and, after all, the Prophet's wife Khadijah had raised four children and buried two infants while she worked. I admired her more than ever. But how was I going to manage it with my business travels?

I decided to figure that out when the time came. It never occurred to me to quit working.

For weeks, I was blissful, going for routine checkups, fantasizing about my two babies, until one day, I began to bleed. We rushed to the doctor's office, and when the scan failed to find heartbeats, the doctor uttered the dreadful words: I had miscarried. I was devastated, and my husband was equally disappointed.

On the way home, Feisal tried to assure me that I would soon be pregnant again. I hung on to his words, set aside my sadness, and focused on the future.

I scheduled a dilation and curettage. In the doctor's office, I asked to see them. I wanted to say goodbye. When the doctor presented them to me, they did not really look like babies, but my heart shattered nonetheless. The doctor tried to distract me by telling me that the next time I was in that room, I would be delivering a baby.

On the way home in the car, Feisal told me that we had to accept God's will and try again. Gazing out the car window, I could not get the embryos out of my mind. I told Feisal that I was amazed at how a tiny piece of flesh could transform into a baby.

Feisal saw the answer in the Quran—it was a miracle of God.

I said I could only pray for a healthy embryo the next time.

"Inshallah," Feisal added. God willing.

Within six months, I was pregnant again. Again I miscarried; again I grieved. My expectations, fantasies, and hopes for this child too were dashed. I then embarked upon what many women who have difficulty carrying a child to term have experienced—the fertility gauntlet. I switched to an eminent female doctor and sat nervously in her waiting room, another woman in a room full of hopefuls praying for a miracle baby. I sat surrounded by walls covered with photos of smiling moms holding beautiful babies—the doctor's success stories. The doctor had a very empathetic approach, but the facts were difficult to process. Men could have children into their seventies while women's fertility fell off after the age of thirty-six.

The doctor said that there was an option—a donor egg. With a donor egg, I could be rocking a baby in my arms within a year. Had we considered this option?

At the dinner table, I asked Feisal if we could use a donor egg. He told me that the Quran mentions conception only within the institution of marriage, and any donor would have to be the wife. Unless the donor egg came from me, the procedure would be prohibited. I wondered, though, if perhaps this was a matter of interpretation. Was it possible to look at the situation from another angle?

Feisal was definitive. He could not have a child using the donor egg of a woman he was not married to. And there were other considerations, he added. What if the child's lineage came into question? What if the donor decided to claim the child? There were many philosophical issues beyond the religious one.

I was crushed. A decision was being made for me. But I wanted children. I did not want to accept myself as a barren woman. I still felt, more than ever, that I was meant to be a mother, a nurturer.

Feisal took my hand as we agreed to exhaust every means possible to conceive the natural way.

In another six months, I became pregnant again. A woman in our spiritual circle, who was known to be a clairvoyant, noticed my glow and asked if I was carrying a child. When I quietly nodded yes, she gave me a big smile and assured me it would be a beautiful baby boy.

The pregnancy was going well until it too ended abruptly, at around five weeks.

I became despondent—not only about the loss, but also over what could have been. I had imagined my children as naughty pranksters like myself and mellow bookworms like my husband. I could not believe that I could not give birth to these children, nurture and teach them, ground them ethically, and mold them into the great human beings I knew they would have been. My hormones went into over-drive, and the only things that kept me sane were my strong relationship with my husband and our faith. For the first time, I was not alone in seeking solace—we were together, and he was an expert guide.

I felt challenged by the hadith that says, "Paradise lies at the feet of the mother." If so, why was God not letting me experience motherhood? Was I responsible for this tragedy? Was I paying for some unknown sins? Deep down, I knew I was not at fault. But how could this be God's plan? I could not understand why God would not bless me with a child, but I knew I could not bear another loss, emotionally or physically.

Feisal was philosophical. Sometimes things happen for a reason, and what may appear to be a bad thing turns out to be good. Perhaps God had a better plan.

Was I being left childless because God was trying to relieve me from parental duties so that I could focus on a greater purpose? As I grappled with the spiritual significance of my childlessness, I turned back to the Quran for guidance. It stated, "God grants whom He wills males and females, and He makes whom He wills barren" (42:50). The line seemed to suggest that my inability to carry a child to term was part of a divine plan. Then I read somewhere that having children is a blessing, while not having children is a mercy.

I therefore sought comfort in the stories of spiritual women, such as Asiya, the wife of Pharaoh, who despite being married to a king never conceived. Khadijah, the first wife of the Prophet, gave birth to six children while married to the Prophet, but her two boys died as children. God did not spare even his own Prophet. I wondered what Aisha, the youngest wife of the Prophet, who never bore any children, did with her life after his death. I discovered that she devoted all her time to spreading Muhammad's message and narrated 2,210 hadiths, his teachings on matters related to his private life and societal topics. She served the Muslim community for forty-four years and was given the honorific "Mother of the Believers."

Although I could not compare myself to these luminaries of my faith, I concluded that God gives different blessings to different people and I had to be content with what came my way. I would utilize the blessings I had for the enrichment of others. Khadijah had been my first role model—she taught me the importance of believing in my husband and the significance of his mission and the need to sacrifice wealth and comfort to carry that mission out. Now I had the chance to emulate Aisha, to contribute as she had toward the advancement of our faith and exemplify Muslim women's leadership.

My miscarriages were an emotional devastation, but they sowed another kind of seed. My four lost children could not have been in vain. They were meant to be, even if they were not to be born. As I realized that God must have had a plan in sending and then recalling them, the tears dried on my cheeks. I could accept that I would not be a birth mother, difficult as that might be. What I could not accept was not having a purpose. I prayed intently for guidance and put all my faith in my creator. But instead of focusing on my own narrow world, my work and my personal life, I turned outward, toward an entire community of young people. I would nurture them and help them grow. And I became, in this way, a mother of many.

A GENERATION OF MUSLIMS WAS COMING OF AGE WITH NEW and challenging issues. Young families were growing. While the mosque where my husband preached was an important place to worship, these young people had other needs. Religion is nurturing, but without a social aspect, it can be isolating, particularly to those of mixed cultural heritage who are trying to find their footing. This I knew all too well. Social activities give context to religion and allow people to celebrate their beliefs with others who share them. Clearly there was a need for networking, meeting others, and establishing continuing education classes to deepen religious knowledge and forge a healthy American Muslim identity that was reflective of American culture.

While the current mosque was a fully functioning place of worship, it was small, which limited its ability to hold social functions and arts programs. As a professional designer, I knew how important space is to people's lives. Simply moving women up from the basement of a mosque, for instance, could change the outlook and attitude of an entire congregation. The prayer area had square footage, but it was a sanctified space—you had to remove your shoes upon entering, and certain social activities, such as eating, were not permitted there. Technology was also not up-to-date.

Feisal and I dreamed of developing an institution that would be devoted to an authentic expression of Islam through cultural and religious harmony. I hoped this might include opportunities for young Muslims to seek mentoring and find community. Historically in America, most religions have gone through a trajectory—they begin by focusing on places of worship but eventually broaden to include institutions like YMCAs and Jewish Community Centers that also offer services such as childcare, gyms, educational courses, and arts programs. In the same way, we Muslims needed to develop local institutions that would give back to the broader community. Feisal and I started to work on this idea, which began to take shape and gain momentum. In 1997, my husband and I founded the American Sufi Muslim Association—later renamed the American Society for Muslim Advancement, or ASMA. ASMA was formed as a non-profit religious and educational organization dedicated to building bridges between the American public and American Muslims through activities related to culture, the arts, and current affairs. In 2000, to acquire our dream community center, we tried to buy the old McBurney YMCA building on Twenty-third Street in Manhattan but were outbid by another buyer.

ALTHOUGH OUR PLANS TO build a community center were put on hold when we lost the bid for the McBurney Y, my husband and I continued to build the community without walls to hold it. We each had a clearly defined role. Feisal was the religious and thought leader, and I volunteered as executive director. But as the imam's right-hand person as well as his wife, I also became a sounding board for and adviser to young women who related to a workingwoman who understood their issues and concerns. They saw in us a modern Muslim couple who were integrated into American culture but had roots in traditional societies. We were living proof that no one had to make the impossible choice of dispensing with their faith to be a true American, an equal partner, an engaged citizen.

One of the first women who approached me in my new role had been forcibly married at a young age, and now she was divorced and having another kind of crisis. She told me she had four children—

but she had known she was gay for her entire life. Was there any hope for her?

I knew she was on a spiritual quest and was looking for unconditional acceptance. I reminded her that she carried the same spark of the divine as everybody else. I then recalled the inscription on Rumi's tomb, which I had seen when visiting the shrine in Konya. Though these words are attributed to Rumi, they were written by a medieval Persian poet, Abu Said Abul Khair (967–1049). To welcome her into our community, I read these words of tolerance to her, which perfectly reflected my feelings about open-heartedness and nonjudgment.

> *Come back, come back, whatever you are, come back.*
> *Be you an infidel, a Magian, or an idle worshiper, come back.*
> *This threshold of ours is not a place for hopelessness,*
> *though you may have broken your penance a hundred times,*
>   *come back.*

>   *—Translation by Behrooz Karjoo*

AS THE WIFE OF the imam, I found myself involved in many community issues. Although Feisal was the one conducting the marriage ceremonies, I was the premarital adviser counseling couples and their families. I also aided in funerals and birth rites. One young woman who sought me out told me she was a lesbian and asked if she could pray beside me. She said she had knocked on the doors of many mosques but had not felt accepted. I was reminded of my own attempts to find a comfortable and safe place to worship. I reassured her that she would be welcome in God's house, where everyone's prayers were equal.

I made myself available to those who wanted to ask very tough questions about their faith. I found I was the one they came to because I had gone through the journey myself. Young women struggling with multicultural issues especially sought me out. Scheherazade, a woman in her early thirties who wanted to wear white at her wedding, reminded me of myself at my own ceremony. She was a first-generation Indian immigrant, and her fiancé was Cuban. "My family said, 'You can wear any color, but not white!'" she told me, adding, "Oh, and they also said, 'And not red! Red is a Hindu color.' My wedding is becoming my worst nightmare!" As completely as I understood how this young woman felt, I also knew that, as she was about to marry a Buddhist who had converted from Catholicism, the color of her gown was the least of the issues she was facing.

Mahida, who had grown up on the East Coast, was referred to me by a friend. She was frustrated because she had not been allowed to look at boys—there were curtains dividing males and females in her mosque; the two sexes were never allowed to socialize and were forbidden to even talk to one another—so she did not even know any Muslim men. How was she supposed to marry one? She sighed in exasperation as she said, "But you are married to an imam, Daisy. You never went through this."

I told Mahida that I had been punished for just waving at a boy from a school bus and that my uncle had made it his life's mission to keep me from dating while I was living under his roof.

At that, she visibly relaxed. We both laughed, and suddenly we had a bond.

Then there was a Muslim man who had spent his whole life wanting to have the last word with every person he ever met, until one day he was stopped cold by a petite, beautiful green-eyed woman—who happened to be Jewish.

This man was my old friend Muz, who called to announce that he had found "the one." Muz was getting married! And he was fine with what he called "the Jewish thing." Helene's family had welcomed him, as had his welcomed Helene. What did I think we could do for the wedding? Was there a way to combine the two traditions? I was thrilled that Muz had found happiness—now I was the one counseling him!

The wedding, a civil ceremony, was conducted by a friend who

was a judge. It was held outdoors under a tree, blending the traditions of the bride and groom. To fulfill their wish to honor both
traditions, they improvised by using cultural symbolism: They
wrapped themselves in a Jewish prayer shawl, and verses from the
poet Kahlil Gibran were read.

Before the wedding, I had asked Muz what was always a key
question in mixed marriages: In what religion were they going to
raise their children?

His answer was simple—no religion. Religion was off the table.
He was confident about that.

Until a daughter was born and, a few years later, she asked him
the dreaded question—what is God? Muz called me, panicked. What
should he tell her?

I suggested he tell her what my grandfather had told me during
our early gardening talks: "God is in everything—the trees, the flowers, the air, and in your heart!"

Muz, the former Mr. Cool, whom not even the Salman Rushdie
affair had been able to ruffle, was a little unhinged by his tiny girl. I
envisioned him pacing the room, clutching the phone as we spoke.
He had tried to keep his daughter's upbringing secular. He never
discussed religion. How had his three-year-old daughter even learned
about God? Why had she brought it up?

I told Muz that he had to face the fact that, unlike him, his daughter was a spiritual being.

The phone line went silent for a moment. Then, my old friend
reminded me of something we both knew—back in Kashmir, his
family had included noted mystics. I laughed when I pointed out
that mysticism, like eye color or musical talent, could skip a generation. For once, Muz had no comeback. I knew—and because Muz
knew me and my family, he very well knew—what might lie ahead.

I DIVORCE THEE;
I DIVORCE THEE;
I DIVORCE THEE

. . .

I was in my office at ASMA in 2007 when I got a call from a distraught young woman in Florida who had found me on the Internet. She said her "older sister" had been verbally divorced by her husband, who "in an angry fit" had unthinkingly proclaimed, "I divorce thee; I divorce thee; I divorce thee." Many Muslim men believe that if they pronounce, "I divorce thee" thrice, they are de facto divorced.

But this woman hoped against hope. Just because he'd said, "I divorce thee" three times, was the wife really divorced? she asked me.

I answered that because we live in the United States, we have to follow the law of the land. In the eyes of American law, the couple was not divorced.

The woman sounded relieved.

I added that a divorce is not a light matter: You must go to court and declare your intent in writing, and only once your papers are processed are you legally divorced. She could tell her sister not to worry.

The next day, the woman called back, sounding shaken. Her brother-in-law had wanted assurance and had called his imam in Gujarat, India. When he told the imam what had happened, the imam said, "Absolutely, you are divorced. She is not your wife anymore. You have divorced her, and that's the end of it. And the only way you can remarry her is if she gets remarried and consummates her marriage and then gets divorced from her husband. Then you may marry her. But she is not your wife anymore."

I pointed out to her that even within Islam there are rules regarding divorce. If someone declaring a divorce is of sober mind, one can argue that the divorce is final. "Was the husband in his normal state of mind?" I asked.

No—apparently, he had spoken in a fit of anger.

I considered this. Then—he was temporarily insane?

"Oh yes," the woman agreed, "he had gone mad!"

If he was temporarily insane, I noted, and said something in a fit of anger, in Islamic law that is not considered to be an enactment of divorce. Of course, I realized that this was counter to what the authority in India had said as well as irrelevant in a U.S. court of law.

But the woman understood my point.

I suggested a simple solution. If the husband apologized to his wife and stated that he did not intend to divorce her, they could simply remain married.

The woman hesitated. She said she believed everything I was saying—but did I know a man who could relay this information? "Because they will only believe a man," she said.

I wanted to say, Really?! But the woman was distraught, and I wanted to help. Besides, I had heard this before. I turned to a young intern in my office, a Christian man who was studying Arabic, and asked him to get on the phone and repeat what I had said to her sister and brother-in-law. He did so, and not surprisingly, because it was conveyed by a male, my message was suddenly legitimized, and the marriage was saved.

GRADUALLY, MY OWN SPIRITUALITY BEGAN TO EVOLVE IN new ways, especially my relationship with prayer.

I have always felt a strong connection between the call to prayer and music. Even before I understood the meanings of the words, I had been transfixed by the melody of the recitation. To me, the call to prayer is the music of the soul. When I had first attended dhikr at the Sufi mosque in Tribeca, the rhythms and words had mesmerized me, and I would find myself repeating them to myself for hours after I had left the service.

Every time my husband did the call to prayer at the mosque in Arabic, I felt a sense of awe and found its meditative quality deeply transformative. Since I had not learned how to read the Quran in my childhood, reciting the call to prayer correctly was a distant ideal. As I observed Feisal, I began to memorize his tempo and replicate the ornamentation and repetition of every Arabic phrase: "God is great. God is great. I bear witness that there is only one God, and I bear witness that Muhammad is a messenger of God. Come to prayer. Come to success. God is great. There is only one God. . . ." When I was able to recite like a cantor would, I felt a deeper connection to my faith, and I felt more spiritually fulfilled. Rather than being an observer, I became a participant.

One day, I asked Feisal if I could recite the *adhan*, the call to prayer, to him. He was taken aback by this request, but I told him I found the rhythm moving and compelling; I recited the melodic passages to him to see his reaction. Where, he asked, amazed, had I learned this?

From him, of course. From listening. Was it so surprising that a woman would wish to access the same deep spiritual connections as a man? The recitation had ignited my spirit and allowed me to reciprocate God's words back to Him. To me, the fact that tradition did not allow a woman to perform the call to prayer was not so much an impediment to spiritualism as a hindrance to the path of leadership.

I struggled to accept that classical scholars were opposed to granting leadership roles to women in mosques. My husband commented that there was no edict that said that only a man could be an imam; what qualifies a person is his or her ability to lead the congregation in prayer and to follow the rules of the recitation of the Quran. Because there was nothing barring me, or any other qualified woman, from leading prayer, he suggested I start with leading women. "If the Quran is silent on a subject," he said, "it is de facto permissible." To encourage me on my spiritual path, Feisal suggested that I do the *adhan* in the house for the two of us, as well as for family and for the women's prayer. So my performing the call to prayer began within a small circle. Until, inadvertently, that changed.

In my mind, the line between what a woman could do in private and what she could do in public was unclear. I said to my eighty-four-year-old father-in-law, Dr. Muhammad Abdul Rauf, a humble, conservative, but open-minded imam who was teaching me how to recite the Quran correctly, "Dad, can I publicly recite the *adhan* as well?" Without hesitation, he answered that women's voices are considered to be *awrah* (their private parts) and, therefore, women's speech could cause temptation. I understood what he was saying— this was the case in other religions as well. But I was not satisfied with the answer and countered by asking my father-in-law, "If God wished women to lower their voice or have no voice, why did he give us a tongue?" To further my argument, I queried him as to why women could recite the Quran publicly but were prohibited from doing the call to prayer under any circumstance. What was the difference? My father-in-law thought I was being provocative. I had no desire to be disrespectful, but I was ready to tiptoe right up to the fine line between spirited inquiry and defiance.

I fervently wished to gain my father-in-law's approval out of my deep respect for him. Yet at the same time, I had to ask myself why, if I was an empowered, independent woman ready to break with thousands of years of tradition and claim equality, gaining his approval was so critical. I thought of Dadaji, whose approval had always meant everything to me—to our entire family. Without his approval, any decision had always felt hollow. Now my father-in-law was the head of my family.

I suggested to him that a live demonstration would prove to him that a woman's call to prayer was as spiritually nourishing as that of a man's. My father-in-law was silent for a moment, then asked me to recite the *adhan*. I knew this was the most important recitation of my life. As I performed the call to prayer, I could tell that he was listening very intently. I expected him to correct my cadences and pronunciation, but instead it seemed as if he had entered a sacred space.

After I finished the call to prayer, my father-in-law stood, kissed my forehead, and proclaimed it one of the most beautiful things he had ever heard.

His approbation was both a spiritual and cultural milestone for me.

Now I pushed even further and asked him to issue a fatwa (legal decree) proclaiming that women could indeed recite the call to prayer. He responded that he was too old and at that point in his life had no desire to upset the tradition himself but that I had his blessing and permission to recite the call to prayer anywhere I wished. Now, with the male spiritual leaders in my family behind me, I felt ready to perform the call to prayer publicly.

In 2003, I was invited to an interfaith breakfast in Washington, D.C., where I agreed to do the call to prayer as an invocation. On the train to Washington, I was concerned that I might make a mistake. I was nervous. There were two hundred people in the room as I stepped up to the podium, covered my hair, and recited the call to prayer in Arabic. After the breakfast, a woman approached me and took my hand. "This," she said, "is the face of Islam that we never see or hear."

WOMEN'S MARCH—
CALLING TO PRAY

...

The year 2016 proved to be a pivotal time for American women, as we watched with shock and dismay as everything women had fought so hard for suddenly came under threat. During one of the presidential debates, Donald Trump referred to Hillary Clinton as a "nasty woman." After another debate he said that one of the moderators, Megyn Kelly, had "blood coming out of her eyes." These remarks spurred a grandma from Hawaii to post a suggestion on Facebook that women organize a march after the presidential inauguration of Donald Trump. Thus the largest protest in U.S. history was born. The more it expanded, the more issues it came to encompass, and the more issues it encompassed, the harder it had to work to be inclusive. The march gave women a way to define their purpose and create a feeling of solidarity and hope, but for it to be truly successful, complete inclusivity was necessary.

Four women, Tamika Mallory, Carmen Perez, Bob Bland, and Linda Sarsour, co-chaired the march. My friend and leadership cohort from Denver, Tony Massaro, connected me to the sister cities coalition, which was keen to accommodate Muslim women throughout the march. From my network of Muslim women, I pulled in Rafath, who enthusiastically shared her commitment with Ceci, Barbara, Sharon, Luan, and Claire, the organizers of the march in Chicago. Rafath said at the time, "It's going to be exciting but more historical. The message will be loud and clear. We will march forward and not be intimidated. We will be fearless and shine with hope and beauty."

The Muslim prayer times on the day of the march were at 12:01 P.M. and 2:26 P.M., so I asked if the organizers would honor the call to prayer and create accessibility and safety for Muslim women to pray. The group immediately responded with an affirmative! Dale of the American Jewish Committee, representing the Sisterhood of Salaam Shalom, arranged for women of other faiths not only to join the prayer but also to create a buffer for the women by forming a circle around them as they prayed.

Muslim women leaders were invited onstage to share the age-old call to worship, a sacred moment, with their sisters. Fifteen years after I had recited the call to prayer on a national television program, the female Muslim chaplain of Northwestern, Tahera Khan, stepped up to the podium and harmoniously recited the adhan, which was amplified on a loudspeaker so it could be heard at a great distance by thousands of fellow marchers.

The display of solidarity among as many as five million marchers around the world was breathtaking. Their genuine desire to make Muslim women feel welcome proved to me that the Women's March was exactly what it claimed to be—a nonhierarchical, grassroots movement. It was inclusive and broad in its appeal, which spread out and attracted people of various genders, races, and generations.

F ROM THE BEGINNING OF OUR RELATIONSHIP, MY HUSBAND
was always of the belief that women could and should be actively involved in becoming a voice for an ethical and spiritual Islam.
He encouraged me to speak on my own about the tenets of Islam.
Perhaps, I thought, a faith-driven woman working for change at
ground level might inspire others. Perhaps I could be that woman. I
was someone women could relate to, a woman who had experienced
some of their same problems. Giving a voice to these issues was
something I felt comfortable doing, and so I began to become more
involved.

In 2000 our friend Michael Wolfe, who was the producer of the
PBS documentary *Muhammad: Legacy of a Prophet,* asked my husband to be an adviser on the film. Much to my surprise, Michael then
asked me to participate as well. Would I be one of the storytellers? I
immediately refused.

Michael was emphatic. My contribution would be my voice.
As a teenager in America, I had grappled with challenges and
contradictions—I'd spanned two worlds, that of being a Muslim and
that of seeking to become an American.

I understood the angle but wondered why I had been selected. I
had no Islamic credentials, I didn't wear a hijab, and I didn't want
people to pass judgment on me. Nor did I want to inadvertently affect this worthy project.

Michael explained that he viewed me as a woman thoroughly engaged with American society and whose face was an expression of Islam that was uniquely American. This was the first time I had been approached to speak as a representative of multicultural American women. In fact, even at the millennium, few Muslim women were approached by the media to share their views on Islam. Would a documentary producer who did not know my husband have approached me out of the blue? Probably not. I was not an Islamic scholar or an academic—I wasn't the most informed resource on religious matters or scriptural issues. But as the wife of an imam and as an advocate for Muslim women's rights, I was in a unique position. Appearing in this documentary would be an important step—for all of us. I had never thought that my bifurcated life could be an advantage, but now I saw that it could be an entry point for others. And, Michael explained, through the medium of film, I would reach a vast audience.

I remembered the dream in which the Prophet had appeared in my room and given me his nod of approval. Recalling the dream and its significance was a deciding factor in my accepting a role in telling his story. Perhaps he had given me his blessing because, through the documentary, someone hearing my voice and relating to my story would feel less alone.

I agreed to be filmed in my role as a mentor in the privacy of my home. My mentees were eight young women: Saleemah, an African American; Naz, a Bangladeshi American; Fatima, a Brazilian Palestinian; and five others. When the time for prayer came, I faced the qibla, toward Mecca, and recited the call to prayer, the *adhan,* in a slow tempo. Thinking only in terms of mentorship, I had not considered that millions of people would be watching me break three barriers on national television: a woman performing the call to prayer, a woman leading the prayer, and a woman being a spiritual mentor while not wearing a hijab.

Since the documentarians were producing a film that portrayed the history of Islam through the life of the Prophet, I had to be prepared to answer correctly whatever questions they asked. I realized I

needed my husband's help to do an in-depth study of the life of the
Prophet and women's status in Islam.

AMONG THE QUESTIONS I asked my husband were those that per-
tained to women as spiritual leaders. Moji had been a spiritual leader,
and scores of Sufi women were shaykhas, but I was not aware of any
woman having led a mixed congregation during Friday prayer. I knew
that the Quran did not prohibit it. In fact my husband told me that the
Prophet allowed women to lead prayers for their families; some even
said he allowed a woman, Umm Waraqa, to lead prayers for her community because she was the most knowledgeable. I felt that, as women
were now looking to me, there must be other women of faith to whom
I could turn for advice or inspiration. But no matter where I looked I
found no accessible female role models or mentors. We women were
all walking as if in a fog with the Quran as our compass—but the
Quran, having been interpreted by men for centuries, did not provide
answers for many modern dilemmas. Still, a close study of the Quran's
verses convinced me that gender parity is part of the divine plan.

As a scholar, my husband never gave an answer directly; instead
he would mention all the sources, pointing to the books and the
leather-bound concordances on the shelves. In the beginning, I had
simply stood beside him and repeated his pronouncements. Gradually, as I immersed myself in the study of the Quran and gained
knowledge and confidence, my own critical thinking emerged.

I felt I was ready for the challenges that the documentary presented. But history intervened.

Although the program was scheduled to air in 2001, its TV pre-
mier was delayed because of the events of 9/11.

PBS FINALLY AIRED *MUHAMMAD: Legacy of a Prophet* in December
2002, a little more than a year after the attacks. But the documentary
now included 9/11 and its aftershock. This was the first time that a
national audience would see how Muslims stood up against the terrorists and refused to let them hijack their religion.

Along with Kevin James, a Muslim firefighter, I became an integral part of the film. After the documentary aired, I immediately received dozens of phone calls, emails, and letters, most of which were positive, but a few were blistering. One email from a male American convert to Islam accused me of being a whore for not wearing a headscarf. Although this was the worst criticism, other conservative Muslims were angered at the notion that I, "a woman without hijab," had been chosen to help portray the life of the Prophet in a national airing. Of course, it was not the first time I'd heard this criticism, nor would it be the last. An older gentleman would approach me in the mosque to beseech me to cover my hair. He would say, "You are so important to our community. If you only covered your hair, you would be a perfect role model." To be honest, there are several conventions and forums to which I am not invited because my hair is not covered. I wish they would look at my heart and not my head.

Muslim women wear burqas, niqabs, hijabs, or headscarves for a variety of reasons. Some genuinely do it out of piety, while others do not want to be objectified. A twenty-four-year-old woman said to me, "I just want to keep my body private." Others are conforming to local customary dress. Some are rebelling against state politics. Still others are making statements about religious identity. Some are required by others to live as invisible beings.

Many American Muslim women wear the hijab as a sign of modesty yet still embrace all the rights and opportunities given to Western women. All Islam requires is that people believe in God; abide in truth, patience, and humility; give alms; observe the fast; guard their chastity; and remember God. This is the mandate. Burqas and hijabs have never been the sixth pillar of Islam. I am a living example of how Muslim women can balance faith with modernity.

After the airing of the documentary, I had expected criticism from some hardliners but was disappointed by the fierceness of their reactions. I was saddened that these reactionaries ignored the battle I was fighting on behalf of my fellow Muslims and focused solely on the fact that my hair was uncovered.

BUT THE PROPHET WAS
A FEMINIST

...

It was thrilling to have the opportunity to meet the formidable feminist Gloria Steinem at a luncheon in 2007. I was surprised to find a very approachable, slim woman, elegantly dressed in black, poised and soft-spoken but with a piercing intelligence. I decided to listen and learn from her interaction with the thirty powerful American women in the room. But after the luncheon, I overheard Ms. Steinem say that patriarchy in monotheistic religions was responsible for women not getting their rights. The three major monotheistic religions—Judaism, Christianity, and Islam—are all Abrahamic. In other words, Abraham is a common ancestor of all of them, with Moses, Jesus, and Muhammad thought to be his descendants. Steinem seemed to be comparing these religions to Eastern religions, such as Buddhism and Hinduism, implying that there was no injustice to women in those religions because there was no sole, all-powerful, assumedly male god to generate patriarchal practices and traditions among their followers. I felt I had to speak up and correct her—privately, when the crowd had left. So I lingered and finally approached her.

When I mentioned what she had said, she reiterated the example of Christianity: Jesus was a man; God is male; there is no room for the feminine.

I told her about my experience as a child in India watching Bollywood movies in which a crowd of men would forcibly grab a young Hindu wife and burn her alive on her husband's funeral pyre. This was done in the name of Hinduism.

Ms. Steinem looked appalled and she said she thought that terrible practice was in the past and had ended.

I told her that Indian women had challenged this interpretation of the scripture and had succeeded in passing legislation to ban the practice. But young Hindu women were still being sent to their deaths because some scholars of the religion justified it in the name of Hinduism—which was not a monotheistic religion.

Ms. Steinem said she had never thought of it that way.

I added my feeling that it wasn't religion that was at fault but the interpretation of it. I explained that fourteen hundred years ago Muslim women had the right to divorce, to inherit, to receive an education, and to own property, yet today, in certain Muslim countries, women were being denied all those rights.

Yes, she told me, she had read somewhere that Prophet Muhammad was the feminist of his time.

Perhaps, I thought, she had seen the article with that title that I'd written for Women's eNews, *the nonprofit news service that covers women's issues. I pointed out that it was difficult to discuss the history of feminism without talking about the Prophet Muhammad and the rights that he gave to women fourteen hundred years ago.*

Steinem then asked how she could help Muslim women.

Would she consider saying publicly that the Prophet Muhammad was a feminist of his time? I asked her. I realized that saying this might be a stretch for her, but it was a true statement, and something I thought America's leading feminist should contemplate. I do not know if she ever mentioned it, but

*at least I had planted a seed. Recently, when Steinem appeared
on Bill Maher's show, in response to Maher's question about
Muslim women, she said, "In his time, the Prophet Muhammad
was a reformer on a number of issues for women." I was thrilled
that my words to her had opened her to a new understanding.*

CHAPTER

25

THE DAY BEFORE 9/11 I WAS SITTING ON TOP OF THE MOST beautiful mountain in Golden, Colorado, while my stepdaughter Zahra was getting married to Bob, a handsome man with golden hair who was brought up as a Protestant but had converted to Islam to show his love for her. My husband had conducted the wedding, and it was truly spectacular—a bright, warm, pine-scented, golden day.

The town of Golden reminded me of my birthplace, the Kashmir Valley, just as beautiful with its majestic mountains, towering pines, and shimmering streams. The bridal party was eating breakfast in the hotel restaurant when someone yelled out, "You better come and see what's on television." We ran to watch and saw the towers coming down, but the event had already taken place—we were on Mountain Time. Watching the collapse of the two towers felt unreal, like watching a sci-fi movie—a gigantic cloud of embers thundered its way through downtown Manhattan, seemingly obliterating everything in its path.

For me the occurrence was deeply personal, because those were my towers. I had worked there for more than four years, and as I saw people jump out of the windows, I was horrified, transfixed. That was my city, my neighborhood, and our mosque was twelve blocks away from the site. I remember nervously telling my husband, "I hope it's not a Muslim."

We immediately knew our lives had changed—if Muslim terrorists had carried out this attack, it was imperative that we distinguish between Islam and the ideology of terrorists.

Back in our hotel room, we started making frantic phone calls, getting in touch with the people we knew who worked in the towers or its environs. Since Feisal was the de facto spokesperson to whom the media turned for commentary, it was crucial that we get back to New York as soon as possible. But we quickly learned that all flights were grounded. The only way to get back was to drive cross-country. Fortunately for us, we had rented a car. Three days earlier—which already seemed like a lifetime ago—I had suggested that we rent an economy-size car because we were in Golden for only two days, but Feisal had insisted on getting a Lincoln. It was roomy, and the four of us—Feisal, myself, my mother-in-law, and my stepdaughter Fatima—could all fit comfortably in it. My father-in-law had remained at our home in New Jersey. "Too old," he had said. The car rental rules were suspended to allow people to drive home. The car rental company would not even charge us for the extra fuel. We started driving east.

The highways were packed with cars of families trying to get back home. People were carpooling, sharing rooms in hotels with strangers. There was a feeling of camaraderie and communal sorrow. In the face of the worst of humanity, the best of humanity was emerging.

Every hotel or motel we stopped at was booked solid. We kept on driving, nine, ten, eleven hours in shifts. We looked through our address books to see whom we could stay with and where we could hear the latest news on television. Feisal had a brother in Kansas. Aisha, a friend of Feisal's, welcomed us in her home in Kentucky, where we sat in her yurt together, grieving for our nation.

The calls started coming in from the media while we were driving. Feisal answered them on a clunky pre-BlackBerry cellphone. They were asking: Why have Muslims attacked us? Why do they hate America? We were on the defensive. We were American Muslims who had to explain the actions of a group of fanatics who had substantively hijacked our religion.

Yet, I thought, we have seen these people. We have seen what they do. I thought of Ramzi Yousef and his mentor Omar Abdel Rahman, the blind cleric, who had tried to bomb the towers eight years before but had failed. If this new attack had been done in the name of Islam, then this time Yousef's coconspirators had succeeded. I felt anger, grief, loss of innocence, confusion, all lumped together.

There were two parts of myself that I was battling—the Muslim part and the American part. I wished that I were just an American without the Muslim label, because it prevented me from sharing the grief as other Americans were sharing it. Feeling the need to push back and defend our religion from those who were trying to hijack it interfered with the ability to simply mourn the loss of lives, the destruction of my city, and a loss of innocence. And then we started hearing stories on the car radio about how a poor Sikh guy in Texas was shot because he was mistaken for a Muslim, about Muslim women harassed because they were wearing a hijab, about a poor guy in some godforsaken gas station somewhere in the Midwest who was beaten black and blue. We heard that there was an Egyptian mastermind among the nineteen hijackers. I remember thinking that if I had not been at the wedding, I would have been on the New York Waterway ferry from Port Imperial in New Jersey to Manhattan that morning, for my usual seven-minute-long commute. I would have seen the planes crash right into the towers. Holy Moses! I would have seen it happen.

As stories started emerging, we realized that among the dead and injured were members of the Muslim community. As our mosque was the closest to Ground Zero, we were an integral part of the Lower Manhattan community, and as such we were needed to provide care and counseling. Among the people of ninety nationalities who had perished, there were sixty Muslims.

While on the road, we received a call from my father-in-law. Although he was in his eighties, not knowing what was about to happen, we had thought he would be okay at home. And of course he didn't watch any television, though he read *The New York Times* from the front page all the way to the last. It took him forever, but he read it religiously every day.

Apparently, Dad was confused. "I was sitting in the living room," he said when he reached us, "and all of a sudden, there was something thrown at the house, and I didn't know what had happened, and then a guy called on the phone and told me to go home, and I said, 'I'm home,' and the guy said, 'No, go home.' And I said, 'Where do you want me to go?' And the guy said, 'Go back to wherever you come from.' And I said, 'You want me to go to Washington?' Feisal, why are they telling me to go home? Do you not want me to stay here?"

My heart sank. *Dad! Oh my God, Dad!*

Dad was home alone, and somebody had thrown something at the house and was harassing him. We called our neighbor Eddie, who had known Feisal for nearly thirty years. Feisal asked Eddie to take the American flag that he flew outside of his house and place it in front of ours. "Please protect Dad," Feisal told Eddie. "Make sure no harm comes to him."

We reached home late at night and were very happy to see that Dad was okay. Eddie had brought him food, visited the house constantly, and guarded it. We discussed the events with Dad. And he was visibly shaken. "Ya Allah! How can they do this?" he said. "How can anybody kill so many innocent people? This is *haram* [forbidden]. This cannot happen. This is not Islam."

ON MY DAILY COMMUTE on the ferry from New Jersey to Manhattan, I tended to stand in the front of the boat, on the bridge, because I loved to feel the changing seasons of New York: the crunching ice under the boat's bow, the smell of autumn in the brisk air, the sun's rays on a beautiful day in spring or summer. But when I returned to work nearly a week after 9/11, I did not stand on or even near the bridge. I couldn't bear to see the altered, smoldering skyline, and when I finally found the courage to confront it, I just couldn't believe the towers weren't there.

In the small ferry terminal, I felt yet another jolt—seeing the photographs of people who were missing or presumed dead hanging on the walls. The terminal had been turned into a shrine. Hand-painted paper hearts with the names of loved ones were pinned to bulletin boards, and large cardboard signs bore messages to departed relatives and friends.

There was an aura of mourning in the terminal. As I walked around looking at the faces on the walls, I recognized some of them: These were people I had commuted with every day. I felt awful. People who professed to share my faith had done this, in the name of my faith, I thought. Therefore, I would be held responsible. In addition to being in mourning, I began to carry this heavy burden of being a Muslim.

I had been away only four working days, and the world had changed. When I walked into my office on Fifty-seventh Street and Fifth Avenue, on that first day back, the grief was palpable. Before this, we had been co-workers, but while I had been away, they had lived through the terrible event and had mourned together. I, on the other hand, had been thrust with my husband into a media storm. I was at a loss for words to share with my colleagues. Fortunately the office manager sought me out to tell me that everyone understood that this was an especially complicated time for me and that they supported me. Any guilt by association that I had imposed on myself dissipated.

The horror of 9/11 helped me galvanize a cadre of young, American-born, college-educated, media-savvy Muslims who knew that the response had to be swift. I enlisted them, along with my friend Zeyba, to help organize an official response to the attacks. Zeyba prepared a statement, which read, in part: "9-11 for us Muslims created a huge tidal wave of human shock and emotion. And for Muslims it really was the darkest hour. On the one hand, we felt America, our land, was being attacked. On the other, we felt we had to be on the defensive."

Fear and distrust rippled throughout the country; no one was left untouched. Though the country agreed that we needed to stand together, no matter what our race or religion, there were so many raw sensitivities.

When there are no words, people often seek solace in art. I believed art had enormous power to serve as a counterpoise to the narrow image of Islam that most Americans were seeing, and I was confident that we needed artists to help touch the lives of our fellow citizens and to help us shift to a transformative way of thinking.

The Muslim artists' response to 9/11 was conceived under the auspices of ASMA and held at the Cathedral of Saint John the Divine, the largest cathedral in America. The event was called Reflections at a Time of Transformation: American Muslim Artists Reach Out to New Yorkers in the Aftermath of September 11.

Brian Lehrer of WNYC, the local public radio station, who had interviewed my husband, graciously agreed to emcee the event. Twenty-two artists—singers, fine artists, musicians, writers—would exhibit work or perform. On January 19, 2002, an impressive tapestry of the Muslim arts community was on full display for the audience of six hundred that filled the cathedral while a full-fledged blizzard was under way. The exhibition stretched beneath Dolly Unithan's canopy of 150 floating doves of peace. The event had a profound effect—not just on the audience, but also on those of us who organized it.

Salma Arastu, an artist and poet, delineated the anguish and confusion she felt in a painting depicting the debris of the towers. On the painting she wrote, *I am humanity . . . lips are trembling, I am shocked . . . , dumb . . . , I am humanity . . . , Insecure . . . , uncertain . . . In the twenty-first century . . . I am helpless . . . , amazed at my own rivals . . . , among my own people.* In his speech, California-born calligrapher Mohamed Zakariya, who designed the U.S. postage stamp commemorating the Muslim holiday Eid, said, "We need to show the soft, gentle side of Islam. Enough with the harshness, the revenge, and the crackpot conspiracy theories. The Prophet has said that 'there shall be no harm for harm, no revenge for revenge.'"

This became the first of many cultural interfaith events I was to conceive of in the spirit of unity.

When Yasemin, a mentee of mine, was interviewed by the media during the event, she proudly said that the exhibition exemplified the spirit of the Muslim community at its best. But speaking to the press was a new experience for her, and although she longed to answer more of the many questions asked of her, she felt ill equipped. So she left her New York job and pursued a master's degree in Islamic studies at the University of London.

While it is true that the events of 9/11 radically changed my life, they also changed the lives of thousands of Muslims, many of whom could have had lucrative careers in law, medicine, or finance but were moved instead to become social activists to explain the true values of Islam. My younger brother Zahid had left Kashmir to escape war and conflict and had moved into his new house two weeks before 9/11. The human toll and destruction caused by 9/11 left the civil engineer shaken. "What is the point of this destruction? Do they know what it takes to construct a building?" he asked me. He seemed shell-shocked.

Feisal's speaking engagements increased ten-, then twenty-, then thirtyfold. Our phone rang constantly, and the demand on him was enormous. He spoke at corporate memorials, in interfaith dialogues, with law enforcement, at churches, synagogues, and think tanks—and I joined him as often as I could. I felt it was important for me to hear people's responses to his comments and also for me to learn how to anticipate questions in case they were asked of me. But the protocol was: He spoke; I listened. He was at the podium; I was in the audience.

All went smoothly until the day I accidentally double-booked Feisal to speak at a Presbyterian church in Princeton, New Jersey— and, simultaneously, at a prominent synagogue in Rye, New York. My husband did not feel we could disappoint either group—and if we did so, they might think we were avoiding the issues. He decided that he would go to the synagogue and I would go to the church.

I wondered if I was ready and equipped to speak, but my husband was confident that I had the necessary knowledge and skills, because I had heard him speak a thousand times. He felt that as his student,

I was ready to take the next step. If I couldn't do it, he said, who could? On the drive to Princeton, I was a nervous wreck. I walked into a church basement to find an audience of about thirty people, almost all senior citizens. I began to speak about what Islam stands for, about its principles, and as I talked, people started nodding their heads, acknowledging what I was saying. Was I actually making an impact? I wondered. Then, as they became comfortable with me, the group began to ask questions.

The first question was "Why is Islam a violent religion?"

I was careful to answer this question the same way that my husband would: Islam is a religion of peace. I responded with all the theological arguments I had heard, every piece of scriptural evidence I knew, and they listened. I explained that what the terrorists did was antithetical to Islamic teachings, that it was more about politics than religion. And I gave examples the way Feisal would—for instance, reminding them that the Crusades took place in the name of Christianity. I said that while the majority of Muslims are peaceful, there's a tiny fraction of that number who are extremists, and they do the same thing that people have done around the world and over centuries—they use religion as a veneer to justify their political agenda. The audience understood that, because I was able to draw parallels within their own faith.

The second question was "Where are your leaders, and why don't they speak out?"

I responded that our leaders did speak out, but we didn't have a central authority in the way that Catholics have a pope. People were speaking out in their individual voices, but they weren't always being covered in the press. I talked about media filtering and told them how my husband had spoken out right after 9/11, for instance, but the story had never come through to the general public. There had been a press conference with interfaith leaders, about fifty or sixty people, including several imams, beneath the Brooklyn Bridge, and although the major media was present, including several TV crews, there was no coverage of the event the next day. I mentioned that the biggest response to 9/11, an event that six hundred people had attended, had received no press coverage. We were speaking out, but our message was not reaching the public. I felt frustrated that the media gave a prominent platform to the terrorists, constantly reporting on their nefarious activities but ignoring the voices and deeds of Muslims who were on the front lines countering them. In truth, I had no good answer for why this was the case. Faith, politics, and publicity are uneasy partners.

Then, just as the meeting was closing, a small, frail-looking woman in her eighties raised her hand. She asked, "What about women? Why are they treated as second-class citizens?"

I launched into my prepared answer—that Muslim women have historically had rights. Fourteen hundred years ago, when these rights were not granted to even Western women, Muslim women had the right to property, the right to divorce, the right to inheritance, the right to have financial independence, and the right to have a career. In Islam, women are equal in the eyes of God. As I continued speaking, the woman held up her hand until I stopped talking, and then she said quietly, "I believe you, dear, but can you explain why that woman with the blue burqa was shot and stoned in a sports field in Afghanistan?"

I froze, because the image of that woman, a mother of five children, who had been falsely accused of adultery, being dragged to the center of a stadium and shot by the Taliban to the cheers of male spectators had so traumatized me and angered me because of my inability to do anything about it. The atrocity was against everything Islam teaches, especially about the status of women—that paradise lies at the feet of the mother. I opened my mouth to respond, but no words came out. There was really nothing I could say.

The woman sensed my distress. She said, "Never mind, dear—just tell me what you are doing about it."

What was *I* doing about it?

That question changed my life. As I drove the hour back home from Princeton, I began to think. Here I was, living in the most powerful country in the world; I was empowered by all the men in my family; I was married to an imam of global influence. That made me, by association, an influential woman. And what was I doing in the fight for women's rights? If not me, then who? It was a question that refused to be ignored, that begged for my answer.

I turned the question over and over in my head. I felt as if a giant pot was boiling inside me, and I was stirring and stirring without a recipe to follow.

ONE OF THE POSITIVE OUTCOMES OF THE EVENT HELD AT
Saint John the Divine was my meeting Sarah. A dynamic
pregnant woman, Sarah was a member of the Methodist Church of
Saint Paul and Saint Andrew. Like me, she came from a strong faith
background—her father was a minister. And she was a force of nature.

Sarah told me that her friends and colleagues at Saint Paul and
Saint Andrew had no Muslim friends and knew nothing about the
Muslim faith. The media seemed to make a point of hitting only the
sound bites, and she believed there was a need to reconcile the gap
between Muslims and people of other faiths. We wondered about the
opportunities to establish a channel for interfaith women's dialogue.
Although I had attended various interfaith occasions, such as interfaith Passover seders and celebrations of Ramadan, and had been
involved in dialogues alongside my husband with rabbis and pastors,
I had never spearheaded an interfaith dialogue on my own. But Sarah
was several steps ahead of me. She was ready to, as she put it, "shatter
the stereotypes" by demonstrating the commonalities rather than the
differences between faiths and their cultures.

The pathway would be through theater. Sarah wanted to take interfaith dialogue and put it on the stage—in the form of a play, with
a goal of creating a visceral, eye-opening experience that would provide a new level of insight. Just hearing the word "theater" filled me
with joy. Recalling my convent days, when I played the role of Henry

Higgins in *My Fair Lady*, I immediately agreed to become Sarah's Muslim partner. We were starting with a blank canvas, our only brush our creativity, and I knew we could let our imaginations go in infinite directions.

Sarah introduced me to Eileen, a tall, slim, brown-haired agnostic Jew in her forties. Like Sarah, Eileen had a background in theater and was an avid social justice activist who had started the organization Jews Against Genocide in Bosnia. Eileen was a jokester who, when introduced to my husband, was delighted by his sense of humor, especially his Egyptian jokes. An imam with wit—who would expect that? Early on, she said to me, "I can't believe how funny you and Feisal are. I love the silliness, and I love how you both get the power of the arts!"

When I repeated this to Feisal, he replied that there is nothing more powerful than personal relationships to break through stereotypes. As a couple, we knew this would be a difficult project for us logistically because I worked full-time, but it was not easy for the other women either. Sarah, after all, was working through her pregnancy, but like most women, we knew that for something important, we would find a way.

And so the plan was set: Sarah would represent the Methodist church, Eileen would represent the B'nai Jeshurun synagogue, and I would represent Muslims. It was humbling and daunting to be one woman representing the 1.5 billion of my faith, but, I reasoned, that is, after all, what each of my fellow Muslims do every day: We are all ambassadors.

We began the process by interviewing hundreds of New Yorkers of the three Abrahamic faiths. The next step was to co-write a script and plan the production, recruiting artists and musicians and assembling a multifaith group of volunteers. We decided to start with nonpolitical issues, then segue to more sensitive questions, such as "What is the path to reconciliation?" The interviews would be anonymous, captured on audiotape—no video, no pictures—and conducted one-on-one in respondents' homes, community centers, and sacred spaces. The interviewees would represent a wide range of voices—liberal, conservative, and orthodox. Their words would form the basis of the play, whose title would be *Same Difference*. The script, we decided, would involve the actual words of people interviewed, interwoven with original music and dance, which would be performed with an eclectic group of musicians.

Despite whatever we three women thought we knew, we had much to learn. An interviewee who wore the hijab recalled one incident in which she was told to "go back home." One of our Jewish colleagues told of being ambushed by an Egyptian woman in Queens who accused Jews of causing 9/11, a fallacy that had been spread in her community. Throughout the process, we each, in some way, experienced becoming "the other." We heard from a suburban Muslim family who went to bed every night fully dressed, expecting imminent deportation. A four-year-old child in Brooklyn told Eileen he was glad the World Trade towers fell, because it meant Jews had been killed. When the boy was told that Eileen was Jewish, the child admitted he had never even met a Jewish person. He was just repeating what he had heard at home. Later, we learned that his Egyptian father had been deported because his immigration papers had not been in order.

As we continued working on the project, we all found that there were many things we did not understand, in spite of our good intentions. But that was exactly the point. With every step we took, we were moving further from our comfort zones—and moving closer to one another.

The play took us into new territory in another way as well—it turned out to be as much a research project as an artistic endeavor. In the course of our interviews, we managed to compile twenty-five hundred transcribed pages; like gestating a baby, the process took a full nine months. As I turned the pages of the interviews, I felt as if I were encountering my own experiences and those of people close to me: women who were not allowed to date, men who were gay and rejected, children of two or more cultures feeling torn between them or displaced. It was impossible to feel alone or isolated when I read these stories. The common thread among the interviewees was a desire to create harmony with those who were seemingly at odds with one another. "What we need is spiritual capitalism," one interviewee said. "Peace is a song," said another. "We're not all singing the same note, but it all fits together somehow. Peace is created within that sense of diverse harmony." We had our leitmotif for the play.

At first, we found the writing process for the play to be overwhelming. The most I had ever written was a speech. The play ended up being a collaborative effort among us three "godmothers" of the production; the professional script-writing team, who worked with transcripts of the interviews; and publicist Meryl Zegarek, who lined up prospective media to cover the event. There were many sticking points, but when the issues were discussed, they were resolved—not always to everyone's total satisfaction, but for the greater good. In one case, during an early read through, an especially prickly incident occurred. I was taken aback by one passage, in which I spotted the *f* word. The writers were enthusiastic about the "authenticity" of language in the dialogue, while I was astounded that they could not see that there was something wrong with using this word in a bridge-building, faith-based play. I could imagine the conservatives—an important audience to our mission—walking out the minute they heard it. Though I had assumed that everyone involved would have the same sensitivities, I was quickly disavowed of that notion, and the process hit a stalemate until a compromise was reached: The line would not be dropped, but the letters *f u* would be substituted. Ideal for everyone? No. Acceptable to the group? Yes. And from there, we moved forward as a team.

Then there was the suggestion to re-create Muslim prayer movements, such as standing, bowing, and bending, in a dance. To Sarah and the non-Islamic production group, this sounded magical. To me, it trivialized prayer. No one could understand my objection until I explained that Muslim prayer movements are designed to mimic angels glorifying God in the seven heavens and that mimicking those movements in a dance would be disrespectful to a sacred rite. Instead, a dance sequence that glorified the veil was created, inspired by Sarah's observations of my preparations for worship—my donning of a robe and a glimmering white scarf, a religious ritual of transformation for women. I asked the group to consider that throughout history it had been common for women of many faiths to wear head coverings. In the Catholic faith, in fact, head-covering for women was a practice mandated for the Latin rite of the church until the mid-1980s.

In January 2003, *Same Difference* opened to a sold-out audience of one hundred at the Church of Saint Paul and Saint Andrew on the Upper West Side, sponsored by the Methodist women's organization. I watched in the darkened theater as pictures from New York City interfaith events were projected on large screens to music, which picked up in tempo until it ended with a prayer call chanted in Arabic by a Sufi Senegalese prince followed by the (Jewish) blowing of a shofar (ram's horn) and then by echoing church bells. One by one, a group of black-clad actors stepped up—a Sunni, a Methodist, a Catholic, an Orthodox Jew, and a Shiite—each with a relevant religious symbol. The artistic scenes and elements onstage encapsulated and honored many traditions from a variety of faiths, culminating in the unifying pronouncement *"Same difference."*

Looking out from backstage, I wondered how many people in the audience had ever made these kinds of connections before. Or how many had questions but had no one to answer them.

The play was a hit, but only after the production had completed its successful sixteen-week run did I learn that Sarah had been discouraged from attempting this project by the National Council of Churches. When she had asked for help in being introduced to some members of the Muslim community, she had been told that no one would talk to her, that there were protocols and channels that took time, and that there was a process that she would need to observe— but Sarah had not been discouraged and had struck out on her own. "I'm happy to see how wrong they were," she told me.

For me, there was also something more—involving a promise to a young girl in Kashmir with a guitar and a paint box. At last, I could tell her that her artistic dreams had been fulfilled in a place that she would never have imagined—a theater on the Upper West Side of New York City.

MU-JEW DILEMMA

...

Muz's daughter, Maryam, was raised in both Jewish and Muslim traditions. From the age of six, she attended Sunday school at the City Congregation for Humanistic Judaism, a progressive congregation. At the same time, she learned about Islam and its ethics from her grandparents during her annual visits to Kashmir. When she was about to turn thirteen, she was excited about her upcoming bat mitzvah, a coming-of-age ceremony for Jewish girls. The City Congregation is a nontraditional synagogue, and so instead of reading a portion of the Torah, Maryam decided to write a series of papers under the guidance of a mentor. For the project, she would explore the roots of both the Jewish and Muslim parts of her family—their histories, values, beliefs, and commitment to helping others.

However, Maryam was not satisfied with going through just the Jewish ritual and asked her dad what the Islamic equivalent of a bat mitzvah would be. He had not heard of any, although a young Muslim comes of age when he or she reaches puberty and becomes accountable for his or her own actions at that time. So Muz and Helene consulted with the rabbi at the City Congregation about creating a ceremony reflecting Maryam's dual identity. He was supportive of the idea and worked closely with the family to create a service that reflected both religious traditions.

Now came the conundrum: Since there was no such Muslim custom, it was unclear what to call the Muslim part of the ceremony. This set Muz on a mission. He asked his relative Dr. Syeed, a linguist, if he could recommend an appropriate term that would reflect the idea of coming-of-age in Islamic society. Dr. Syeed suggested that Maryam reaffirm the shahada, *the declaration of the Islamic faith.*

Muz called me for my advice, and I suggested we simplify it: Since Maryam had never done the shahada, *I suggested that instead of "reaffirming" the* shahada, *she could simply "affirm" it. I had helped converts to affirm their* shahada, *and this would be similar. Maryam was excited to be coining a new expression: "affirmation of* shahada."

Since the family wanted to hold the ceremony in a neutral setting, they rented a theater. Surrounded by 150 family members and friends, Maryam looked radiant in an ivory dress. She read a statement she had written that reflected both traditions and included the history of the Jewish and the Muslim people, while music from both traditions played in the background.

Then my husband asked Maryam to step forward to affirm her shahada, *"There is no god but God, and Muhammad is the messenger of God," which she recited flawlessly in Arabic. Immediately afterward, I presented a package to her, the contents of which would prepare her for her life as a Muslim. This gift included a prayer rug, a scarf, prayer beads, and a tiny velvet box with a chain and locket. As I put the chain around her neck, I explained to her that the inscription on the locket, the "Throne Verse," called* Ayat-ul Kursi *in Arabic, was from the Quran and was meant for her protection. Simi and Paul, an interfaith couple whose wedding ceremony I had conducted, were among the guests. They thanked me for creating the ceremony, saying they* looked forward to the day when they could have an "affirmation of shahada" for their two boys.

Maryam has evolved into a remarkable young woman with a complex understanding of her dual identity. She is at peace with herself while many kids her age struggle with their sense of self.

Maryam is a freshman at Brandeis University. She has taken this sense of duality to her campus, where she both attends Hillel services and is active with the Muslim Students Association. She is studying writing and writes frequently about how she came to integrate within herself the values of both her religions. In a recent blog post, she sums up what both religions mean to her: "[It means] growing up celebrating the Sabbath with my family, talking about the highlights of our week, and watching the candles melt away. It means my aunt coming over and making a Passover meal and my father cooking a Kashmiri lamb dish at the same time. It just means a safe place and an accepting community. Just trying to do what you can do to better the world, which is both a Jewish and a Muslim value." She ends her post by quoting Hillary Clinton: " 'Do all the good you can, for all the people you can, in all the ways you can.' This is at the core of my identity."

WAS BECOMING ADEPT AT RAPIDLY RESPONDING TO ISSUES CON-
fronting American Muslims, but I began to realize that there was
a more endemic problem. The media was portraying the inevitability
of a divide between Muslims and Western civilization when a young
Muslim scholar commented to me, "Then this must mean I am at
war with myself! Am I not the West?" I overheard the concerns
among the younger people in my community, and I recalled those
moments after the Iranian Revolution when I was conflicted, trying
to reconcile my Muslim and American identities.

I began to worry that if our next generation was feeling this
sense of powerlessness, the sense that the world was against them,
then they were taking these feelings of vulnerability and isolation
to bed with them every night and would be unable to cope with
the enormous challenges being thrown at them. I had traveled this
arduous journey before and wondered what I could do to enrich and
enliven their sense of belonging. From my own experience, I knew
that the easiest cure was talking and listening, beginning a dialogue.
Remembering Moji's saying "By bundling sticks together, you will
gain strength," I decided to bring together young Muslim men and
women and empower them by creating lasting bonds between them.
I was certain that this demographic of young, urbane, professional
American-born youth was key to mending the relationship between
Muslims and others as they straddled multiple cultures.

In 2004, I founded Muslim Leaders of Tomorrow (MLT) and invited both Muslim men and Muslim women nationwide, ages twenty to forty-five, to a weekend retreat.

We assembled 125 women and men at a contemplative center in Garrison, New York, amid towering, fragrant trees and overlooking the tranquil Hudson River. We faced our very first challenge when we asked the group to envision a shared picture of the future they wished to see. Samina, a Californian woman, was on the panel "Pluralism in Islam." The panelists had been chosen from among different sects and strands, Shia, Ismaili, Sunni, Sufi, Salafi, progressive, conservative, and liberal. All were asked to hear each other out and try to develop a methodology for improved communication.

When Samina spoke, she nearly choked. "At lunch, I conducted an informal survey of how my colleagues felt about Shias, and I was shocked at the vitriol and intolerance I heard in response," she began. "When they were talking to me, they did not know I was Shia." As I listened to her, I wondered how we could possibly move forward as a collective before Muslims themselves learned to respect their differences. Her comment shook many people; even among the enlightened attendees, people were still stereotyping one another.

Ahmed, a young man in his twenties, said, "We need to better understand the needs of the entire spectrum of the Muslim community."

Next, we asked the group to look inside themselves to see how they could create change. As the conversation continued, it became heated at times, but through this process of expressing frustration and difference openly and in a safe space, we moved forward. A woman yelled, "I am tired of women being treated badly and men passing judgment!" A conservative Arab male responded, "I am concerned that Muslims might turn away from the accepted practices, norms, and proscriptions of their faith, particularly in the progressive movement." All in all, I knew we succeeded, because the conversations that took place were necessary bumps in the road toward a stronger Muslim community. Many attendees felt the first panel was unprecedented, as it had allowed a previously taboo conversation to occur.

This retreat was just the first of what we hoped would be a lasting network of the brightest young minds in our community. An African American woman said that it was exciting to see Muslims becoming more liberal and tolerant. Others worried about hatred, backlash after terrorist attacks, and security issues in the United States, and most shared the concern of a Pakistani American woman who said, "I don't want the extremists defining the Islamic agenda for the rest of us." I also heard comments like "I love the new networks and friends and hearing about other people's work and feel hopeful about where this is going." It didn't hurt that we ended with a hilarious comedy routine by Azhar Usman of Allah Made Me Funny.

To capitalize on the momentum, in 2007 we expanded MLT to Europe, and in January 2009, it went global, becoming the largest global network of young Muslim leaders. Unfortunately, due to the uproar surrounding the Muslim community center in the spring and summer of 2010, we lost funding and were unable to continue the program. In spite of that, deep connections were made, enabling many of the participants to become leaders in Muslim communities around the world: youth like Eboo Patel, who has defined interfaith leadership; Reza Aslan, author of many books including his best-seller, *Zealot: The Life and Times of Jesus of Nazareth;* Wajahat Ali, a *New York Times* columnist; Mona Eltahawy, an Egyptian American media commentator; Irshad Manji, who became a lightning rod with the publication of her book *The Trouble with Islam;* and Samina Ali, whose TED Talk on hijab received 1.8 million views. I routinely bump into MLTs in the U.S. and around the world. They always thank me for connecting them to individuals who have become their lifelong friends and want to know when the next MLT gathering will be. I smile and think, The umbilical cord is already cut, and you are strong enough to be on your own.

STONING AND THE
SLEEPING CHILD

. . .

On March 22, 2002, Amina Lawal, a thirty-year-old Nigerian single mother, was convicted to death by stoning by the Nigerian court for committing adultery. The proof of her transgression was a child, born out of wedlock, though of course, Lawal could have been raped. She was scheduled to die in January 2004. Her story received a great deal of media attention, and once again Muslims were ill equipped to respond.

I myself did not understand the issue, so I hosted a gathering of young emerging women leaders on October 2, 2002, and invited Dr. Azizah al-Hibri, a professor of law at Richmond University in Virginia, to explain the legal basis for this accusation. She began by saying that there are different schools of Islamic law and that in most of them, the act of intercourse is defined as penetration. But four witnesses to the act are necessary for the accusation of adultery to be substantiated.

Dr. al-Hibri went on to say that this requirement makes it near impossible for anybody to be convicted of adultery. She cited the story of Aisha, the Prophet's wife, who was left behind in the desert while her caravan went on without her. She was found by a stranger and brought back home to the Prophet. People's tongues started wagging, and she was accused of adultery just because she was alone in the company of a man. The

Prophet was very pained by the accusations, and people told him to divorce her. Aisha, distraught, went to stay with her father. Then God sent a revelation exonerating her: "And those who launch a charge against chaste women, and produce not four witnesses [to support their allegations], flog them with eighty stripes; and reject their evidence ever after: for such men are wicked transgressors" (Quran 24:2).

Dr. al-Hibri pointed out that these tough standards for the accusation of adultery came about almost as a way for women to avoid slander and as a protection from their own failings in the eyes of the community. In Islamic law, being pregnant without being married does not automatically mean that adultery has taken place, since a woman may have gotten pregnant by means that were considered beyond her control, such as rape.

In fact, I was astonished when Azizah continued by saying that "if a woman is separated from her husband for as many as seven years and she gives birth to a child, this is called a 'sleeping child' who belongs to the husband despite the separation." This interpretation exists to protect women whose husbands were away for extended periods of time, during which the women could have been raped or pressured into having sexual relations.

Amina Lawal's lawyer, Hauwa Ibrahim, successfully defended her using just this argument of "extended pregnancy" or sleeping child, which eventually resulted in her acquittal.

Dr. al-Hibri's comments made me realize that it was necessary not only to know the law but also to understand the basis for it and how at times it can become distorted. In that moment a seed was planted in my head as I realized that Muslim women need to act upon their convictions rather than expect others to do it for us.

Now that I had been energized by the creation and success of MLT, my focus shifted. As more and more women sought my counsel and told me their stories, I saw more clearly how much their pain seemed related to issues of faith that were based on outdated mores or men twisting religion to legitimize their actions. For example, Latifah, an elegant African American convert, called me sobbing one day, because her husband had taken a second wife. I asked for the details, but she was too distraught to answer. I told her to name the person who had officiated the marriage and tell me where it had taken place. "He conducted the ceremony himself," she said, "on the Internet—she was an out-of-state bride!" Then I asked her who the witnesses were, and she said he had told her that "the angels were his witnesses."

When I heard that, I laid down the law. First, Latifah needed to tell her husband that virtual angels and dot-coms don't qualify as witnesses—witnesses must be human. Second, she needed to tell him that we have laws in this country that must be obeyed by all its citizens, and we have laws and contracts in Islam that he had broken. If her husband gave her a hard time, he was to call me directly. I never heard from him.

As the wife of an imam, I was an authoritative source in spiritual mentoring and marriage counseling. With marriage, there was a whole continuum of conflicts that drove couples and their families to seek my counsel. Interfaith couples would come to talk when they began thinking of marriage, and I often found myself intervening when tensions flared up between families. I would try to mediate disagreements around the marriage ceremony over things like who proposes at the altar; I was asked my opinion on freezing eggs, what birth rites and names should be considered, what children's books couples should buy. My work supporting my husband, which had begun as private and often intimate counseling conversations with women, now evolved into a more visible role. I was still working under my husband's wing, but I was also increasingly stepping forth on my own.

Sammy, an Egyptian investment banker, wanted my husband to perform his marriage to Cindy, his Christian American bride. My role was to give premarital counseling on how to raise their children in an interfaith marriage. As the date of the wedding neared, how-ever, the couple surprised me by saying that they wanted me, not the imam, to conduct their marriage.

I could not believe what I was hearing. I understood that our counseling sessions had led to a bond of trust that the couple wanted to continue as they took their marriage vows. They were comfortable with me and were intrigued by the idea of a woman performing their ceremony.

What Cindy was asking me to do was a definite breach of tradi-tion—I had never heard of a woman performing a Muslim marriage ceremony. I wasn't sure how Feisal would react, and it was with no little uncertainty that I went to him to discuss the issue.

Feisal surprised me by saying that there was no specific prohibi-tion against a woman performing the *Nikah* (Islamic marriage). Still, I was not convinced. I felt certain that people would criticize my husband for allowing me to perform the ceremony. Would they not say that this was his role, a man's job?

Feisal was confident and also realistic in his answer. Yes, we had to be prepared for criticism, especially the first time. But soon enough, he said, people would get used to it, and before we knew it, other women would be following in my footsteps. This was how change happened. Feisal promised to write the sermon and the actual words for the ceremony. All I would have to do was deliver them, in the way I had seen him do so many times. I thought of the important traits my husband shared with my father. Like Papaji when I was learning to swim in the lake, Feisal wanted me to succeed on my own in an area rarely explored by women of our culture. He knew I might struggle, but to give me confidence, he had tossed me a lifeline.

Plans for the marriage moved forward smoothly—until the groom's uncle Faris learned of the arrangements. He was outraged that a woman was performing his nephew's ceremony, and he went on a rant: It was not allowed! He could not be part of something that was *haram* (forbidden). He would not attend the wedding!

Now the groom's brother Muhammed chimed in. If Uncle Faris needed to be convinced, they would have to consult with a higher authority. They would call al-Azhar University in Egypt, the ultimate Islamic seminary and authority on Islamic affairs. The seminary maintained a hotline for religious legal questions and decrees (fatwas). With his list of questions in hand, Muhammed dialed the phone number while the whole family looked on nervously.

"Salaam alykum," he began, and then politely said he would like to speak to a mufti (jurist) about a matter that needed a fatwa. He was told to go to the university's website—fatwas were now issued online.

Digital fatwas? For a moment, everyone was astonished. But this was a sign that things were, indeed, changing. The groom's sister grabbed the phone and jumped straight to the point. Her brother was getting married, she said, and his family wanted to know if a woman could perform a marriage.

"Naam, naam, naam," she was told. Yes, yes, yes. "We have no objections. We already have *mazoonas* [woman officiators] in Egypt."

The thought that Egypt was ahead of the United States in advancing women's roles in Islam was disconcerting, but it didn't lessen the enormity of what I was about to do. On the day of the wedding, I was so nervous that I practiced my delivery repeatedly and directed a barrage of questions to God. Why am I being put in this position? I asked. What else do you have in store for me? I had become comfortable at last with my relationship with God and was doing a lot of community work, but why was I suddenly being thrust into a role that was traditionally relegated to men? Still, I realized it was important for me to fill the gap in the community.

Stepping up to conduct the ceremony, I noticed Uncle Faris sitting in the front row, just waiting, I was sure, for me to make a mistake. But when the bride and groom approached, I quickly focused my attention on the couple. As Sammy and Cindy looked blissfully at each other, I delivered my husband's sermon. I then asked the bride to propose marriage to the groom, following in the footsteps of the Prophet Muhammad, whose wife Khadijah had proposed marriage to him. The groom wholeheartedly accepted. The rest of the ceremony went as planned, and I pronounced the couple husband and wife. As the family and guests rose to congratulate the couple, I was relieved and pleased with my performance, until Uncle Faris sidled up to me and whispered that I had surprised him—he had been expecting me to make a mistake and was glad I had not, but he had to correct me on one thing. The bride should not have proposed the marriage.

I replied that she was following in the footsteps of Khadijah, the Prophet's wife.

Uncle Faris rolled his eyes. Who had told me, he demanded to know, that Khadijah had proposed marriage to the Prophet? My facts were surely wrong.

Now I was disturbed that this man was willing to rewrite history because it did not suit his way of thinking. As Uncle Faris was still peering at me with more than a little disdain, a weathered man in his eighties, a respected elder among the guests, approached me and shook my hand. Gripping it tightly, he commented that he had lived in this country for fifty years. He had been expecting a bearded man with long robes and a *kakula* (imam's hat) to conduct the marriage, and when he saw me instead, he could not believe what he was seeing. The ceremony I had performed was the best he had ever seen in his life, and he had attended many, many weddings. Today he was happy—now he could die in peace. "Because with you leading Islam in America, I know we are in good hands. May Allah always bless you." Only then did I see the animosity on Uncle Faris's face fade.

NO COMPULSION
IN RELIGION

. . .

Meira, like me, was a workingwoman in corporate America. We became very close friends. Meira was usually lighthearted, so I was surprised when she approached me worriedly for advice. She was concerned about her daughter, Sanah, who was in love. Richard was a delightful young man, Meira said, and seemed perfect for Sanah, but he was not Muslim; therefore, Meira's husband, Salem, would not agree to the marriage. Meira was concerned that a Muslim woman could not marry a non-Muslim. And Salem was not budging, causing a lot of stress in the family.

Meira sighed in frustration. She asked me to talk to Salem. "I cannot explain to my daughter why a Muslim man is allowed to marry a non-Muslim woman while our women cannot do the same thing," she said.

I acknowledged that, yes, the prevailing view was that Sanah should marry a man of the Muslim faith, but I suggested that there was another way to interpret the issue. I explained that the rulings on which this view was based were made by scholars who lived in patriarchal societies in which the man was seen as the dominant party in a marriage. At the time of the ruling, scholars had been concerned that a Muslim woman's religion might be compromised if she married into a Christian or Jew-

ish family, or, worse, that she might be coerced to convert by the family. In addition, there were concerns that a Muslim woman's child would be raised in a non-Muslim father's faith. But those concerns were not applicable in today's nuclear family, in which both husband and wife contributed in the decision-making process. Sanah would not allow Richard to undermine her faith, and if she and Richard agreed, they could raise their children as Muslims. If we could address these two major objections, then the prohibition would have no grounds.

I also assured Meira that Richard did not need to convert; there is no compulsion in religion according to the Quran. In fact, neither husband nor wife can force a religion upon the other. As a Christian, Richard believed in God, and if he also believed that Muhammad was a prophet, then he already accepted the core message of Islam.

Meira worried that the couple would need to agree to raise their children as Muslims. Was that necessary? she asked me. I told her that that was ideal, of course. But since a Muslim believes in Christianity and Judaism, and has regard for both, couldn't the children be raised to respect and appreciate the father's faith, traditions, and holidays? I said. But she thought the kids might grow up confused. So I reminded her that she and I had both gone to Catholic schools where we said the Lord's Prayer every day—and had that confused us? I repeated to her the saying I had often heard, that all religions are from the same source; they are like rivers streaming into the same ocean—the ocean that is God.

Meira smiled. Yes, she understood—but how would she convince Salem?

I told her that the solution was staring at us right in the Quran, which explicitly allows Muslim men to marry "believers," that is to say, Christians and Jews, but prohibits them from marrying nonbelieving women. On the other hand, the verse below does not specifically prohibit Muslim women from marrying people of the book, that is, Jews and Christians. Scholars have stated that when the Quran is silent—meaning it doesn't state something explicitly—the issue it is discussing is open to interpretation and the action is possibly permissible. This is particularly significant in modern times, when Muslims are grappling with dilemmas that were not of concern in seventh-century Arabia.

"Do not marry unbelieving women [idolaters] until they believe; a slave woman who believes is better than an unbelieving woman even though she allure you. Nor marry [your girls] to unbelievers until they believe: A man slave who believes is better than an unbeliever even though he allure you" (Quran 2:221).

As the Quran puts it, the issue is the distinction between believer and nonbeliever and not of a particular religion.

I suggested she tell Salem that today the majority of American Muslim men are marrying non-Muslim women and that there are simply no eligible Muslim men left for girls like Sanah to marry. If their daughter had found her soulmate, Salem should accept him wholeheartedly into the family and expose him to the Islam they knew and loved. The rest would follow.

In this case, it took some time for everyone to see things the same way. After months of family conversation and several counseling sessions, I heard that Salem had agreed to the marriage of Sanah and Richard—with one special request: Would I do the family the honor of officiating at their wedding?

M Y LIFE CHANGED RADICALLY AFTER 9/11. IT WAS THE
woman's question at the Presbyterian church in Princeton soon after 9/11 that was a clarion call for me to accept the mandate that was being thrust upon me. The question—what was I, Daisy
Khan, doing about the status of women in Islam?—simmered within
me for several years as my priorities began to shift. I felt that I needed
to make a change. I had always worked in a structured corporate
environment, but slowly I came to the realization that there were
others as equipped as I was to do my day job. I was increasingly feeling the responsibility of what it meant to be a Muslim woman—an
educated Muslim woman who had been empowered by all the men
in her family and was already heavily involved in the work of her
husband, a religious leader. It was time to examine ways in which I
could help. I knew the time had come for a life-changing decision,
and so I turned to God for guidance. I followed the teachings of the
Prophet, who had taught his followers to do an *istikhara* prayer, in
which you supplicate to God and request His guidance in making a
decision. It involved waiting for an answer in a dream or opening the
Quran to find the answer in the first verse you see. As if God Himself
was leading me on my new path, the Quran responded with "A condition of a people does not change unless they change what is in
themselves." I felt as if this verse was speaking directly to me, saying,
Nothing will change unless *you* get involved. I was apprehensive, but

I knew what I had to do next. I told Feisal that I wanted to quit my corporate career and devote myself to building community. I asked for his support. Without hesitation, he smiled and said, "If you are doing God's work, don't worry. He will provide!"

I was excited about the opportunity to mobilize my inner resources to raise consciousness about Islam, a religion that had inspired millions of people and that my role models Moji and Dadaji had exemplified. Yet I knew it would not be easy; my religion had been used to justify the killing of innocent people and the exploitation of women, both in my own community and across the globe. But I took comfort in my scriptures, which affirmed gender equality as an intrinsic part of Islam. Since I had not been able to find a female mentor to turn to, I thought that perhaps I could start with myself—a faith-driven woman working for change at ground level, who might assure others. So after quitting my job in 2005, I devoted my energy to developing a blueprint for change. A structural change. I started with identifying the constraints and challenges of my community. I found that the deep diversity among American Muslims had resulted in balkanized structures that hindered our ability to work with one another. To rectify this, we needed high-level thinking from which innovation could spring.

I focused on Muslim women. It was time for us to elbow our way into the discussion and fill the space. To me, this did not seem like work but rather like a mission—something I wanted to do, loved doing, and was increasingly compelled to do. I wasn't sure where to start, but my almost twenty-five years of corporate career experience enabled me to find solutions. I studied social movements that had succeeded in the past and built on them. I began a year of research and fact-finding to learn about women's rights and leadership. I was fortunate to have been introduced to Helen LaKelly Hunt, who had written a book called *Faith and Feminism: A Holy Alliance*. Until I read her book and learned about the suffragettes and how they had used faith-based arguments for equality, such as women being created in the divine image, I had not known how to reconcile feminism with the Muslim faith. Although gender equality is guaranteed in my faith, over the past centuries, these rights had been stripped away from us. When I read *Faith and Feminism,* I realized that, historically, women's struggles are one: Our challenges are the same throughout the world, and our histories are one.

The suffragettes had certainly never come up in Kashmir, and I had missed that phase of American history in high school. Now I made up for lost time and undertook an intensive study of how the suffragettes had propelled both the British and the American women's movements to achieve voting equality. The long history of the struggle for women's rights was daunting, but every sentence I read made me feel connected to it, a part of something, coupled at last to a larger cause. Organizing, of course, took leadership, but it also took resources and a community.

To help, I enlisted my friend Mino Akhtar, a member of our community. I had a unique bond with her, as we were both South Asian baby boomers, both spiritualist career women who had worked in Fortune 500 companies and were interested in all things Islamic. She was an activist for women's issues, and I knew she would be able to lend her organizational skills to help me develop a sustainable platform for Muslim women.

On a beautiful April day in 2006, Mino, Feisal, and I finished a hearty breakfast at my home. Before he excused himself, Feisal blessed us. "You ladies have to get to work to change the world. I know great things will come out of your kitchen table discussion today, and I will pray for your success," he said.

Mino and I began by listing all the problems plaguing Muslim women. We agreed on four focus areas: First, there was the need to change the perception in the minds of the public that Islam treats its women as second-class citizens. For this, we needed to showcase female scholars, mystics, and jurists, both historical and contemporary, who had deliberated, argued, and pondered questions of spirituality and equality. An essential part of this struggle was to demand that their voices be at the forefront of the debate about women's rights, responsibilities, and status.

Second, we had to explain the varied cultural landscape of Islam, since the realities of women in Malaysia are not the same as those of women in Saudi Arabia, Afghanistan, or America. For example, Muslim women had been heads of nations in traditional societies such as Pakistan, Bangladesh, Turkey, and Indonesia, and yet in other Muslim nations, they were virtually invisible. Third, we had to tackle barriers to Muslim women's advancement by examining the nexus of custom and religion.

Finally, it was necessary to build solidarity between fragmented groups of Muslim women who were divided along geographic, ideological, and socioeconomic lines. This was not uniquely a Muslim issue; for example, there is little cooperation between Orthodox and Reform Jewish women or between Catholic and evangelical women. However, for Muslims, division and suspicion between camps of hijab wearing versus non–hijab wearing and spiritual versus secular would derail any movement attempting to create a better present-day reality for women. To create a cohesive and unified movement, we needed to foster cooperation among divergent and sometimes opposing groups. This meant we had to be inclusive of women with perspectives ranging from traditionalist to secular feminist to spiritualist to revivalist to progressive to literalist. Mino and I knew we had a big dream, but we could not wait for the day when Muslim women would unite and breathe life into gender equality.

We were wrapping up our meeting when a thought popped into my head. Where will we get the money to do this? I wondered. And as if Mino had read my mind, she quoted an Indian philosopher: "As soon as you formulate an idea or a goal, all sorts of people will come forward to help you realize it."

WOMEN BORN WEAK?

...

In 2005, when I was in Jeddah, Saudi Arabia, accompanying my husband to a conference, the daily newspaper Saudi Gazette *asked to interview us at their headquarters. Surprisingly, upon arrival, I was separated from my husband and ushered through a special entrance marked* WOMEN ONLY. *There I was greeted by a cadre of young women who spoke fluent English. I was introduced to Sabria, the editor; local reporters Maha and Shroog; and Rahla, a features editor. They were amused that I continued wearing the* abaya—*the overcoat that most Saudi women wear in public. "Take the* abaya *off," they told me. "There are no men here!"*

Though of course I had attended an all-girls school, an absolute segregation of men and women in the workplace was wholly unfamiliar to me. As the shock wore off and the women concluded interviewing me, we began to share common concerns regarding Muslim women around the world. Clearly these women were highly educated and were at the forefront of bringing progress to their country. I wanted to comprehend the restrictions placed on them since, despite being at the top of their game, they had to seek consent from their male guardians for all of their activities. Without a guardian, they could not represent themselves in court, register a business, apply for a

new passport, or travel abroad. In extreme cases, a divorced
mother had to seek the permission of her son, who was considered to be her male guardian.

Discussing these issues with Saudi women was a double-
edged sword. The subject hit a nerve with them, since on the
one hand, they are coddled by their own society, but on the
other hand, women around the world scorn them for not standing up for their rights. While I was waiting for my car, Shroog
stunned me with her answer when I asked her how she felt
about needing a guardian. She matter-of-factly replied, "Women
are born weak. We cannot defend ourselves. That is why we
need the protection of our male guardians." She had learned
this in her school, she said, and knew it to be true for all Muslim women.

I then told her about the world I grew up in. I said that
women in Kashmir work the land, toiling side by side with men;
they venture out into the pasture without needing the permission of their fathers or husbands. I told her about women in
Egypt, the home of Islam's prestigious al-Azhar University. "Do
you think Egyptian women are not Muslim because they go to
the Nile without their husbands' permission?" I asked her. I
also told her about the female heads of state of Pakistan, Bangladesh, and Turkey. Muslim men had voted for these women
to lead their nations. Finally, I reminded her about her own history going back to the time of the Prophet, when women rode
camels and were fiercely independent. As a reporter, I asked,
shouldn't she inquire about her own history and investigate
who had instituted these restrictions?

I knew I had confused her, and I doubt I changed her mind,
but it was not her fault. This was what her school curriculum
had taught her, and unless the curriculum was altered, more
women would continue to think they were born "weak."

In 2006, I invited the editor of the Saudi Gazette *to the WISE conference, along with Fatin, a businesswoman I had met at the Jeddah Chamber of Commerce. Fatin had decided to run for local election, and since she attended the conference, her guardian was clearly supportive of her women's empowerment work. Sabria, the editor of the* Saudi Gazette, *did not attend; I was never told why. For more than a decade, we in America had been hearing about the frustrations of Saudi women, including their not being allowed to drive. But women in Saudi Arabia knew the root cause of their disempowerment was guardianship, which not only curtails their day-to-day mobility but also limits their very agency.*

In 2011, I saw a flicker of hope when women began to be appointed to decision-making positions. The late King Abdullah gave women the right to join the Shura Council, and thirty women became members. Women were given the right to run and vote in the 2015 municipal elections.

Then in 2017, a sea change began to occur. Women who had been working for decades to remove the requirement of guardianship were elated when a royal decree—a magic wand of sorts—suddenly recognized "the right of a woman to be her own guardian and take care of her official matters." Many believe that the law was introduced to satisfy the U.N. Commission on Human Rights in relation to the international conventions to which the kingdom had acceded. However, the gutsy new prince, Mohammed bin Salman, referred to as the power behind the throne, is credited with pushing a litany of social-change maneuvers like ending the ban on women drivers. The 2017 landmark decision by King Salman is part of a vision to increase the number of women in the workforce and reduce unemployment by 2030.

Saudi advocates for the empowerment of women instantly

hailed the announcement. My friend Maha Akeel, who had at-
tended our WISE conference and is the director of communica-
tion for the Organization of Islamic Cooperation, commented
in one of Saudi Arabia's largest daily newspapers, Arab News,
"[Male guardianship] has always been an obstacle to women
and demeaning because unfortunately some guardians abused
their authority over women and took advantage." Suhaila Zain
al-Abideen, a senior member at the Saudi-based National Soci-
ety for Human Rights, said, "This means male guardianship
has been lifted and the legislations that demand a male guard-
ian have been amended." She also affirmed that guardianship
had no basis in Islamic law: "Shari'a law does not necessitate
male guardianship of women, because we are perfectly compe-
tent."

A younger Saudi woman, Lina Almaeena, whom I had met
while she was still attending college, used an American collo-
quial expression: "We've come a long way." Then she added, "I
think it's a fantastic step. Every day we hear of an improve-
ment. A lot of things are changing. Not only at a woman's level
but at so many levels." Almaeena is sure these changes will in-
clude work permits, which would make unnecessary the pres-
ent law that requires women to get consent from their guardians
to work.

The kingdom is resolving big issues with respect to integrat-
ing women into its society: Just this year, it appointed three
women in the male-dominant financial sector to the positions
of the chair of the Saudi stock exchange, and surprisingly,
women finally received the right to drive. I look forward to em-
powering women, including raising their awareness of their
own rights—and especially helping them to unlearn what they
were taught in school, that women are weak!

CHAPTER
30

WE NOW NEEDED TO GIVE OUR WOMEN'S INITIATIVE A name. We wanted a unique name that also conveyed a sense of gravitas. The name also had to communicate some key ideas: faith, wisdom, spirituality, and equality. I asked a bright young male intern from Boston University, Shafiq Walji, to come up with a name for us. In a few hours, Shafiq showed me a handwritten acronym: WISE, for Women's Islamic Initiative in Spirituality and Equality. As soon as he said the words, everyone in the office spontaneously applauded. We had a name!

I had met Shqipe Malushi, an Albanian American woman, at a Faith and Feminism Dialogue that my friend Mino had invited me to, and where I had been asked to give an opening prayer. When I recited the first chapter of the Quran, Shqipe was visibly moved and inquired about my work. I shared my dream for Muslim women with her, and Shqipe offered to guide me when it came to fundraising. Now together we pitched proposals to foundations and women's groups.

Shqipe reintroduced me to Helen LaKelly Hunt. "Meet Daisy Khan, a Muslim woman with a big dream," Shqipe said to Helen, who listened as I shared my vision.

Helen surprised me by saying, "I believe in you and your vision, and I will be the first one to give you twenty-five thousand dollars!"

With the Sister Fund seed fund behind us, we were able to get another foundation director to provide funds to bring in international participants, but she suggested we start small. I was ecstatic—their grant would enable us to unite American Muslim women with women from around the globe. I was about to agree when Shqipe blurted out that we Muslim women had always been told to stay behind, be seemingly invisible and silent, and now she thought that we should hold the conference in the epicenter of commerce, somewhere people would notice. We needed to make a high-profile statement.

Shqipe's forthrightness and aggressiveness embarrassed me, and I was sure we had lost the grant, but instead the foundation director nodded enthusiastically. We decided to launch our initiative in the heart of New York—at the Westin hotel in Times Square. We were a bit nervous about staging an event in the huge ballroom, but we were immediately oversubscribed. And so, in 2006, WISE was born.

As I was preparing the launch for WISE that fall, I asked my husband if there were any red lines I should not cross. He advised me that if I was to be effective, I had to learn to not overstep my boundaries. As his wife, I was already in a position of authority, accustomed to mentoring, advising people on personal matters, and resolving marital issues. But now my stage was enlarging, and he felt I might find it difficult to restrain myself. For example, in spite of the wealth of knowledge I had acquired, I was not a scholar, so I should not profess to be one. I should err on the side of caution, deferring to people who knew more. But, I wondered, how was I to respond if, for instance, someone asked me about the stoning of women? Would I be expected to restrain myself then and say, "No comment"?

Feisal had more experience by far than I did, and he was aware, long before I was, that someone, somewhere, was always going to be opposed to something. He was simply alerting me to this. But the fact was, I knew my limits all too well. I wondered if any layperson could hope to master the complex subject of Islamic theology. Feisal reminded me that I could look to tradition for an answer. Lay jurists are self-taught scholars who can persuade people if their arguments are sound. They are not unlike apprentices, people who have studied extensively and understand religion and the content of the Quran. They are able to interpret the Quran and what the Prophet says about an issue, the consensus among scholars, and any analogy that can be drawn. Based on these tenets, a range of rulings can be made by lay jurists.

My husband pointed out that I could also rely on the jurists' encyclopedia, *The Distinguished Jurist's Primer*, authored by Ibn Rushd, an eminent scholar who had lived in Córdoba, Spain, and who started writing in 1157, when he was thirty-one. In the West, he is known as Averroes and is famous for his commentaries on Aristotle and Plato. I trusted this source because I had read that Ibn Rushd believed in the principle of women's equality, that women should be educated and allowed to serve in the military, for, after all, they might be tomorrow's philosophers and rulers.

And yet I still had questions. I didn't want to rely on the old scholars who hid behind the opinions of their medieval forerunners. I wanted to come up with opinions that were relevant for our times. Feisal directed me to *ijtihad*—the reinterpretation of scripture— where the reader exerts his intellectual ability to find a solution to a legal question. This, he said, was a rich part of our tradition. I was confused because I had heard that the doors of *ijtihad* were closed in the tenth century when jurists had argued that all major matters of religious law had been settled and people needed to follow the traditions that were already established.

My husband didn't see it that way, however. Nonsense, he said— the doors were always open; it was people's minds that were closed. He explained that I was "to open them further, through knowledge." We laid out a plan for me to follow so I could stay on firm footing. Feisal explained that whatever I did must be in the best interest of women and the community and promote the public good.

We discussed creating a body of work that spoke for women not dictatorially or hierarchically but with a collective voice. In Islamic law, there was *ijma*, or consensus, which was the basis of *shura* councils. This idea shimmered with possibilities, and I found myself wondering if in fact there had ever been a *women's shura* council. The idea was not only innovative; it was also contradictory to tradition, as historically it was men alone who held the social and religious advisory roles. Was a women's *shura* council even possible?

Feisal assured me that this concept was within the appropriate boundaries, even if it had not been previously tried. Then, as he knew me so well, my husband reminded me that it was better to walk through a door that was already cracked open than to break the door down.

My grandmother Moji had shared with me a famous Kashmiri folk story of a nobleman who had eleven sons. There was discord in the family, and the sons began to fight one another. The nobleman summoned all eleven sons and gave them each a stick. Then he told them to sit in a circle and break the sticks. Puzzled, each man easily broke his stick. The father took eleven new sticks, tied them up in a bundle, and said, "Now break this bundle of sticks." The sons tried mightily, but they were unable to break a single stick. The nobleman said to his sons, "When you stay together, you will gain strength from one another, and no one can hurt you."

This story was on my mind when the WISE conference first gathered a diverse group of women from over twenty-five countries, major influencers and policy shapers, both Muslim and non-Muslim. Almost everyone we asked accepted our invitation. I felt confident that our speakers, presentations, and discussions would inspire the group and lead us somewhere interesting. Most of all, I believed that when we women came together, we would be unbreakable.

AT THE 2006 WISE CONFERENCE, I was approached by an unassuming, dark-haired woman who asked if she could speak at the podium for only five minutes. She wanted to check in with her sisters about something that she believed was important to them. Every moment of the day was already scheduled, but I recognized her name—she was Laleh Bakhtiar, a renowned Iranian American scholar who had authored dozens of books on spirituality and told me she was undertaking the first English translation of the Quran by an American woman.

After she was introduced, Laleh announced to the assembled crowd that she had recently discovered that verse 4:34 of the Quran had been misinterpreted for over fourteen hundred years. She said that while translating the Quran, she'd come upon this verse, which, paraphrased, says that if a man is having problems with his wife, first he must speak to her gently and try to explain the situation to her; then, if the conflict continues, he was to leave her bed; and if that still doesn't work, he should hit her. The room froze. Laleh told us that when she came upon this verse, she was so distraught that she stopped working on her translation project to wonder how a God who is merciful and compassionate—a God who says that marriage is all about harmony and love, who says that women and men are garments for each other—how this God could say that men should beat their wives. She questioned whether she could even continue with her work. And that was when she decided that, as a scholar, she had to dig deeper and find out what these words of the Quran actually mean.

For those of us in the audience, hearing that a woman was interpreting Quranic text was truly revolutionary and inspiring.

Laleh went on to tell us that she had researched and found that the word "*daraba*," which is used for "to beat," has many meanings including "to leave" or "to go away." So why was the word "beat" used in most English translations? Was this translation actually an issue of patriarchy? Laleh sought the opinion of about thirty scholars— imams, sheikhs, ayatollahs—and asked them: First, was the Prophet a walking Quran—meaning, did the Prophet do whatever is in the Quran? They all agreed that, yes, the Prophet was a walking Quran. Second, did the Prophet ever hit his wife? And everyone said, oh, no, he was never, never known to hit his wife—wives, actually, since he had multiple wives, and it was always known that he had many conflicts with them. And what did the Prophet do when he had a conflict with his wives? Laleh asked. "People said he would just leave the house," she was told. So, Laleh said, in that case, why was the word "*daraba*" translated in this verse as "beat" and not as "leave," when the action of our Prophet himself was to leave the house?

The audience was transfixed as Laleh informed us that "leave" was the correct translation, because if the Prophet was the walking Quran and he walked away and did not beat his wife, then the meaning of this word was not "to beat" but "to go away."

On hearing Laleh's logic, the women in the room broke out in deafening applause, cheering and whistling, and some even leaped up onto their chairs. There were cries of "It's about time somebody did this!" and "Why didn't we know this before?" and "Domestic violence and even beating women to death has been done in the name of an error of interpretation!"

At that moment, it became clear to every person in the room that it was imperative that women be involved in interpreting the scriptural text.

LALEH'S PRESENTATION CHANGED THE tenor of the conference. Scholars and academics, religious leaders and ordinary women, women from every part of the globe, suddenly opened up, sharing feelings that ranged from the most general to the most intimate. Some of the stories told were unbearable to hear, but their horror was transformed by inspiration; horrendous events had motivated these women, and now it was up to those of us at the conference to do something, to care, to act. It felt impossible not to.

A Nigerian lawyer told the harrowing story of Amina Lawal, who was sentenced to death by stoning in Nigeria because she was falsely accused of adultery. Years before, this story had precipitated my hosting a Quranic study group in my apartment, and now the room was listening to this courageous and inspiring firsthand account from a lawyer who had helped overturn the conviction.

Dr. Nafis Sadik, an adviser to the secretary general of the U.N., told of delivering significant policy papers on family planning, only to have the men in the room comment on her dress.

Unflinchingly, a meek-looking Pakistani woman named Mukhtar Mai recounted being gang-raped at the order of her village elders, subjected to tremendous pain and humiliation before her community and the world. But instead of retreating into a dark hole, she had turned her tragedy into a mission. She described how she had raised funds and then opened a high school for girls in her village, as well as crisis control centers and clinics for both boys and girls. She ended her remarks by reading her motto: "Our only hope is the fight for justice. End oppression with education. To remain ignorant is a crime. To remain apathetic is a crime. . . . To remain silent about a crime is a crime."

The majority of the women agreed that the biggest barrier to their advancement was the distorted interpretation of scripture. Being an imam's wife, I knew how people could manipulate scripture for advantage. I had seen, firsthand, religious leaders manipulate concepts such as polygamy, honor killing, and forced marriage to their own personal advantage. When Laleh put forward the idea of establishing a more egalitarian approach to the scriptures, I was thrilled, because I knew that this would create a seismic shift in the lives of women around the world.

Due to the many different sects in Islam, there is no central authority. This allowed the two hundred women at the conference to authorize WISE to establish the first Global Muslim Women's Shura Council to examine issues that Muslim women of all sects were facing worldwide. Although we had a majority in favor of such a council, there wasn't instant unanimous agreement—a number of women were wary. Several hands went up, and there followed questions about what this entity would do.

I explained that the purpose of this council would be to use Islamic law to promote legitimate and equitable positions on issues that Muslim women were facing—Afghan girls being forcibly married, Pakistani women being wrongfully accused of adultery, Saudi women being restricted from travel because of guardianship, honor killings being practiced in Jordan, female genital mutilation in parts of Africa, and the right to education being denied to girls in many Muslim lands. There was a disconnect to contend with. In spite of the Prophet Muhammad's being considered by many as the ultimate feminist—a man who honored his wife Khadijah, gave property rights to women, abolished the pre-Islamic practice of female infanticide, scrupulously helped with chores, and sought his wife's advice on community affairs—the reality for Muslim women often does not match the ideals set forth by him. In his last sermon, the Prophet even emphasized this point by saying, "Treat your women well and be kind to them, for they are your partners and committed helpers." When I cited the Prophet, heads nodded in agreement.

The hard work that lay ahead of us was to restore the God-given rights of personal fulfillment, justice, and equality to Muslim women and to remove the limits placed on them under the banner of false Islamic traditions. We discussed how, wherever obstruction has been encountered by women, it has not been by Islam the *faith* but by local *traditions* and *customs*—and interpretations mandated by men in the name of faith, as Laleh had so passionately demonstrated. My quest for truth always led me back to the Quran, and there I found the answers I sought. In AD 640, Umm Salama, the first Muslim woman who dared to question the Prophet Muhammad, asked, "Why does Allah [God] only address men in the revelation [Quran]?" The Prophet remained silent, but her question was so sincere that it reached the divine throne, and God himself sent a revelation, which affirmed the embrace of women in the faith, their equality, and their importance:

> For Muslim men and women,—for believing men and women, for devout men and women, for true men and women, for men and women who are patient and constant, for men and women who humble themselves, for men and women who

give in Charity, for men and women who fast (and deny themselves), for men and women who guard their chastity, and for
men and women who engage much in Allah's praise,—for
them Allah has prepared forgiveness and great reward.

—Quran 33:35

If we found that scripture was being distorted in a specific way, we
would reinterpret the Islamic text. With the support of this council,
women would no longer have to rely on the interpretation of male
scholars with outdated attitudes toward women.

Still, everyone did not agree. One conservative woman challenged
me. Who, she asked, had given me the authority to create a Muslim
women's *shura* council?

My answer was to point to the sky. I cited the Quran 42:38–39:
"Those who respond to their Lord, and establish regular prayer,
whose affairs are conducted by mutual consultation [*shura*] among
themselves, and from what we have provided them, they spend, and
who, whenever tyranny afflicts them, defend themselves." I also explained that there were *shura* councils dominated by men all over the
world. And there were no barriers to us women creating one ourselves.

With an overwhelming mandate, we agreed to establish the council, with the purpose of increasing awareness of Muslim women's
advancement in Islamic and Western societies. It would take a number of years to create an effective working structure for the *shura*
council. Its thirty members would be culled from women who had
attended the WISE conference, and it would include women from
different nationalities and with divergent views. Council members
would include scholars who were well versed in Islamic law as well as
activists with comprehensive knowledge of contemporary issues facing Muslim women.

Helen LaKelly Hunt had been writing a dissertation on the suffragettes, who, during their first convention, made clear that they

opposed the evil of slavery, which was upheld by Christian churches. In 1837, they wrote a resolution that called upon women to "stand pledged to each other and the world, to *unite* our efforts for the accomplishment of the holy object of our association, that herein seeking to be directed by divine wisdom, we may be qualified to wield the sword of the spirit in this warfare; praying that it may never return to its sheath until liberty is proclaimed to the captive." We too knew we had mighty work to accomplish! Through our new *shura* council, the women of WISE declared our conviction that the Muslim woman is worthy of respect and dignity, that she is a legal individual, a spiritual being, a social person, a responsible agent, a free citizen, and a servant of God. Therefore, we affirmed that she holds fundamentally equal rights to those of men to exercise her abilities and talents in all areas of human activity.

I was especially pleased with the conference because my parents and my sister Gudi attended. Papaji recalled, "When you could not command respect as a girl, you would put on my trench coat and go back into the room pretending to be a man." Then he said, "Not much has changed: Even then you were turning things upside down—the only difference now is your arena is much bigger." They were extremely proud of me. There was an irony to this. Gudi, who had been raised under the tutelage of Moji, had become a doctor, a healer, while I, the carefree artist, was following in Moji's footsteps. Gudi must have read my mind when she commented that she had never realized that Moji had had such a strong influence on me. Mummy, on the other hand, was thrilled to watch Moji's prediction unfold before her eyes, and Papaji was ecstatic that I had pulled out the boxing gloves. We had taken the first step—a first but giant one. I suddenly understood that this would be my life's work.

IT'S ALL IN
THE INTERPRETATION

...

In 2010, years after our first WISE conference, at which Laleh Bakhtiar had opened our eyes about ijtihad, *independent reasoning, the power of interpretation, I heard of a child custody case brought by a Polish American Muslim woman against her husband, a Muslim doctor from India. She claimed that her husband had hit her for "disobedience" and withheld a household allowance, causing her to deplete all of her money from before her marriage. She had avoided going to the police because her husband could have lost his medical license if he was convicted of a felony, and as a housewife she was dependent on him. With no other recourse, she took her husband to court to fight for sole custody of her four children.*

The judge presiding was a woman, and she asked the husband what his reasons were for beating his wife. He opened a translation of the Quran by Marmaduke Pickthall and pointed to verse 4:34, where daraba *was translated as "scourge." He told the judge that clearly his religion allowed him to beat his wife, and by using this justification, he was seeking protection under the First Amendment, the religious freedom law.*

Later, his wife took the stand and opened The Sublime Quran, *Laleh Bakhtiar's English translation, to where it says to "go away from them." She told the judge, "You see, there is a* difference of opinion about this verse, so it is not that a husband can beat his wife."

That evidence helped her win the child custody case. This also demonstrates the power of ijtihad, especially when applied to modern dilemmas.

I N September 2006, a month before our WISE launch in New York, a Danish newspaper, *Morgenavisen Jyllands-Posten*, published twelve cartoons, most of which depicted the Prophet Muhammad as a terrorist. The newspaper maintained that its aim was to contribute to a critical debate about Islam. Danish Muslim organizations disagreed. They objected to the depictions and petitioned the Danish government to act. But when the judicial complaint against the newspaper was dismissed in January 2006, demonstrations erupted on the streets in some Muslim countries.

On October 18, 2006, I was pulled into the conversation. The organization Intelligence Squared invited me to participate in a debate with the theme of "Freedom of expression must include the license to offend," and I would be pitted against a master of words, the late self-proclaimed atheist Christopher Hitchens. I told my team, "I will lose this debate. I played team sports—hockey, basketball—but I was never on a debate team." Regardless, I agreed to participate so I could share my point of view. The event was held at the Asia Society, with approximately five hundred people attending. I spoke for twenty minutes, but below is a brief excerpt from my argument.

The motion of today, where freedom of expression must include the license to offend, is in a sense . . . a moot question. . . . The freedom we have to express ourselves does in fact enable us to offend.... The appropriate question to ask is whether freedom of expression is absolute and limitless, or should it come with some social responsibility....

...There are, however, certain kinds of speech that undermine the very values that liberty of expression is meant to advance. Take, for example, the infamous Danish cartoon protest. To put it into context, we live in an environment—and this is especially true of Europe—where Muslims constantly face xenophobia. While the overwhelming majority of the world's 1.2 billion Muslims do not partake in any violent actions in response to these political cartoons, a tiny, minuscule minority has grabbed the world's attention and apparently now has absolute command of how Muslims are to be perceived....

Clearly, we're living in a very tense time. In such a situation, for a right-of-center Danish newspaper to come out with cartoons that show the Prophet of Islam with a bomb in his turban, with a sword in his hand, and with a menacing look on his face does nothing, absolutely nothing, to advance desperately needed dialogue or enlighten people in any positive way. If it does anything at all, it serves to suppress constructive dialogue by fueling extremist sentiments.

I had been coached by my friend Rabbi Michael Paley, who was the scholar in residence at and director of the Jewish Resource Center of the UJA-Federation of New York. He was the one who told me, "Daisy, it all starts with a cartoon." He was referring, of course, to the terrible caricatures of Jews in Nazi Germany. I realized he was right.

Fueled by Rabbi Paley's wise words, I continued my argument:

The issue is whether there's any wisdom in showing the Prophet of Islam with a bomb in his turban, no less. This is the sort of thing that furthers that familiar yet dangerous and unsound argument: Some Muslim men are terrorists; therefore, all—or even most—Muslim men are terrorists. . . .

. . . Ultimately, the question to ask is: Do we use our free speech to insult an already marginalized people, or do we use it to advance and enhance a desperately needed discourse between people living in an increasingly interconnected world?

As I'd predicted, Christopher Hitchens won the debate, but a decade later the very same conversation continues.

Sherin Khankan, who had just attended the 2006 WISE conference in New York, found herself squarely at the heart of the debate too. Born in Denmark, as a teacher, activist, columnist, and public speaker, she specialized in contemporary Islamic activism and in 2001 had founded Forum for Critical Muslims, the first organization in Denmark that promoted female Muslim leadership. In October 2006, she published a book, *Islam and Reconciliation—A Public Matter*. Earlier that year, when the cartoon crisis exploded around the world into a full-fledged international crisis, with street demonstrations, boycotts, and fatalities, Sherin and I had discussed the need to bring a coherent conversation to the debate. Then I had recalled the MLT retreat after 9/11 and how much good that had done. This was a moment ripe for MLT's expansion, so on July 7, 2006, which marked the anniversary of 7/7, the coordinated suicide bomb attacks on the trains and buses in London, ASMA brought MLT to Copenhagen, where the cartoon controversy had started. We assembled 120 young male and female Muslim leaders from seventeen countries, under the theme "Muslim Integration in the West." The topics of the sessions ranged from issues facing 28 million Western Muslims to the need for women to be given more prominent roles in mosques to determining who could speak for Islam given our lack of central authority to, finally, how we could unite, given the multiplicity of beliefs and ideologies among ourselves. Mino, who had agreed to facilitate the MLT sessions with me, was as amused as I was at the similarities of the challenges to those we had discussed when we first sat at my kitchen table to talk about women's issues.

I had invited Flemming Rose, the editor of *Jyllands-Posten* responsible for commissioning the cartoons of the Prophet Muhammad, and asked him to directly engage with our young Muslim leaders. Rose had never spoken to a group of Muslims about the cartoon crisis and was concerned for his life, so I asked Mona Eltahawy, a contributor to *The New York Times* who was in touch with him, to intervene, and with her assurance of his safety, he agreed to attend.

Rose entered the packed room visibly nervous. When he settled in, he began to hear from the other participants. One French man objected to his national loyalties being questioned. Then Rose heard from an American Muslim writer, Jamal, who confided to the group, "I am afraid to speak against my own people, who stifle my critical thinking."

Rose was surprised at the openness of the dialogue and said, "I wish I had met Muslims like this group before," referring to the civility and mature discourse among the young leaders. When asked what he had learned from his recent experience, he said what everyone in the room also understood: "Freedom does come with a price, and knowing what I know now, I am not sure I would have done it."

Every decade seems to have its own problems, but I have never been disappointed when I have offered an artistic response to clarify what matters for us all in a moment of global upheaval. On this occasion, I presented Rose with a set of cartoons meant to clarify, not to provoke. They were drawn by the famous Turkish American cartoonist Salih Memecan, who had flown in from Turkey, he said, "in the interest of increasing cross-cultural understanding." Rose was so tickled by the notion of "one cartoon arguing another cartoon," as he put it, that he agreed to publish them in his newspaper.

SAVE THY HONOR

...

I received an invitation in 2005 from the Goethe-Institut to speak about honor killings. My co-panelist was an avowed secularist, Gunel Ateş, a Turkish German lawyer advocating for a law to ban forced marriage in Germany. She spoke about her harrowing experience in advocating for victims of honor killings, for which she was regularly receiving death threats. When she passionately implied that Muslim men honor-killed their sisters or daughters because Islam justified it, she got my attention. I had heard many non-Muslim advocates blame Islam for honor killings, but to hear it from a Muslim woman was a matter of deep concern for me.

Gunel had been in great personal peril. As a younger woman, she had set up an office in Germany to help women with domestic violence issues, and when she was twenty-one, a man came to her office and shot her. She survived, but the person next to her did not. The shooter wanted to make an example out of a woman trying to defend women. Years later when an infuriated husband of a client tried to attack her, accusing her of fighting against Islam, she soldiered on. But when her three-year-old daughter was threatened, she closed her office.

I felt sad and concerned for Gunel at the same time. Here was a courageous woman on the front line of saving girls, and because she was ill informed about Islam, she was not an effective advocate. I decided to educate her on the subject so she could fight her battles more powerfully. I explained to Gunel that honor killings were un-Islamic. This practice is not sanctioned in the Quran—there is no verse that says you have to kill an individual to preserve family honor. In fact, I informed Gunel, honor killing is not a religious issue. It exists across many continents and cultures where women are oppressed. In these societies, communities feel strengthened by viewing women as property, and men justify their crimes as punishment against women's perceived immoral behavior.

In 2009, Gunel attended the second WISE conference, in Kuala Lumpur. She confided in me that she had learned an important lesson—that in order for women to persuade people to listen, we have to find reasons within Islam to convince them of our arguments.

N 2002 A WELL-KNOWN TV PRODUCER, ANISA MEHDI, APPROACHED
me with a request: Would I participate in a documentary called
Inside Mecca? She was filming the hajj and wanted me to be one of
the storytellers. Naturally, I was honored by the request and was
thrilled to deepen my understanding of one of the five pillars of
Islam. I turned to my husband for help, and he directed me to "Pilgrimage to Mecca," an article published in 1978 by *National Geographic* that he had helped his father write.

I learned that the Kaaba, the simple cubic structure, was called the
"house of God" and was built by Abraham for the worship of God.
More than two thousand years later, the angel Gabriel would bring
the same message of the one God in a revelation to the Prophet Muhammad, a native of the town in which the Kaaba was built.

The producer asked if I could relate the "striving" story, one of the
main rites of the hajj, which centers on Hagar, an Egyptian slave who
gave birth to Abraham's first son, Ishmael. Both Hagar and Ishmael
were left alone in a desolate valley by Abraham with some dates and
water. But soon enough, the water ran out. When her infant son was
writhing with thirst, Hagar desperately began to search for water.
She had asked the departing Abraham, "Has your Lord instructed
you to leave us here alone?" When Abraham answered affirmatively,
she said, "Then God will not abandon us." With this conviction, she
ran between two hills, Safa and Marwa, looking for water, and in-

deed, God did not abandon them. Zam Zam water miraculously gushed forth, quenching the infant's thirst.

In the film, I described how Muslims reenact this event through a rite called *sa'ee*, or "striving," in which they rush back and forth seven times between two hills that are over a thousand feet apart. This ritual honors Hagar's sacrifice and serves as a reminder of our struggle.

The more I learned about Hagar, the more I was inspired by her determination and bravery. I also found it reassuring that Islam recognizes the struggle of a woman. I found it ironic that some men on the pilgrimage who ardently reenact Hagar's fearlessness and courage consider women to be the weaker sex. I had heard that some women were forbidden by their husbands to walk fast because they deemed it immodest. Those men who think women are incapable of making decisions and must always be accompanied by a man, who believe a woman has no role in shaping destiny—I wonder if they ever think about Hagar. Left behind with a child, all alone, without a man to protect her, she nevertheless shaped their destiny.

Do such people ever wonder why God chose a woman for this role? What if Hagar had not submitted to the will of God as conveyed by Abraham—would the town of Mecca have flourished? Would the Prophet Muhammad have received a revelation? It was a woman's belief and self-sacrifice that are ultimately behind Islam's holiest shrine.

Feisal and I decided to go to Mecca to perform a mini-hajj, called Umrah. I felt it would be powerful to carry out a ritual that would take us back to the time of Abraham, the patriarch of Judaism, Christianity, and Islam. Abraham introduced the concept of human equality to all three monotheistic faiths.

It is said that when you first glance at the Kaaba, whatever prayers you make are granted, so as soon as I arrived in the city of Mecca, I headed straight to the Kaaba, which is situated within the bounds of the sanctuary called Masjid al-Haram. When I set my eyes on the cubical structure, I was transfixed by its simplicity. The striking cube is made of stone and encased in intricately woven black cloth decorated with gold calligraphy. The Prophet Muhammad was driven out of Mecca, a pagan society that did not accept his message of the one God. He migrated to Medina, where he preached for over eight years. By then, his message had spread far and wide, and he was able to return to Mecca, at which point his teachings were accepted. The first thing he did was remove and dispense with the idols from the Kaaba, except the statue of Mary, as she is considered a prophet in Islam, since prophets are those with whom God communicates. For fourteen hundred years, the Kaaba has remained vacant, a stark reminder that humans should bow to nothing except their creator.

As I approached the Kaaba, I saw men draped in white cloth so there was no way to distinguish the rich from the poor, symbolizing the unity and equality of all humans. I felt transformed by the unification of people from diverse cultures and ethnicities, all reconnecting to the one God. Malcolm X was also clearly affected by this experience. After praying with blue-eyed, white-skinned Muslims, his own militant views changed.

As Feisal and I circumambulated the Kaaba seven times, I felt at one with the sea of humanity glorifying God individually and collectively. I thought of the rotations of planets orbiting the sun, feeling part of a larger order. Then, in the bustling flow of the crowd, I was separated from my husband. I found myself thrust in front of the Kaaba; I reached my arm out and touched it. In that moment, I sensed a continuum of energy connecting the present to the past. I imagined Abraham standing here with his son Ishmael, Hagar rushing between two hills to look for water, the angel Gabriel pronouncing Muhammad as Prophet. I was standing in the city where Khadijah, a tradeswoman, offered marriage to a young Muhammad; where Bilal, a slave of African descent, was freed by Muhammad to exemplify human equality; where Fatima, the daughter of the Prophet, and Ali, his son-in-law, endured hardships; and where Aisha spent years spreading the message of the Prophet. These people, my spiritual ancestors, had walked this path, and while I stood where they had once walked, I realized that what unites us is our collective spiritual quest.

In 2006, a well-respected Saudi woman sent out an email to her network with an urgent call for Muslim women. "There is a proposal to move the women's prayer area from the Holy Kaaba and from out of the Mataaf [circumambulation area]," she wrote. "History is being reversed. Women and men have prayed in this space called 'haram' [sanctuary] since the seventh century and now some clerics want to push us to the fringes. What would the Prophet say!!!"

I immediately circulated the email to my WISE network of women to see what we could do. I received an instant reply from Aishah Schwartz, a convert to Islam who founded the Muslimah Writers Alliance. *"Astaghfirullah; astaghfirullah,"* she wrote—God forbid; God forbid. "I will get a pot of coffee ready and stay up all night if I have to fight this." The next morning, as promised, Aisha's petition landed in my in-box. She had targeted the petition at the authorities in the kingdom and named it "Grand Mosque equal access for women project." Like a pebble in a pond, it started a reaction that rippled outward from an inner circle to the global sphere. Within days we received more than one thousand signatures, as well as comments such as "Follow the prophet's example," "There will be a mutiny," and "This is OUR holy site."

I forwarded the signed petition to the historian in Saudi Arabia who had requested help, expecting that this would be the first step in a prolonged campaign. To my surprise, her response was quick: "Petition delivered to the King. He is pleased to receive signatures from women from all over the world." My friend had realized that the signatures of women asserting their rights would be the best ammunition for the king to use to stop the proposal in its tracks. Journalists from the Associated Press reported on the validity of this proposal. Why was it being considered now? they asked. A Saudi woman, Aziza al-Manie, reported in *Okaz* daily, "Women are not all young beauties that rush to the mosque with an aim of seducing men." Pressure mounted from all sides. Almost immediately, the issue of moving women from Masjid al-Haram was dropped. In that moment, I felt as if our foremothers Hagar, Khadijah, Fatima, Aisha, and Maryam were applauding us for remaining steadfast in our courage and faith in God.

When the call to prayer sounded, I took my rightful place in full view of the Kaaba. I looked at the women behind me, beside me, and in front of me praying humbly to God, asking Him for favor. They came from all corners of the world and never imagined that the perimeter around the Kaaba might be prohibited to them. I felt honored that our small efforts had restored our rightful place in full view of the house of God.

QUEEN OF SOCIAL MEDIA
AND QUEEN OF HEARTS

. . .

In 2007, I was invited to participate on a panel of international opinion leaders convened by Her Majesty, Queen Rania of Jordan. I was eager to see her impact firsthand. I already admired the young queen, as she had used her position to advocate for various social issues. The queen was born in Kuwait to Palestinian parents, and because she had not been born to royalty, for much of her life she had experienced the world from a non-royal vantage point. She had been educated at excellent schools and had held jobs at Citibank and Apple before she assumed her role as consort of the monarch. She had deep respect for her traditions, but as an educated contemporary Muslim woman who had functioned independently on multiple continents before her marriage, she thought globally, tried to merge the best of East and West, and was not afraid to engage in new conversations.

Those of us on the panel, facilitated in Jordan by Professor Carol, an American academic, were asked to share our views on ways the queen could help in bridging the East-West divide. At the onset, Queen Rania made it clear that this was to be a working group, and all lines of thinking were welcome. The queen was an excellent listener. Everyone was given a chance to speak and be heard. I mentioned that hearts and minds are changed at the grassroots level and said that Her Majesty, as a Muslim woman in a leadership role, had the ability to dismantle stereotypes about Muslim women.

A few months later, Queen Rania did something unprecedented for her station. She announced that "debate is part of the dialogue" and engaged the public directly through her "send me your stereotypes" YouTube channel. One of the questions posted to the queen that triggered strong discussion was "How empowered are Arab/Muslim women?" Queen Rania is much admired for her stylish beauty, but her intelligence and fortitude more than match her looks. Though she married into her role in life, she also reinvented it and made it her own, much like her predecessor, Queen Noor, whom I met at Aspen Ideas Festival in Colorado. This independent-minded queen was so fascinated by cross-culturalism that she married the King of Jordan, uprooted herself, adopted a new country, and instead of being a figurehead queen, she focused on global peacemaking, improving the educational system, and promoting women's rights. Like me, she got her start in architecture and planning and continued to use her design skills for the betterment of society—the preservation of Jordan's cultural heritage. When King Hussein passed on, she used her natural gift as queen of hearts to be an excellent orator who lectures widely to help Americans better understand Muslims, Islam, and the Middle East and their compatibility with American values. I thought about other women, like myself, who had similar, if far more modest, opportunities and challenges. When is a woman's role not a stereotype? When she decides that it is not.

N 2009, YASEMIN, A DYNAMIC NEW YORKER LIVING IN DUBAI, invited me there to speak on Muslim women's issues at "Live It Up Conscious Dining," a monthly gathering of young professional women. As I was sharing how the Global Muslim Women's Shura Council had issued a statement against child marriages by providing an egalitarian interpretation of the Quran's text, Yasemin immediately saw an opportunity. "We need to do the same for adoption!" she declared. "Its permissibility is in question even though the Quran instructs Muslims to take the orphan into our home and raise them as our own child." I recalled from my hadith study that the Prophet Muhammad once knotted his two fingers together and said, "No other action will get you closer to me than taking care of an orphan." Yasemin added, "If the care of orphan children is compulsory in Islam, why do sheikhs make a blanket statement that adoption is *haram* [forbidden]? Why do they spread misinformation?"

The issue of adoption had never come up with my community members, but I knew in my heart that it could not be forbidden. Moji had practically adopted Gudi, and the Prophet Muhammad, an orphan himself, was raised by his uncle. The Prophet took his cousin Ali and raised him as his own son. "Why are the sheikhs objecting to it?" I asked Yasemin.

She replied, "Their prohibition is born out of ignorance. They are incapable of finding a viable solution to rules of jurisprudence on issues of inheritance, segregation, guardianship, paternity—there is no public pressure for these scholars to find modern-day solutions. Muslims prefer that the government take care of the orphans, and all they say is 'I will give a check.' Others have imposed restrictions on themselves, saying things like 'I can't take on another child' or 'These kids have mental and psychological problems.'" Then she said to me, "We need to challenge all this, for the sake of the children."

Aasma, a divorced lawyer, was listening intently. She now spoke up. "As a single Muslim woman, I want to adopt a child. Can I?" I told her I did not see any reason why not. The next day she wanted me to see her commitment to adoption, so she walked me up to the second floor of her villa. As she opened the door to a room, her face lit up. "This is the nursery for my two children!" she told me. I was awestruck at the sight of a fully furnished nursery with two sets of bedding and toys. Seeing the empty cribs left an indelible mark on me. I knew I had to do my part to help these women realize their dreams, and to give countless parentless children a chance at life.

Remarkably, a few months later, Muz's wife, Helene, who worked at Spence-Chapin, an adoption agency based in New York, called WISE's *shura* council seeking religious consultation about facilitating the adoption of Muslim children from Morocco in the United States. I knew this was no coincidence.

Although the *shura* council was initially reluctant to accept this challenge, when it heard the staggering statistics—that there are around 132 million orphans in the world, eight hundred thousand in Iraq alone—Farheen, a member, spoke on our behalf. "These facts and our impulse as mothers and nurturers compel us to take this on," she said. Over the coming months, we deliberated, and in 2011, we published our position paper, entitled "Adoption and the Care of Orphan Children: Islam and the Best Interests of the Child." It stated that the best interests of the child are primary in adoption. Families considering adoption needed to strive for a balanced combination of transparency, justice, and compassion. Adoptive parents had to refrain from obscuring the adoptive child's biological lineage, and they had to strive to help the child flourish in all areas of life. The just division of wealth among biological and adoptive siblings of each family had to be ensured. In other words, open adoption is not only permissible in Islam; it is also an obligation.

We announced our new partnership with Spence-Chapin. I informed Yasemin and Aasma about our plans and asked if they would be part of our pilot project to place children from Morocco into caring and loving American Muslim families. Aasma, who was working in Dubai, was willing to come back to America—"What can be better than giving a parentless child a chance to grow up with a family?" She said all plans were progressing well when, unexpectedly, a false rumor spread in Morocco that the children being adopted by Americans would be converted to Christianity or other religions— consequently politicizing these children's lives. The pilot program came to a halt, leaving us all disheartened.

When Yasemin remarried and returned to the United States, she informed me that there was a growing interest in adoption among Muslims. She said that the *shura* council's statement, which was the result of a credible body of research, had compelled her to pursue a doctorate in the jurisprudence of adoption. I was astounded by her passion when she told me that she had become a licensed foster caregiver. "The first child I am caring for is Carliyana, a four-year-old," she said. When she saw the look of "wow" in my eyes, she added, "Muslims have to raise the bar. Carliyana is a Latina child who needs a family. When I took her into my care, I made a conscious decision not to distinguish between her and my daughter. They are both my babies."

Aasma continued to work in Dubai and live in the rented house, where an empty nursery marked her continued quest to adopt a child. In 2015 she discovered Mrs. Edhi of the Edhi Foundation adoption center in Karachi, Pakistan, who had reversed her previous position and now allowed single ladies to adopt. Aasma filled out an application for a child, any child. She persisted for months, and finally her pleas won Mrs. Edhi over. One day, Mrs. Edhi placed in her arms a

six-day-old infant boy (called Jhoula) who had been left in a swing
outside one of the centers. Many months later, after fighting in court
and in bureaucratic offices where a father's name was insisted upon
(but did not exist), Aasma finally walked up the staircase of her home
in Dubai to the second floor, opened the door to her nursery, and
placed her baby boy in his long-waiting crib.

> *Your children are not your children.*
> *They are sons and daughters of Life's longing for itself.*
> *They come through you, but not from you,*
> *And though they are with you yet they belong not to you.*
>
> —*Kahlil Gibran,* The Prophet

Aasma followed the central principle of the Quran regarding orphans: "Making things right for them is better." And she walked in
the footsteps of Asiya, Pharaoh's wife, who took infant Moses from
the basket and raised him to be a prophet prince. In her determination, Aasma has become an exemplar for single women seeking to
give their love and energy to a parentless child.

LAISA ALAMIA, A WOMAN from the Philippines, was determined to
make a difference. And her work, in turn, inspired another woman to
act. Fed up with domestic violence committed in the name of Islam,
Alamia asked an imam to deliver a sermon refuting the abuse. The
imam replied that if she would write the sermon, he would deliver it.
Alamia, an Islamic scholar, had never written a sermon before, but
she agreed. The sermon was very well received, so the imam then offered to deliver other messages on social issues. So she started writing ... and writing ... and writing sermons, until the imam had
delivered sixty of her sermons. This extraordinary woman told her
story at the second global WISE conference, held in Kuala Lumpur
in July 2009.

Jamila Afghani, an educator, had taken copious notes as Laisa spoke. Jamila, from Kabul, had a limp, as she had contracted polio as a child. Every aspect of her life thus far had been a fight, a challenge to overcome. She had earned a college degree in spite of her family's opposition; her brothers had felt she was dishonoring them by getting an education, which had only increased her determination. She then went on to start a home school in Kabul.

After three months of fact-finding and speaking with local residents, she contacted me and told me that she now believed that a larger program of training imams could be a successful tactic in promoting women's rights in her country. This would be a completely new, ground-level approach, and we agreed to partner with her.

The idea was to train the imams by presenting scriptural evidence from the Quran, with a goal of promoting women's rights. Since Muslims consider the Quran to be the highest authority, if we could present evidence by using verses from the Quran, our argument would be impossible to ignore. Together with Jamila, WISE designed a holistic, gender-sensitive training program for Kabul, which she implemented. We translated booklets that incorporated scriptural evidence to prove the rights of women in Islam regarding marriage, inheritance, property, education, and mobility. The aim was to train twenty imams who would deliver khutbahs (Friday sermons) in twenty storefront mosques that had deep, influential roots in the local communities.

Because we were concerned about the tradition-bound male imams accepting training from a woman, we devised a stealth strategy. Jamila would remain behind the scenes while her husband would serve as the face of the project. Jamila would coach him on how to answer any questions that arose in the workshop. During the actual training sessions, she would listen and take notes, watching to see what teachings resonated most, trying to anticipate the issues.

We hoped these materials would elicit a more open approach from the imam community and legitimize a new perspective for today's world. We trained male and female student monitors to observe the reactions of the imams and to learn on-site. Because of the po-

litical realities, however, we decided that WISE would remain a silent partner—we were aware that if the imams saw any American
involvement, the project would never get off the ground. It wasn't a
perfect approach, but results were what counted. And if we could
help change the course of the life of even one woman, we would consider the effort a success.

When the training of the first twenty imams ended, one imam
asked some questions that Jamila's husband couldn't answer. Things
had gone so well up to this point, and since Jamila was in the room,
he commented that his wife was also an Islamic scholar. He gave her
credentials and then suggested asking Jamila if she had an answer.
The men looked at Jamila dubiously, but when she began to speak,
the imams were stunned by her scholarship and knowledge. That was
when Jamila's husband admitted that all the papers and documents
in the reports had been prepared by his wife. But words in booklets
and presentations—or any academic material—we knew could go
only so far. The most powerful learning occurred when the imams
began to appreciate and respect Jamila. And through her, to respect
women.

Jamila continued with the program, rolling it out one neighborhood at a time. A young man who wanted to know if his sister was
allowed to go to school asked an imam who had been trained by
Jamila. The imam responded, "Of course, it is her right. The Quran
says, 'Oh Lord, increase me in knowledge'" (20:114).

The next step was convincing the imams to allow women to come
to the mosques. If women weren't encouraged to attend the mosques,
they would not learn what their rights were; their line of communication would be secondhand, from their husbands, who might come
home and repeat what they had learned—or might not. The imams
were reminded that every woman is accountable for her own actions.
If a woman doesn't understand her religious responsibility, how can
she possibly teach her children?

Jamila approached one forward-thinking imam who believed that
women had the right to pray on Friday in a congregation, and he

agreed to carve out space for women in his mosque. "After my mosque, others will follow," he said, and he was right. Ten other mosques opened their doors to women and children. A woman leader was also assigned in each mosque to monitor progress and provide a channel of communication between the imam and the women worshippers. With these changes, the mosques began to feel like communities, places for families rather than boys' clubs.

In 2012, WISE decided to go to Afghanistan ourselves and meet with the imams; we felt that the program had progressed far enough and been successful enough that it was time to do so. I charged Fazeela Siddiqui, a WISE program director, with the assignment. As anticipated, when Fazeela met with the local imams and told them about our involvement, they were shocked.

"Your sisters across the pond happen to be Muslim and, yes, also happen to be Americans," Fazeela told them.

There was a tense moment. Then one of the leading imams lectured us that Americans should not have spent $7.5 billion on warfare. He informed her, "You Americans should have only spent millions on training us imams, and we would have been a shield against the Taliban—and you Americans would not have to shed your blood for us."

Sometimes, change feels slow, merely a steady drip from a faucet rather than a waterfall of momentum. But even a stone, when subjected to water and time, will become smoother. What started in 2009 as a group of twenty has expanded to over six thousand imams who are now training one another to preach and teach about the importance of the dignity and empowerment of women and girls within Islam.

One imam who was appreciative of Fazeela's presence smiled and stated that seeing other imams who were involved gave him courage. He then prayed that all Muslim women around the world would find their united voice in equality as provided by our faith.

An imam from Kabul gave this analogy: "Your booklet *A Jihad against Violence* was to our society as treatment is to a patient." He took his human accountability to God very seriously and acted on his conviction. He set out to recruit people away from the Taliban. By reading the Islamic rules of warfare to them, he was easily able to convince them not to kill noncombatants and civilians, destroy property, commit suicide, or engage in cheating and treachery; not to commit rape or terrorize populations; and never to wage war against other Muslims. The scriptural evidence for nonviolence provided in *A Jihad against Violence* enabled him to convince eighty Taliban fighters to lay down their arms, he claimed.

Eventually, however, the Taliban became aware of the imam's work and threatened him with a car bomb. Yet he fearlessly continued his work. In time, the extremists carried out their threat. A bomb went off in the imam's car while he was traveling with his two sons. His eldest son was killed, and his second son lost both his legs. The imam continues his work, undeterred by tragedy.

If we had not intervened with the imams, would one man be alive and another have both his legs? Or would the eighty Taliban fighters have killed eighty more innocent people? Or two hundred? Must peace always come at such a price? I think of these things when I sit in my office stirring my coffee, or on a plane, or when I am laying my head down at night on a strange pillow in someone else's country. When I give a speech to a room full of activist women, sometimes I wonder—which of us in this room will not be safe tomorrow? We work toward unity, but the irony is that the ultimate unifier, which has brought us together, is also the deadliest divider, and that is violence.

In 2017, the Taliban began the targeted assassination of imams and scholars. I received an email from Jamila's organization. "With deep sorrow we came to know that one of the active member[s] of NUA, Mr. Maulana Abdulghafoor of Logar province, was brutally killed by the Taliban. He was active in spreading the message of Moderation, Tolerance, Social Justice, Balance and Participation." This heroic man paid the ultimate price to help Muslim women find their voices and uphold their rights. It's a great loss for Afghanistan.

Jamila has been threatened as well. She lives every day in fear, and we on the other side of the ocean can only pray for her life. To help her, I approached an American government official to try to get her a special visa, but to no avail. Yet she and the imams continue their work. Once the imams recognized Jamila as the face of the project, they came to value her and feel indebted to her, as her trainings in public speaking and intergenerational dialogue had made them better leaders. It is said that when Jamila walks into the room they rise to their feet to honor her.

DRAWING THE LINE

...

A workshop we held on ending child marriage yielded immediate results. An imam who had just finished his training was asked to officiate a marriage. When he arrived at the wedding party, he saw a thirteen-year-old bride sitting next to her fiancé, weeping. The imam asked the bride why she was crying.

She replied, sobbing, that she did not want to marry.

In Islam, consent is a necessary part of the marriage contract. Was she saying that she had not given consent?

She had not; she was being forced into marriage.

The imam asked the girl what she wished to do, and she told him she wanted to finish school.

The imam then made an announcement to those present: He could not conduct this marriage, because the girl had not given her consent—she had actually refused and was being forced into marriage.

Both families then tried to bribe the imam to continue with the ceremony. This incensed him, and he informed them that he was accountable only to God. He again decreed that this marriage could not take place. With that, he left the premises.

During the following Friday prayers, the imam gave an impassioned sermon, beginning with the question of why we forc-

ibly marry our daughters off when Islam forbids coercing anyone into marriage.

After the service, an old man who had been sitting in the corner approached the imam and grabbed him by the collar, as if he were a small boy being chided. Why had the imam not told him this before? the man asked. No one, the old man shouted in fury, could help him now. Time had passed. He had already committed all sorts of violence against his daughters. He had taken the walwar *(bride price) for each of them, stopped them from getting an education, and forced them into marriages. The old man was now convinced that, in the name of mistaken beliefs, he had caused his daughters suffering every day. Why hadn't the imams spoken about these issues before?*

The imam responded, "I know it is too late for you, but it is not too late for all the others who are here!"

T WAS ALWAYS CLEAR THAT WISE WOULD NEVER HAVE ENOUGH money to carry out all of our goals. But one thing we did have was passion. We saw that our grassroots project of training the imams directly was having more of an impact in changing people's beliefs about Muslim women's rights than any other program or action I was aware of. And this ignited an ember and, from that, hope.

One of the position papers issued by the *shura* council dealt with female genital mutilation (FGM). I of course had heard about FGM, and although I was certain that it was not an Islamic rite, it was nevertheless being performed in certain African countries, including Egypt. I discovered that approximately 200 million girls around the world have undergone FGM. The reasons are varied. Some claim it's a rite of passage for a girl to transition into womanhood; others think it is a crucial custom that has been practiced for a long time. I decided to travel to Egypt to go into the field with our local partners and learn more about this practice.

In Egypt, I met a barber who reminded me of the barber in Kashmir who used to come to our house to cut the men's hair. His shop was just a little shack with a plastic chair, a tiny sink, one mirror, and a bunch of blades—that was it. Except that this barber cut more than hair. He was a practitioner of FGM. For him, it was an issue of supply and demand. "You know, people need a service, so they come here. They ask me, and what am I supposed to do?" he said. "There is nobody else for them to go to." The work also provided much-needed additional income.

The path to the Egyptian barbershop had begun with research. We needed to know why the practice was still happening in Egypt despite being legally banned. Were men perpetuating this horrific practice? It turned out that they were not—in fact, it was usually the grandmother, the family matriarch, who was the enforcer.

Because it was illegal, FGM had gone underground, and people were having midwives and barbers perform the procedure—and as a result, girls as young as thirteen were dying of infections. In order to succeed, we had to stop the practice at the source—the practitioners.

This barber had been identified to me by an Egyptian NGO, the Egyptian Association for Society Development, as a practitioner to approach in the first effort of our collaboration to end FGM.

The moment he heard the word "illegal," the barber became very concerned. It was clear that he thought we were from the authorities. He said, "So what do you want me to do?"

What would it take to make him stop?

He shrugged. If he were making enough money just being a barber, he would not need to resort to this practice.

What would happen if we set him up with a new and improved barbershop that could attract more customers? We had received a grant from the Dutch foreign ministry to end the practice by working with practitioners, so we invested in the barber. We underwrote a brand-new shop with a modern, adjustable chair; a TV; a sink with running water; a blow-dryer; and a mirror with lights—everything new. The barbershop was now the envy of the village—and the barber became a champion of the cause of stopping FGM. He signed a contract agreeing that he would refrain from performing the practice, and he told us the name of another practitioner. There were seventeen FGM practitioners in this village alone. We approached them one by one with the same message and a plan for each of their businesses—a convenience store, a tuk-tuk (a small scooter taxi) service, and a poultry shop.

The next step in our crusade was to convince and convert the families. We had studied the foot-binding of Chinese women, trying to discover how the Chinese had ended that disabling practice, which was based on hundreds if not thousands of years of tradition. We heard of one instance where a noble family had announced that they were not going to bind their daughter's feet and that they had an agreement with a family whose son promised to marry her even if her feet were not bound. We wanted to use the same model for FGM. We hoped to convince some prominent families to come forward and declare: We will not cut our daughters! And we hoped to have a young man's family come forward and say that they would accept such a woman, that their son would marry her regardless, because the family did not believe in the practice.

I met and enlisted a prominent imam from Cairo who had seen the adverse effects of FGM firsthand. "Every time a couple comes to discuss their sexual problem, FGM is behind it," he told us. "We must stop this practice. I am ready to help you!" I was thrilled that a religious leader of his caliber was willing to stand with us. He was so passionate that he made a further pronouncement: "Let me be very clear: FGM is not a Muslim practice. It precedes the birth of both Islam and Christianity. It is not mentioned in the Quran—on the contrary, the Quran promotes mutual pleasure during marital sexual intercourse, which FGM severely limits." When I asked him if he was willing to become our champion and go public with these pronouncements, he said, "Of course. It is my religious duty to prevent this harmful act. It has caused long-term damage to too many families—sadly, some have broken up because of it."

A year later our partners on the ground informed us that there were, in fact, some thriving examples of our success. It was important to share these stories to show what was possible, so I traveled once again to Egypt.

After trekking through the crowded, dusty streets of a small village near Giza, accompanied by members of the local NGO, our WISE team was introduced to a weathered, black-draped woman as she pushed two clean-cut young men forward toward us. She introduced them proudly as "future businessmen!" The woman was none other than Aisha, a former FGM practitioner, now the proud owner of a small, newly refurbished, open-front chicken shop.

Aisha's poultry business was a model of success for the program. In her shop, beside a wall of live chickens in metal cages, a small black-and-white television flickered proudly on a metal cart, attached to an extension cord. The two young men were Aisha's new assistants. She was now an entrepreneur.

I thanked Aisha for her work, and she gave me a big hug. She said, through the translator, "Now I sleep soundly at night. I don't hear the screaming girls." The conversation momentarily paused. Then she continued, "I have everything I could wish for. I am not harming anyone, and I can relax because I only work five days a week now—and I have peace of mind because my income is reliable." She thought further for a minute, then added, "Except, I think I would like to have machines to help butcher the chickens."

"She's ready to automate!" said the translator.

Aisha picked up a chicken and held it out to me. I thought she was trying to give it to me as a gift, and I wondered how I would get a live chicken through customs, but she picked up on my confusion and waved the chicken around.

"Or-gan-ic!" she announced in English, beaming. She had learned the word just for me.

At our headquarters in New York City, there is a photograph of Aisha standing in her chicken store beneath a large WISE sign, flanked by her two assistants. She has a successful small business, a new perspective—and her pride.

Our project was successfully in place, and we were poised to expand it when the riots in Tahrir Square erupted and the Egyptian revolution unfolded. At that point, we and our partners were unable to continue our work on the ground. It was a crushing blow—but it did not deter us from our ultimate goal. When plans are interrupted in this way—which they inevitably are—activism needs to be flexible. You must already be thinking ahead so that you don't lose momentum.

Our team regrouped. And as we reconsidered our strategy, news emerged that thirteen young girls had died from genital mutilation in Egypt. I felt helpless, but I could not permit myself the luxury of discouragement, because I knew that my path now was to transfer my energy, and my team's, to yet another place where our work was still needed.

A breakthrough occurred in 2011 at an academic colloquium of religious leaders held in Mauritania. It was particularly noteworthy that this took place at a meeting in Africa, because the practice of FGM is most prevalent in parts of that continent. Dr. Adriana Kaplan-Marcusán, a scholar who lived in the Gambia, had met me at the 2009 WISE conference. She was so committed to eradicating female genital mutilation that she had urged our *shura* council to issue a position paper against the practice. In 2011, Dr. Kaplan-Marcusán walked into the colloquium in Mauritania uninvited and asked for the scholars' and imams' attention.

The religious leaders were speechless—this simply was not done, and certainly not by a woman.

But Adriana spoke respectfully to the audience. "I just want to share one thing with you, and then I want your opinion," she said, and proceeded to read the one-page statement on FGM that the Global Muslim Women's Shura Council had issued at her urging.

One of the senior sheikhs took the paper out of Adriana's hand and read aloud that the "Quran makes no mention of FGM; on the contrary, it strongly condemns acts that negatively affect the human body and promotes mutual pleasure during marital sex. Moreover, no women in the Prophet Muhammad's household were FGM'ed, and even in conservative Saudi Arabia, FGM is unknown."

Faced with these proof points, one of the sheikhs said, "We are convinced by the Islamic argument that you have presented—and today, right now, we're issuing a fatwa against this practice. We should ban this practice forever."

Adriana shared her joy with me, and over the years she has kept me posted on her progress. Recently, she informed me that she was organizing an international conference in the Gambia in February 2018 in honor of the U.N.'s International Day of Zero Tolerance for Female Genital Mutilation (FGM) and invited me to attend.

In her invitation to me, she made it clear that our collaboration had enabled her to help eradicate FGM by simply changing hearts and minds. "As you know," she reminded me, "the rigorous and pedagogic document on FGM from WISE has been disseminated in all my conferences, workshops, classes, etc. In Mauritania, in 2011, during a colloquium on FGM and Islam for religious leaders organized by U.N. agencies, I presented the document as well as our clinical studies, and they came out with a fatwa against FGM." I am thrilled Adriana is using the secret weapon of the soft power of women to break down harmful ancient rituals. When she invited me to attend the conference, I felt so proud of her and of the scholars who were helping to end this social ill, as well as elated for the girls who will not be harmed anymore, that I am packing my boxing gloves and boarding a flight to the Gambia to join them.

AMERICAN-TALIBAN
TANGO

...

*By December 2012, thanks to a grant from a Belgian organiza-
tion, we were able to bring three prominent women from Afghanistan to participate in a congressional briefing on Capitol
Hill. Massouda Jalal, former Afghan minister of women's affairs, had had the courage to run against President Hamid Kar-
zai of Afghanistan; Suraya Pakzad, recipient of the International
Woman of Courage Award, had founded the Voices of Women
Organization, an Afghani group that provides shelter, counseling, and job training for women, working undercover during
the Taliban regime; Sadia Begham, a young activist, had run an
underground school for girls during the Taliban era. All testi-
fied that the years before the United States was to withdraw its
forces from Afghanistan were crucial in developing methods to
empower Afghan women and create resilient communities that
could continue to independently counter extremist regimes.*

*I wondered if the members of Congress fully understood
that a critical measure of success in Afghanistan would be what
women and girls could accomplish after the U.S. troops left.
The Afghan women pointed out to the legislators that if a
woman remained free to vote and a girl was free to get an education, then more than twelve years of American engagement
would not have been in vain. A strong Afghan woman is a de-*

feat for the Taliban. I hoped the legislators would leave the room with a new view of who Afghan women really were and what they were capable of. It occurred to me that this briefing with these women in front of nine members of Congress, although far more impactful and sophisticated, was not so unlike the presentation I had given to Mr. Greene's high school class years ago in Jericho. Both were introductions of sorts. Both exposed stereotypes and changed minds.

After the briefing, California congresswoman Barbara Lee contacted our staff for assistance in writing an addendum to a bill labeled the Afghan Women and Girls Security Promotion Act. It would train Afghan women to become policewomen who would provide security for female government officials. Six days later, however, Nadia Sediqqi, acting head of women's affairs in Laghman Province, was shot by the Taliban on her way to work—five months after her predecessor was murdered in a bomb attack.

On January 3, 2018, Saifullah Maftoon wrote a positive news story at Pajhwok.com. He reported that the city of Ghazni had hit a record number of fifty women on the police force. One policewoman, named Fatima, said, "After my husband was killed, no one helped me, thus I joined the police." Zahra, a resident of Ghazni, expressed happiness over the increasing number of policewomen. "It is a good initiative for women to address their own problems and help others," she said. Six years after our congressional briefing in Washington, D.C., Afghanistan has five thousand women serving in its police ranks nationwide.

IN THE HIMALAYAS, THE CLIMATE IS TRICKY. VISITORS OFTEN think the climate is uniform, but in fact, it is quite the opposite. The weather in one area may be mild at the same time as another area nearby is hit by towering clouds where the airstream hits the steep mountain slopes, pushing the air upward in a roiling pattern until the wind and clouds cascade toward the interior regions and the valleys. Then the weather explodes with a vengeance, unleashing torrential rains and snowstorms. I thought I was familiar with and prepared for these patterns of reversing winds and torrential storms. But I was not when they came to New York City in the turbulent aftermath of 9/11.

In 2009, eight years after the attacks of 9/11, a small building ten blocks south of the mosque where my husband had preached for twenty-seven years came on the market. It was also two blocks from Ground Zero.

Soho Properties chairman and CEO Sharif el-Gamal had been attending the Friday services at the Tribeca mosque. Many new immigrants were flocking to the mosque for Friday services, creating severe overcrowding issues. To comply with the fire codes, we created three twenty-minute services. We knew we needed a bigger space, and Sharif agreed. He also bought into our vision for a community center like a JCC or YMCA. He understood the need for one because he was a member of the JCC uptown, where his children were learning how to swim. When the property became available, we saw the opportunity to build the community center we had dreamed of since 1997. Mr. el-Gamal purchased the property with the pooled resources of a handful of investors, including my husband.

In October 2009, Sharaf Mowjood, an MLT who was studying journalism at Columbia University, attended our Ramadan *iftar* event, where we announced the acquisition of the building by our community. He first mentioned the story on his radio show and was urged to also write an article about our plans for the community center for his school newspaper. After the paper published the article, someone forwarded it on to *The New York Times*, which deemed it newsworthy enough that they assigned a seasoned reporter, Ralph Blumenthal, to the story. I knew Ralph from previous interviews he had conducted with my husband and urged Sharaf to ask that he be a co-reporter. The *Times* agreed. Ralph met Catherine McVeigh Hughes, a member of Community Board 1, at our Friday service at the newly purchased building, where prayers were being held to meet the demands of overcrowded congregations in a makeshift mosque. Catherine told Blumenthal that she had known Imam Feisal well for years, that he had been in the neighborhood for decades and was known to her father from the Chautauqua Institution, where he had lectured at interfaith events.

On December 8, 2009, an article titled "Muslim Prayers and Renewal Near Ground Zero" appeared on the front page of *The New York Times*. The article was very positive and stressed that there was a great deal of support for the project from interfaith allies such as Rabbi Arthur Schneier, the 9/11 Memorial & Museum, and the Reverend Joan Campbell. It barely raised an eyebrow. I was interviewed by Laura Ingraham on *The O'Reilly Factor* on Fox News. When she heard my description of the project, even she had no problem with it. But unbeknownst to us, in January 2010, opposition groups began working behind the scenes, trying to get landmark status for the building that we had purchased. Their strategy was to get the building tied up legally so that the project would get tied up in landmark legalities and bureaucracies and die a natural death by never coming to fruition.

Since I had a background in design and architecture and understood building codes, I knew that the landmark issue was a serious impediment to our project. A landmark attorney advised us to present the project to the community board first and get their support. This would influence the landmark decision-makers.

On April 26, we met with the community board's financial committee to describe our vision for the community center, which would serve as a place to create understanding and increased dialogue between all faiths. Most important, it would help revitalize Lower Manhattan. We emphasized that our intent was to have this community center serve the needs of the broader community—not just Muslims.

After reviewing the plans, the board made a few recommendations that we agreed with, including a 9/11 memorial and a senior citizen space, then unanimously passed a resolution approving the proposal. The center would be named Cordoba House and would be sponsored by the Cordoba Initiative, the multifaith organization led by my husband.

The meeting was wrapping up on a positive note when, out of the corner of my eye, I noticed a man with a large-lens camera taking photos of the slides of our presentation. He told me he was a reporter from the *Daily News* and was doing a "little story."

The next day, the "little story" ignited a furor when it prominently featured the headline 13-STORY GROUND ZERO MOSQUE. The *New York Post* jumped on the bandwagon with an editorial piece headlined MOSQUE MADNESS AT GROUND ZERO. The opposition seized on this and branded it as a "Ground Zero mosque" and a "mosquezilla." This unleashed a tidal wave of Islamophobia, starting with a full-force initiative by a group called Stop Islamization of America. Suddenly we were under attack, being painted in the far-right media as extremists. Among the accusations leveled against us: that we were building a victory mosque *in* Ground Zero and that we were wolves in sheep's clothing armed with hidden agendas—to build a caliphate and institute Shari'a law in the United States.

MY HUSBAND AND I had taken our roles as citizen ambassadors very seriously, and we had worked hard to further understanding between Americans and Muslims abroad. Before our plans for the community center were made public, the U.S. State Department had organized a lengthy speaking tour for both of us in four Gulf states.

It was a worthy initiative, but the timing was terrible. I was concerned that, given the media storm we were now embroiled in, our absence might be misconstrued. I intuitively knew that going on this tour was not the right decision and that it would have serious repercussions. We decided that only one of us would go, but I continued to be worried that if my husband left, critics would say that he was trying to avoid responsibility and that he would be branded as the "imam who fled the scene." Feisal felt compelled to keep his commitment.

When you are in a crisis, you never know how it will turn out. I had my ear to social media and the community, and I could see vitriol already emerging.

I sensed a tsunami was headed our way. It would be years before I again slept soundly through the night.

UNTIL NOW, MY HUSBAND and I had made our decisions together, but I had to face it: I could no longer influence my husband's decisions. Crisis experts stepped in, and other voices were influencing Feisal. I was losing my husband's ear. After all those years as a partner and collaborator, I was relegated to the role of wife. I accepted this—not just because I had little choice, but also because, after all, these were "experts."

During the month that my husband was away in the Gulf, the crisis at home mushroomed. If the media called, I had to respond. If questions arose, I had to answer them and tell myself to conquer my

fears, that this was for only one month. Then, suddenly, I found myself thrown in front of the media. A regular stream of interviews took
over my life—CBS, NPR, *Democracy Now!* It seemed that every
media outlet wanted to speak to me. The ABC anchor Christiane
Amanpour convinced me to participate in a debate that she would
moderate titled "Should Americans Fear Islam?" on *This Week.*

When I arrived at the makeshift studio, the line for admission
was snaking around the block—the debate was overbooked. After
hair and makeup, I was moved to the greenroom, where evangelical
preacher Rev. Franklin Graham sat. I introduced myself, and to my
surprise, Reverend Graham bluntly said, "I want you to know that I
don't believe in Islam! I don't believe a word of it. I do love Muslims,
but your religion is not real."

I was dumbfounded at his rudeness and appalled that he called
himself a Christian. This couldn't be the same religion that the nuns
of my convent school in Kashmir had practiced. I felt as if Sister John
might leap out of her grave and tell me to "go sock it to him." I
looked him straight in the face and said, "I want you to know, I went
to Catholic school for eleven years and have recited the Lord's Prayer
more than three thousand times. Jesus is close to my heart, and your
words do not represent the teachings of the Jesus I know."

Amanpour sat in the middle of the highly charged town hall debate with three women on her right: me; Azar Nafisi, bestselling
author of *Reading Lolita in Tehran;* and Donna Marsh O'Connor,
who had lost her pregnant daughter in the World Trade towers.
Franklin Graham sat on Amanpour's left along with Robert Spencer,
a fervent Muslim basher, and next to him was the father of a man
who died on 9/11.

I felt like a gladiator on the floor of a Roman amphitheater, the
lions charging from all directions.

Amanpour turned to Graham and said, "You call [Islam] a 'wicked'
religion."

With sanctimonious pride he denigrated Islam on national TV in
front of over three million viewers. "I don't believe in Islam. I don't

believe a word of it," he said. It's true that Christians and Muslims view the divinity of Jesus differently, but his calling Islam a false religion was baseless. I wondered why he had chosen to remain actively ignorant. If he'd read the chapter of Mary in the Quran, would he have responded differently?

Azar Nafisi challenged Reverend Graham when he lumped all Muslims together. "Reverend Graham, who is a Christian?" she asked. "The gay Episcopalian bishop is a Christian. The Methodists are Christians. The Baptists are Christians. Sarah Palin and Barack Obama and Bill Clinton are all Christians. Who is to say which one is more Christian than the other? And that is the point about Islam."

Donna Marsh O'Connor said, "I think Americans should fear criminal behavior. I think we should do the best we can to control criminal behavior. But I can't raise my two remaining sons to fear the people who live next door to them. That is not what my grandparents came to America to escape."

Amanpour took her concerns about our community center back to me, asking, "Do you think that you should move the center?"

I replied, "No, I think that American values have to prevail."

That night at home, when I took off the TV makeup, part of me felt sad realizing how much we had to rebuild as a community, and part of me felt hopeless in the face of this kind of opposition. Although my faith was greater than my fear, it was the first time I realized that we might not be able to withstand the onslaught. Perhaps, I thought, we had reopened the very wound we were trying to heal.

SUKKOTH PREDICTION

. . .

In 2010, *my friend Rabbi Burt Visotzky of the Jewish Theological Seminary invited me to the seminary's celebration of the
Jewish holiday of Sukkoth. Even though I was overwhelmed by
the pressures surrounding the Ground Zero controversy at that
time, I decided to join him, especially since the seminary had
supported us as we sought to build our community center.
When I arrived at the Jewish Theological Seminary and approached the sukkah, the temporary shelter built for the holiday, I was surprised to find all of the tables empty except for
one with a half dozen rabbis and Jewish leaders seated around
it. It became clear that the rabbis wanted a private meeting.*

*They welcomed me and asked how my husband and I were
holding up. I told them that under the circumstances we were
surviving. Then they held out an envelope. "This is a small contribution from all of us. Right now, there are many demands on
your organization, and this is one way we can help."*

*Just as I finished thanking them for their kindness, a rabbi
turned to me. "You are keeping the fight up, aren't you? Don't
back down!" he told me.*

*I was feeling somewhat resigned and replied, "I guess we
are."*

"No, no," he shot back. "You don't understand. You must

keep this fight up. You are not only fighting for yourself; you are fighting for all those who will come next!"

Another rabbi looked me straight in my eyes and said, "You are fighting for us too! One day, they will come after the Jews!"

Was I hearing this right? Surely the Jewish community did not need my protection. And what could I, a Muslim, do to safeguard them?

Then they made me promise that I would keep fighting—not just for myself, but also for other groups, "Hindus, Sikhs, and Buddhists, and then again for us Jews."

My experience with the rabbis left me unsettled. But I naively never expected their prediction to come true.

In 2017, anti-Semitic hate crimes and Islamophobia spiked more than 60 percent. Hundreds of Jewish tombstones were vandalized, and Jewish Community Centers across America had to evacuate because of bomb threats. As a response to the rise of hate crimes, the American Jewish Committee formed the Muslim-Jewish Advisory Council, which I joined. On February 1, 2017, we met with Democratic and Republican lawmakers in Congress. We urged them to intensify the country's response to the increase in hate crimes across the United States, especially those targeting Muslim and Jewish communities.

Around that time, I received an email from Rabbi Joy Levitt of the Manhattan JCC, in which she wrote, "I am actually terrified for all of us and would love to talk about what we can do." The moment is seared in my memory: During the 2010 mosque controversy, Joy stood by my side on national television and supported the building of a community center. She said, "The opposition to the mosque feels very familiar. In the 1600s, governor of New York Peter Stuyvesant did not allow a synagogue to be built in Manhattan, and two centuries later it

took an act of Congress, by the newly formed American government, to allow a synagogue to be built in Washington, D.C."

The desecration of the tombstones was so offensive to Muslims that Tarek el-Messidi, a thoughtful Muslim activist,
started a fundraising campaign that raised $160,000 to help re-
store the cemeteries.

The support I received from my Jewish friends and the Muslim community's response to the hate-fueled desecration of the
tombstones are powerful statements of unity in the face of religious intolerance. Only if we stand together in support of each
other will we prevail. For as Joy told me, if we do not protest
injustice, who will protest when they come after us?

ON MY HUSBAND'S RETURN FROM THE GULF TRIP, LAW
enforcement warned him that there was a credible threat
against him, and he was advised to find a safe house. When Feisal
called me from the car, he provided no further details, only asked me
to pack a bag for him—he would make a brief stop at home to pick
it up. I suspected from the measured tone of his voice that he thought
his calls were being monitored.

I realized that the only thing to do was to switch to survival mode,
which meant going on autopilot. I mindlessly busied myself packing
his essential things—the "good wife" response—and when he arrived
to pick up his bags, we made small talk.

Feisal's stay at the undisclosed location lasted months, during
which I saw him only periodically, mainly during staged media interviews or at community meetings. It was like being married to someone in the Witness Protection Program. I turned to the one group
that I knew I could depend on—my family, who were both supportive and frantic. They were convinced that my life was in danger and
begged me to leave the house and come stay with them. My brother
Zahid rushed to my house to assess the security. He stressed that I
needed to be very careful, that there were crazy people out there who
could harm me. Months later, when a brick was thrown at our basement window, I was grateful that my brother had installed a first-rate
security system.

While Zahid was dead serious, my brother Abid maintained a sense of humor. Abid, who as a child had eaten our mother's lipsticks, was now a psychiatrist living with his family on Long Island. He would follow the news coverage and then would call and read aloud the worst of the headlines that involved Feisal and me. "So, Daisy, it looks like you've done this or that horrible thing! Ha!" He'd laugh hysterically. "So now you're really in the frying pan! Ha! This is what they are saying about my sister!" And I would yell at Abid, both of us reverting to our childhood roles. Still, I appreciated his attempts to point out the ironies and humor of the situation. Perhaps it was his coping mechanism.

My husband and I had collaborated on all fronts since 9/11, and now, of all times, when we should have been working as a united couple, discussing things, sharing the stress, we found ourselves separated because of circumstances beyond our control. How had our intentions become so terribly misunderstood? I was certain our phone lines were tapped, even at home. Every word we spoke in our infrequent conversations was purposefully superficial. There was no time, no place, for real emotions. I continued to work at the office and tried to set a strong example for our young workers, but the truth was, sometimes I felt afraid to even breathe.

Meanwhile, I was bombarded by the media, which were demanding to know where the imam was. Suddenly, Feisal and I were a front-page story in the *New York Post* and the *Daily News,* and I had to step in and appear on TV and radio shows as a spokesperson. During one interview, Fox News drilled me with questions like "Is Imam Rauf hiding behind his wife's skirts?" Arfa Auntie called all shaken. "I never imagined that *our* Daisy would be on national TV every night. I get so angry because this is all very unfair. You have sacrificed so much. You gave up your big-salaried job, gave up your comforts, tried to bring normalcy to this crazy world, and this is how you are treated. If you want to come home, the door is open."

People threw eggs at our house while I was inside, alone. Feisal's ex-wife and his musician daughter were being hounded by the tabloid press looking for "dirt." I was terrified of involving my family or my young staff members, who seemed numb. Post-9/11, everyone had been walking on eggshells. Now I felt as if those shells were cracking under my feet. We were in the news for six months consecutively, from May to October. Faroque Chacha provided a clinical metaphor for assurance. "This attack on both of you is not personal! The opposition groups are tapping into a deep resentment among the anti-Muslim folks. This is like in chemistry when you use an enzyme that creates a catalytic reaction and everything at the bottom bubbles up to the surface," he said.

I had always looked forward to opening the mail, but now the pile that arrived each day became an ugly, unpredictable paper monster. I might open an envelope and find my face staring back at me—in the form of an image cut out of a recent magazine profile, pasted in the center of a hand-assembled collage captioned: *Daisy (the new face of terror) Khan=another whore of Muhammad. Americans! Don't fall for the lies of this bitch and other Muslim leaders!*

Death threats started pouring in at my home and my office. The New York Police Department assigned a hate crimes unit detective to me. At first, this seemed excessive, and I told him we really didn't need to worry about anything; it didn't make any sense that somebody would want to harm me. But Detective Rodriguez did not agree and informed me that most assassinations were carried out by mentally unstable people who didn't think rationally and that his team needed to secure our office and train our staff on how to handle security issues. That was a sobering message.

It was time to establish a new, security-minded protocol for our office, with hidden cameras and an intercom. They told us that, going forward, Bernadette, our office receptionist, had to wear plastic gloves to open all mail. When I asked about the threatening phone calls and emails, the response was blunt. The department said that any hate calls would need to be digitally recorded; we needed to forward to them all hate emails so that IP addresses could be pursued. By this time, we were happy to comply. It seemed there was a protocol for handling hate. Hard copies of documents had to be inserted into plastic covers and put in binders. We had one binder full of hate mail and two binders full of support mail. The most vituperative messages were directed at either my husband or me personally. We knew that the intense level of hatred being projected at us was really meant for terrorists, but the terrorists were dead, and people didn't know whom else to unleash their anger at. We were visible public figures. In the office, it was almost impossible to do any real work, and I noticed the staff trembling when they saw hate mail. I can't imagine how the young people, in particular, found the courage to come to work every day, but to their credit, they never once let us down. One day, when they were trying to keep their composure amid the barrage of negative publicity, I wanted them to know that trials can also be blessings in disguise. I shared the following prophetic story with them.

Every time the Prophet Muhammad would walk with his companions through an alleyway, a woman would open her window and insult him by throwing animal entrails at him. She did this so often that the Prophet could predict when this would occur and was able to duck. One day as he was passing, there was no garbage thrown at him. Surprised, he asked his companions, "What happened to her?" When he heard that she was sick, his reaction shocked his companions. "I will go see her," he said. When he arrived, she was so moved that he had come to check on her despite her hostility toward him that she told him, "Muhammad, you are a good man, and I will follow your message."

I had used this prophetic wisdom to reassure my young team that negative news coverage was the equivalent of modern-day animal entrails and that we, like the Prophet, must find means to avoid them. Every morning, all the media entrails were piled on one desk, then meticulously placed in clear sleeves or recorded in an e-spreadsheet and filed away.

One day, Bernadette, in her plastic gloves, handed me a different kind of message. It was a crumpled five-dollar bill, accompanied by a note: *I am unemployed. Please accept this $5.00 bill, it is all I have right* *now.* I read it aloud to the team. Occurrences like that kept us going. We realized that the loudest, most raucous voices were not necessarily the voices of the haters.

During the days, I managed to stay focused within the hurricane, running the office, but when I came home at night, I missed having my husband there by my side, being able to turn to each other and ask, "What's happening to us?" It felt empty, not having him to hug for reassurance, but when I was lonely, I remembered verse 58:07 in the Quran, which explains that no matter how few or how many we are, God is always there. So when two people are together, God is always the third party, and when we are alone, God is no less with us. These words gave me solace and reassurance. Even though on the surface the opposition appeared to be an obstruction, the Quran provided me with hope: "Indeed, what is to come will be better for you than what has gone by" (93:4). My faith was now more important than ever, because it was not only my purpose; it was all I had to cling to.

CHAPTER

37

*I*AM BACK IN *KASHMIR RIDING MY BIKE, LAUGHING WITH HALIMA and her American cousin Peter. The sun is out, and my hair blows free. The scent of roses is in the air.* Then I wake up. The day is dark. There is no sun. There are no roses. I had had this dream several times recently. I rubbed my eyes and thought how far away those days were, in time, space, and circumstance. I imagined this is a throwback dream, a longing for that simpler time. Perhaps it was stress that triggered this dream.

There are many books and experts available to tell women how to handle a marriage crisis. But where do you turn when the crisis is a 360-degree life crisis? When you are living and breathing it, when your challenged relationship is not just with your husband but with a community in free fall, people in disbelief and fear, and your primal source of security, your own faith, is a target? I was precariously balanced on a high wire, praying the wind would not be too forceful. It was all I could do. I constantly reminded myself that so many had suffered so much more, that this was relatively minor compared to their tragedies.

On May 25, 2010, after weeks of negotiations and standoffs, a key community meeting was scheduled. Though I had not thought it possible, the community meetings had become increasingly turbulent. Within weeks, the controversy had escalated to the boiling point, and Feisal and I were both flanked by security as we were led to the meeting. A crowd of about three hundred jeering protesters swarmed the building, waving signs and shouting, *"No mosque here! Go home! No Shari'a!"* Someone held up a poster of my husband's face with rifle crosshairs on it. We were rushed inside.

Jeers and hostile epithets filled the room as my husband spoke. The community center was now branded by the media as the "Ground Zero Mosque." Our Jewish and Christian friends immediately circled the wagons. "We have seen this before," they told us. Rev. Kevin Madigan reminded the Christians in the room, "When St. Peter's Catholic Church was built only a few blocks from here, the surrounding community wanted to burn it, and they had to put a fence around it."

Yehezel Landau, a Jewish scholar and a bridge builder, had traveled from Hartford, Connecticut, to vouch for our commitment to interfaith dialogue. Talat G. Hamdani, whose son was a first responder on 9/11, reminded the audience that Muslims had given their lives too. Rev. Chloe Breyer, head of the Interfaith Center of New York and daughter of Supreme Court Justice Stephen Breyer, told us she was shocked by the vitriol and hatred we were being subjected to. Rev. James Forbes, the pastor of Riverside Church who had walked with Dr. King during the civil rights marches, showed up for us, despite his age. "In moments like this," he said, "you need to show support. I am right behind you." Walter Ruby, a Jewish advocate, stood firm and announced, "We are your friends."

Muz and his family understood the importance of the community center; it was being built for his children. His daughter, Maryam, had prepared her own remarks for the community meeting, but when she saw the jeering from the crowd, she was so shaken that her mother took her away. But her father read her statement:

> My name is Maryam, and I am a sixth grader at the Gateway School. I am honored to talk about something so important to me and to other kids like me. My mom is Jewish, and my dad is Muslim. I consider myself to be both Jewish and Muslim. I have always had a place to go in the city to learn about Jewish

history, culture, and traditions. I don't have a similar place to go to learn about what it means to be Muslim. I think that in a city as big as New York, we should have a place that can be a community center for Muslims that welcomes people of all different religions and backgrounds. I'm sure that most kids, as they are getting older, want to figure out who they are and what they are as a person. For kids like me with different backgrounds, it would be great to have a place to come together and talk about what we care about as kids—not as Muslims or Jews or as Christians—and share our stories, our experiences, and our values. I think the Cordoba House could be that place. Thank you.

After all the speakers for and against the resolution had spoken, it was the last speaker, Marc Ameruso, a member of Community Board 1, who became the deciding voice. He said he had done his own research about the "visionaries" behind the project. "As someone who's served in government and understands security, I picked up the phone and called all the people I knew in intelligence. I was told the following: 'This is the Kiwanis Club of the Muslim community. If you can't work with them, then who will you work with?'" His supportive words gave the necessary assurance to those who were on the fence.

Immediately after all remarks concluded, Julie Menin, the chair of Community Board 1 passed a resolution, with twenty-nine in favor, one opposed, and ten abstentions, approving the Cordoba House project, a community center with a five-hundred-seat performing arts center and lecture hall, a culinary school, an exhibition space, a swimming pool, a basketball court, a library, and childcare. The resolution went on to say that programs and facilities would be open to the general public and would be very helpful in meeting a number of important community needs and that the project would create over 150 full-time and over 500 part-time jobs and would involve an investment of over one hundred million dollars in infrastructure in the Financial District. There was one caveat, though: The board took "no position regarding the religious aspects of or any religious facilities associated with the Cordoba House." In addition to Community Board 1, politicians including Mayor Michael Bloomberg, Rep. Jerrold Nadler, Manhattan Borough President Scott M. Stringer, New York State senator Daniel L. Squadron, Assembly Member Deborah Glick, and Council Member Margaret Chin supported the project.

ONE OTHER THING OF NOTE occurred at the community board meeting, something that shook me to the core. Of course, we still had our detractors, who remained violently opposed to our project. It seemed that every constituency in the city of New York had a point of view. Feisal and I had no time for any personal discussion; we were like two colleagues who worked for the same company but lived in different cities. How easy it would have been to walk away, to give up, to buckle under the pressure.

From the beginning, one of the most formidable opponents of the center was a man named Lee Hanson. He sought me out at the community board meeting and introduced himself.

Looking at me intently, he asked if I remembered my friend Halima.

Naturally, I did. Halima and I had remained close over the years, as she had also moved to the States and then enlisted in the U.S. Army. Yet we had barely spoken since 9/11.

Mr. Hanson then said, "I am her uncle Lee. Don't you remember me?"

Uncle Lee? I flashed back to that idyllic summer in Kashmir with Halima, Peter, and Kathy, bicycling, swimming, stuffing ourselves with ice cream. And I definitely remembered Peter and Kathy's parents—Uncle Lee and Auntie. How could Mr. Hanson, our project's archenemy, be Halima's beloved uncle, the same Uncle Lee who had taken us for ice cream so long ago in Kashmir? An older woman, her eyes red and swollen with tears, stepped forward. It was jolting to see Halima's aunt, as she reminded me so much of Halima's mother.

Auntie took my hand as she pleaded with me not to build the center in the proposed location. She was speaking not for herself, she emphasized, but for her son. I was confused. What were they doing there? Then they told me that Peter and his wife, Sue, and their two-year-old daughter, Christine, had been on the second plane that hit the towers. She was the youngest of the 2,977 victims.

I felt the blood drain from my body—it was a physical sensation, and I staggered. As I offered my sympathies, I was choking internally. Why had Halima not told me? I asked.

Suddenly Uncle Lee seemed like a very old man. I was so shaken, I thought I heard Uncle Lee say, "Muslims had hijacked the planes. How could she tell you?" Which made me wonder, was it too painful for her to come to terms with this tragedy and the loss of her cousin, or was it because her family had been torn apart by this trauma? I was certain she was angry at the terrorists who had not only hijacked the planes but also hijacked our religion.

But Halima's father is a Muslim, I wanted to say. Had she distanced herself from her heritage? If I had known, I would of course have reached out immediately to her and the family. I thought back to Kashmir during the Pakistani conflict, when my friends had chosen sides on the playground. It had come to this. My oldest friend's extended family and I were now on opposing sides.

But was there even a "side"? Did there have to be? Why was anyone an "enemy" here? Faltering, I said, "Uncle Lee, I'm so sorry; I didn't know that Peter died. No one told me. Let me introduce you and Auntie to my husband." I guided the Hansons to a corner of the room where Feisal, shaken by the hostility of the crowd, had stepped to remove himself from the fray. He was sitting alone, trying to meditate, his head bent over his prayer beads. I gently tapped his shoulder and introduced them, then explained to Feisal that Uncle Lee's son and family had perished on 9/11.

Feisal expressed his deep sorrow and said he would pray for their souls. He reached out, took Uncle and Auntie Lee's hands, and started praying. I envied my husband his inner resources, but I felt conflicted. I knew these people, and their pain felt like my pain. I weighed my quest to build the community center against the pain being experienced by the Hansons and by others like them. The last thing I wanted to do was cause them more sorrow. But I also knew that nothing is black and white, that every point of view is a kaleidoscope, with the pieces falling into different patterns depending on how you hold it.

After speaking with Uncle Lee and Auntie, I immediately reached out to Halima. I had been not only stunned but also hurt that she had never told me about Peter. I said that I was devastated about him and his family, that I had had no idea that Lee Hanson was Uncle Lee, that her uncle was now our biggest opponent.

Halima had acquired a soft Southern accent while attending college in Berea, Kentucky. But now her voice hardened. What did I expect? They were opponents of the project, not of me personally, she said.

I confessed my helplessness and asked what she thought I should do.

Different people process grief differently, she told me. They were still grieving. She hadn't known right away herself that Peter and his family had died, because she had been deployed in Germany as a base commander. When word came of 9/11, it had been her job to secure the base. She returned from this job to be given the news about Peter and his family. She had served in the army, risked her own life during Desert Storm fighting for her country. Her mother was American. She was American. And yet, because her father was Muslim, he and their Muslim relatives and their fellow Muslims were under scrutiny in their own country. Halima's voice, previously so assured, wavered.

I asked if there was anything I could do for Uncle Lee and Auntie. I felt desperate to help, to make amends in some way—for what, I wasn't sure.

Uncle Lee and Auntie had changed, Halima said. We all had. We talked about the way we tended to shut each other out when we needed each other most; how one could be Muslim, but also be American; and how painful it was to now be told, "This is not your tragedy."

Halima begged me to look at the situation from the Hansons' perspective. Maybe because she was the product of two cultures, she always seemed able to see both sides of the issue.

The media continued to ask for interviews. Reporters tried to catch me unaware, hoping for a controversial sound bite. I could not imagine why what I thought interested anyone, since I was not a public figure.

Then someone in the media pointed out that actually I was now a public figure, and everything I said and did was of public interest.

There were many nights when I would come home, turn on the TV, and find some talking head discussing my husband and me. The media strategy seemed to be to put a face on the controversy—our face—and put us under a cloud of suspicion personally, questioning our organization, our funding sources. Once, I turned on CNN to find a reporter holding up a copy of our annual audit statement. Some of the accusations were so absurd that I had to laugh at them, but no training had prepared me to handle something like this, especially now that it had turned into a months-long siege. I just knew I had to stay strong.

But how to do that? Rumi said that the true smell of a seed comes out only when you grind it in a millstone, by which he meant that the true character of a person comes out when we go through life's vicissitudes. I felt that I was in a grinder. I remembered my grandfather saying, "Make the Khan name proud." I recognized the expectations of others, but I had also set high expectations for myself. But it was the words of Kashmir's rebel saint, Lal Ded, that helped me regain my confidence:

> Let them jeer or cheer me;
> Let anybody say what he likes;
> Let good persons worship me with flowers;
> What can any one of them gain, I being pure?

If the world talks ill of me
My heart shall harbor no ill will:
If I am a true worshipper of God
Can ashes leave a stain on a mirror?

—*From* Daughters of the Vitasta,
by Prem Nath Bazaz

ONE DAY, RABBI MARC Schneier, who had founded the Foundation for Ethnic Understanding and had worked with both Feisal and me, came to the office to show his support. "Where's the imam?" he asked me.

I told him that Feisal was at an undisclosed location.

He looked concerned. I was all alone, then?

I told him I was, but I was holding up.

The rabbi pointed a finger at my face. I expected him to lecture me on personal security the way the NYPD had. Instead, he told me he was speaking to me as a brother. I was *not* to allow anyone to become a wedge between my husband and myself. These, the rabbi warned ominously, were the moments that could lead to a divorce!

The rabbi's statement left me shaken. I could no longer deny that my marriage had reached a crisis point; there were many stresses that could tear us apart. If I was being honest with myself, I had to admit that fighting for the community center had effectively meant I had made the decision to table my personal life and focus on my mission of faith. As the mission had grown to national and even global proportions, my husband and I working as a team had in fact divided us—physically and emotionally. As I was no longer the "partner," I needed to become more of a person in my own right.

Moji's dream for the frail baby girl had become reality, but Dadaji's dream for the woman had prepared me for this life. One of my husband's favorite Rumi poems seemed to define my own path: "Two birds can't fly if you tie their feet together, just because they have four wings."

So I decided not to fall or flutter but to fly. Now we would fly side by side. I was ready to become my own person.

OH NO—*NOT* JAPANESE INTERNMENT AGAIN!

...

When Lisa's grandparents were released from the Japanese internment camp, her grandmother was angry. But her answer to what had happened to her was not to disengage, but to fight for a seat at the table. She began writing letters to members of Congress. She told Lisa's father and uncle, "When something bad happens, engage more." Lisa's father had told her this story repeatedly during her childhood. As a mixed-race child—her father is Japanese American, her mother is of Irish descent—she felt enriched by her Japanese and Irish cultures, but life wasn't always easy. During her teenage years, she was shy and remembers being confronted with racialized stereotypes. During that time, she said, "I became aware of the stereotypes about how Asian women are 'supposed' to behave. People would assume that I was passive, or always agreeable, that I spoke 'Asian,' among a lot of other ignorant things. It woke me up, because I could see that they were perceiving me as an Asian woman, but there was a whole other half of my identity that people just didn't see."

When Lisa started studying at Vassar College, she took classes on religion and particularly Islam. She learned about the "Ground Zero Mosque" controversy from her professor Max Leeming, who had attended Friday prayers at our mosque *and was shocked when the controversy erupted. Max knew us personally and had vouched for us during the debate moderated by Christiane Amanpour on ABC. While watching the town hall debate, Lisa had felt deeply conflicted. On her father's side, her Japanese American grandparents had been interned during World War II. Yet she also understood and empathized with those on the other side of the debate: On her Irish mother's side, her uncle had been killed when he was working as a firefighter on 9/11.*

However, it was that very town hall debate that persuaded Lisa to find out more about ASMA and the proposed center, and that led to her decision to intern for us that summer. At her interview she said, "When I heard an opponent of the mosque question Ms. Khan, asking, 'How do I know you are not lying to us?,' I thought that was so unfair. Just because she identified as Muslim, suddenly he could not take her words at face value. That really led me to put my foot down and to say, no, we cannot allow the tragedy of 9/11, which unjustly took so many lives, to then be used as an excuse to violate the most fundamental freedoms for other people, because then we're just perpetuating this cycle of fear and divisiveness, and to what end?"

During her internship, however, things were not easy. Lisa lived with her Irish relatives and knew how painful the tragedy was for them. Every day she came home to her loving family, yet every day she also experienced their loss of not having their father and husband, her uncle, around. She knew that if she told them she was working for a Muslim organization, they might be offended, so she provided them scant information about her internship.

After her graduation Lisa's parents told her, "Try to find a job where you're serving others—that is the most valuable thing in life." This ultimately brought Lisa back to New York to work

full-time with WISE. Today, she is my right hand; she under-
stands both sides of an issue and is effective at repairing frac-
tures and navigating perceived differences and disagreements.
When we look back on our first meeting, she recalls the "dra-
matic thought" of Japanese internment and how the possibility
of Muslim internment had felt so remote. Today, we have a
Muslim ban, hate crimes on the rise, people preventing mosques
from being built, visas being revoked, and families being sepa-
rated from their children.

But I have faith in our future. There are millennials like Lisa
out there who prefer creating social change over material gain,
are increasingly engaged, and refuse to back down.

"WHAT DOES ISLAM SAY ABOUT EVOLUTION?" I ASKED my husband once, and waited eagerly for an answer.

My husband's expression changed into that of a lecturer as he lifted one finger and said, "If there is one thing I will teach you, it will be that you learn how to think for yourself." And then he continued to lecture me. "If you are going to speak as a wife of an imam, then you need to understand that Islam is not a person or an institution that talks or makes declarations. Islam is an action, a verb, a thing you do. It is 'an act of submission to God's will.'"

He proceeded to clarify his statement. "The correct way to ask a question is 'What does God say in the Quran?' Or 'What did the Prophet do or say? What are the opinions of the scholars on this matter?'" Then he laid down the ground rules. "I will never give you a simple black-and-white answer," he told me. "You need to first explore the various meanings in the text, its context, and then study the multiple interpretations that exist. Only then will you become adept at teaching others."

Seeing the look of bewilderment on my face, he assured me, "Don't get me wrong; I am happy to guide you, but you have to exert your own energy first. Look around you. You don't have to go far." He pointed to our bookshelves, which held hundreds of books, encyclopedias, and concordances.

This was the greatest gift my husband gave me, the gift of learning the nuances of my religion not by emulation but by reason, inquiry, and intense critique. I was gaining confidence, and I even had a safety net: Although I was making a lot of decisions on my own, I always knew I could fall back on my husband. With the two of us flying side by side, the supersonic tailwind propelled me forward into territories unimaginable.

AND YET LIFE BRINGS unexpected changes. All relationships evolve, but my husband's and mine had been transformed by a tsunami. Our dreams for the community center were once again put on hold, our voices drowned out by opposition activists. Our marriage had gone through a firestorm. We no longer talked about our work as much as we had when I was under my husband's tutelage—my apprenticeship had ended. But in other ways, this made for a healthier relationship.

Now I defined myself not so much as an imam's wife and work partner but as a spouse and life partner. My focus shifted to my own work, and my husband supported this. We both realized that marriage is an ebb and flow, and if you are committed and in it for the long term, you have to be flexible enough to adapt to change. Every couple has their crucible. The community center had been ours.

When our relationship had been of a partnership solely devoted to religious and community work, we had had very little time for everyday activities that other couples take for granted, and I wondered how we would reconstruct our life together. But in the end, I slid into the new role quite comfortably. In this new phase, we were still both very busy independently, but when we were together, we were able to prioritize our relationship. On free weekends, we continued to host spiritual gatherings in our home, entertain family and friends at brunches, or watch a Netflix movie in our living room. Feisal likes food shopping; I like gardening and cooking. I read the newspaper in hard copy; he reads it on his iPad. He loves to read books while I am on social media so I can stay current, and together we listen to music for relaxation. If all this sounds perfectly normal—it is, and it isn't. The new normal for many people of our faith since 9/11 is that there is no normal.

I identify with Umm Salama and her search for clarification. Because of her, light shone on the fact that Muslim women can say with certainty that gender equality is an intrinsic part of our faith and should become a mainstay of our future.

The ideas that are passed from one person to another, that can be heard and experienced firsthand, are often the most effective agents of change. When people ask about our strategy, I answer that it has been not about PowerPoint presentations or management by objectives but about management by belief—by moving forward at the grassroots level, on the ground within communities, where women traditionally have shown great strength. Taking the long-term view involves gradually opening hearts and minds and building from there.

When the Global Muslim Women's Shura Council met in 2009 in Kuala Lumpur at the second WISE conference, it presented its first position paper, *A Jihad against Violence,* a condemnation of domestic violence and terrorism. We all agreed that Muslim women had everything to gain by speaking out—and much to lose by remaining silent. We can speak; we can illuminate; we can act. In these ways, we can change. Where I see inspirational stories that have been primarily about men, there is always a women's side too—one that has inevitably received far less focus.

But beyond our personal relationship, in 2013, after the community center controversy had subsided, both our organizations, the Cordoba Initiative and ASMA, including ASMA's programs MLT and WISE, were severely impacted as our detractors continually referred to us as a couple as if we were one person. They continued to refer to us as the "Ground Zero couple," and by linking us, they were undermining the work we did independently of each other. We were the most visible Muslim couple in America, and their goal was to taint us and thereby taint the community. Some of our supporters began to worry that all the work we had done over the years was in jeopardy. At the minimum they thought we should restructure so we were no longer seen as a mom-and-pop shop. The ASMA board began to discuss ways to create a clear distinction between our respective roles and work. They thought I would be pleased.

On the contrary, I was filled with trepidation. After all, Feisal and I had accomplished so much by working together, and by continuing that way, we could do so much more.

Most of the women board members were surprised. They had assumed that because I was accomplished I would be delighted to move forward independently of my husband. They felt we both would benefit from the separation, and one well-wisher tried to convince me by saying, "You will fly on your own."

But I was already flying! We were not in the business of commerce. We were creating conversations! We had succeeded in building common ground and developing constructive spiritual and theological debates. Since when did one clap with one hand? I could not imagine creating deeper conversations without my second hand, my husband.

I was conflicted for months; my spirit was vehemently against it. No true dreams appeared, as I'd hoped they would, to clarify the decision. I believed that my marriage was a result of divine intervention, that my children were never born because I was meant to be a mother to many, and although I had accomplished a lot without my husband's involvement, I knew something deeper was holding me back from feeling comfortable letting go. My husband analyzed it this way: "You have become root-bound with me, but you will not grow under my shade any longer! You are not being asked to step aside. The sun simply needs to shine on you directly."

Because I did not understand my reaction I began to search my soul. I came up with several obvious vulnerabilities. First, my husband had always lent an air of credibility to my religious work. I recognized that I had leaned on him for support and that over time he had become my crutch. My fear was that if I did my work independently of him, I might fail. And yet, I knew, I might also flutter or fly.

In addition, my public persona was so rooted in our joint work, and I worried about the impact our splitting our work into separate organizations would have on our constituencies. Our success was their success. How would they perceive the separation? Would it disappoint them, or would they see it as a healthy development? My inner woman's voice was nagging at me. What will our children, our tribe, our supporters, and our people think? I asked myself.

As for our detractors, I was sure this would be a cause célèbre. I was certain that they would claim victory for having divided us.

While I was agonizing over this decision and trying to arrive at a conclusion from deep within myself, those involved were frustrated at my perceived delay tactics. I needed help, and I needed it now.

The life of a public figure is a lonely one. Your family and friends always agree with you, and there is only a handful of people whom you can trust with your inner thoughts. I needed a friend, a confidante, an arbitrator, a truth teller! I reached out to Mino, who had known Feisal from his undergrad years at Columbia University and who had helped me found WISE. As a board member of ASMA, she had been part of the conversations early on. As a change management professional, she had guided us through these discussions. Although she did have her own perspective, I knew she was the right sounding board for me. I was sure I would walk away with clarity.

Mino told me she had watched with fascination as my leadership evolved from the earliest of days. She recapped it this way: "When I first met you, you were an avid student of Imam Feisal in terms of your faith and spirituality. When 9/11 happened, it was the first time I saw you put your stamps of art and activism and spirituality together to create the art tribute to 9/11, and to me, that is when you started to emerge with your unique style of leadership. It was like a flower had bloomed with varieties of petals. Feisal gave you the spirituality petal to add to your art and activism petals!

"When you started MLT and I helped you with it, you were

working as a team with Feisal, but he was perceived as the leader, even though you and I designed and facilitated the sessions with great success. Then we put our ideas together to launch WISE, and there you clearly were the leader; as women, we were reluctant to give Feisal too much room on the floor. We needed to keep our women engaged and respected as independent scholars who didn't require a man's voice to legitimize us. I am sure that was a bit tricky for you as the wife! Even I felt anxious as an old friend of Feisal's!

"While ASMA, which had spawned MLT and WISE, was expanding, the Cordoba Initiative, with Feisal at its helm, had emerged as a multifaith initiative to build bridges. This is where it was clear that you and Feisal had different expressions of leadership—his leaned more on scholarly research and educating about Islam, whereas you were more on the ground, more grassroots, activist oriented.

"As a couple, you have had to continually parse your private and public roles, to redefine and change them as different initiatives were launched to respond to the needs of the day. You have had to manage the internal emotional needs and bruises that are a given in such a situation. But that is again where your faith, and the larger picture, became the overriding context and cause, not petty egos, which fight for the spotlight, for recognition, et cetera. Your Sufi discipline of negating the self has played a key role in keeping that context front and center and letting everything else go.

"The lessons you have learned can benefit others. You can provide great advice for future women leaders—as balancing our public and private roles is so challenging, no matter what religion you are. You can help others on how to handle their unique circumstances, on how to build a better future. Most importantly, you can teach them on how to always keep separating ego from freedom!

"If you don't hold back, your talent will explode, and you will be thanked—the universe always rewards actions. Go forward, and offer your unique gift to the world."

The internal voice that had held me back had been trapped in a circumscribed sense of "what I do," but after speaking to Mino, I felt ready to use this unique moment to birth something new, to become who I wanted to be.

In 2015, I stepped down from ASMA, an organization I had nurtured and loved, and handed it to my husband. ASMA was renamed Cordoba House. And my husband and his executive director, Naz Ahmed Georgas, created a cutting-edge curriculum that placed a strong emphasis on a child's personal spiritual development and on the practical application of Islamic values in a modern-day context. I stand behind them, cheerleading, for their commitment to plant the seeds for the next generation.

And in 2015, WISE was born all over again, this time as its own organization, where I have been leading women to promote human equality, restore their rights, and create a peaceful environment for us all. One of the first things I realized in my new role was that focusing on my own mission meant I was able to revisit many conversations about my work with women and move them to the global table. Since WISE had formed the Global Muslim Women's Shura Council, we had made huge headway in a fractured environment, with the limited funds we'd been able to raise. We'd learned that shifting the status quo is not an easy journey. Historically, every step women have taken forward has been met with what at first appeared to be a concrete wall of opposition. But we have seen that, with resilience and fortitude, possibility can convert to actual change. At WISE, we are committed to being ambassadors for the changes that can open up opportunities in the lives of all women, regardless of religion or geography. We are focused on those who seek the light that comes through the crack in the window, those who open the windows to empowerment. From small steps, a journey happens.

THE NINE-YEAR-OLD
RUNAWAY BRIDE

...

The parents of a nine-year-old girl arranged a marriage for her to a man in his thirties. Regularly beaten by her in-laws and raped by her husband, the girl managed to escape two months after the wedding. With the help of her father's second wife, who put her under the protection of a judge, she immediately sought a divorce. The judge took it upon himself to give the girl temporary refuge and had both her father and husband taken into custody.

Nadia al-Sakkaf, editor-in-chief of the Yemen Times, *used her role to spearhead a campaign against child marriage in Yemen, helping to push forward legislation to ban the practice. While she was reporting on the divorce described above, a young tribal leader became irritated by the daily reports and contacted her. He wanted to meet the girl and verify her story for himself. In Yemen, tribal leaders wield a lot of influence, so Nadia invited the man to a birthday party for the young girl. When he arrived, he scanned the premises, trying to identify the bride. The organizers pointed to a large birthday cake flanked by three little girls in pink party dresses, one of whom was the birthday girl. The tribal leader was so shocked that he blurted out, "But she is like my little daughter! We can't have this!" He*

threw his full support behind al-Sakkaf's campaign to pass leg-
islation to increase the minimum marriage age in Yemen.

In Islam, intellectual and physical maturity and a woman's
consent are prerequisites for a marriage to be valid. Yemeni law
used to allow girls of any age to wed, but it forbade sex with
them until an indefinite time when they were considered "suit-
able for sexual intercourse." In court, this girl's female lawyer
argued that this marriage had violated the law, since the girl
had been raped and was clearly not of age. The lawyer rejected
the judge's proposal for the girl to resume living with her hus-
band after a break of three to five years, and ultimately the
court granted her a divorce.

The girl returned to school in the fall of 2008 with future
plans of becoming a lawyer.

At one of our WISE conferences, Nadia al-Sakkaf told our
group how she and the Yemen Times *subsequently successfully*
ended the early and forced marriages of young girls by influenc-
ing the Yemeni government to repeal laws permitting such mar-
riages. Later, Nadia became the first woman to be appointed as
information minister in Yemen.

CHAPTER

39

ONE DAY I WAS SPEAKING TO A COMMUNITY GROUP WHEN a question was raised: "What can we do about ISIS?" At the time, al-Qaeda, not ISIS, was at the forefront of the conversation on terrorism. Unlike al-Qaeda, however, ISIS had tentacles that reached into communities, homes, and the intimate psyches of women and girls—and the group grabbed hold of physical territory that enabled and empowered its platform and appeal, as well as magnified the potential danger.

It was 2014, and ISIS had declared itself a global caliphate. Claiming succession to the historical caliphate leaders going back to A.D. 632, the group attempted to establish itself as the leader of a worldwide Muslim movement that would unite Islamic territories. The world has now witnessed its unyielding and cruel ideology in action.

As we had done with other issues, we asked ourselves if there was anything further we could do to address the increasing global threat posed by extremists and prevent further extremist recruitment. Globally, women often hold critical traditional and contemporary roles in their families and can leverage this influence toward building more peaceful and resilient communities. Perhaps most important, mothers are frequently the first ones to detect a behavioral change in their child who may be tending toward extremism, but mothers often lack the tools, resources, or know-how to get their children out of an extremist mindset. Perhaps the community activism that we had de-

ployed so successfully on the ground in Egypt and Afghanistan could
be leveraged in the United States and beyond to propel cultural understanding at a time when the world was rocked by confusion and
misunderstanding. Could we help people understand—group by
group, community by community, whether it be in mosques and Islamic centers around America, in a women's mosque in California, at
the United Nations, or in the halls of Congress—that ISIS is not
Islam? The thread of violence is insidious. Like needlework on a
quilt, it surfaces, recedes, unravels, then knots, only to continue to
retreat and resurface again and again along the seams of a fabric that
is destined to be rent, torn, patched, ripped, then smoothed into place
as just an illusion of order. To gain perspective on my role in this new
world order, I envisioned myself as a square in this quilt, the stitching
pulling me sometimes gently, other times tightly.

In 2012, a global counterterrorism conference in Singapore had
illuminated for me the seriousness of ISIS's tactics for luring young,
impressionable women into joining their cause. Then in 2016, Afra,
my associate from the WISE Shura Council, arrived with some
news: The Syrian community in the U.K. and Canada was stunned
that one of their own had recently left to join the caliphate. This
woman was not an impressionable youngster but an eminent professor of Islamic studies—a PhD working at a university in Saudi Arabia. She had come from a prominent Syrian family of scholars
steeped in Islamic law. She had abruptly left her family, her job, and
her entire life to join ISIS. Afra described the note the woman had
left behind for her family, which informed them that throughout
their entire lives they, as Muslims, had been waiting for a caliphate
and that ISIS was the only group that had actually established one.
She believed the group needed her scholarly talent to help build its
state.

Educated or not, this woman was in for a reality check. We had
learned of the many atrocities that she was likely to encounter—
children being forced out of school to watch beheadings, women
being raped and enslaved, and those who refused to follow dress

codes and be fully veiled being publicly whipped. But this highly educated woman clearly undertook this action with a level of awareness of the consequences. Significantly, elite individuals are often the forerunners of a trend.

As Afra spoke, I set my shaking cup down so hard that the tea sloshed onto my oak table and began to seep into the wood. The tea struck me as a metaphor for what we were talking about—something that had been quietly contained but that was now encroaching beyond its confinement, creating a stain that might be indelible. The Quran reminds us that those who practice evil think they will get the better of us—so guarding against evil-mongers is a religious obligation. I thought then of Jamila, brave Jamila—of the threats to put a pipe bomb in her car, of the threats against her daughter (*Just like a flower, she can be plucked*, they'd warned in a note).

Determined to become fully familiarized with the extent to which ISIS was using online tactics to lure young men and women to their cause, our WISE team attended a debriefing session at a law-enforcement headquarters. The topic was digital tactics of extremism. As we walked in, I was surprised to see Elise, a young woman who, just a few years before, had been an intern in my office. Proudly handing me her card, she explained that her role was expert adviser to the counterterrorism unit—she helped them bridge the gap between the Western world, Islamic culture, and issues of extremism. For much of the presentation, Elise led the discussion. It was a proud moment for me—now I was learning from her.

Sitting at the head of the large conference table, Elise played some startling videos—startling, that is, in their normalcy. We watched one video that looked like Disneyland—but it was ISIS land. Gamboling kittens and amusement park rides—Woodstock for extremists, at least as ISIS depicted it. Most of the women who were recruited from the West were young, some only teenagers. These videos were specifically targeting them. The movement was called the "cupcake jihad." The music on the video swelled. Cut to a hot young militant with an assault rifle slung over his shoulder, his long hair

blowing in slow motion. "He wants to meet you, girls!" a voice en-
thused. "He wants you to become the wife of a soldier like him—
a bride of ISIS."

There was no happy ending to be had here. A few young girls
were known to have escaped, Elise said, but for the most part, these
girls vanished from the radar screen and found themselves isolated in
an uncertain and unstable world about which we had more questions
than answers.

We examined a glossy magazine called *Dabiq*, which was published by ISIS to promote their ideology. I had to admit, it looked
slick—which was the point. The front of the magazine resembled
Vanity Fair magazine, with profiles of thought leaders and prominent
cultural personalities—both male and female—as well as editorials.
The back pages of the magazine, though, were more like *Popular Me-
chanics*, with ad after mail-order ad for explosives and weapons, and
how-to tutorials for bomb making. Chapter titles included "Earning
Money," "Transporting Weapons," and "Bomb Making."

Elise pointed out that even if these extremists were people who
lived on the margins, even if they had failed in the wider world, they
were lionized within the ISIS culture. In a twisted way, they then
became role models to recruit others.

A new and frightening kind of social phenomenon had emerged,
which Elise called the "echo effect," with these trendsetters providing
a template for other aspirants. When I heard this, I recalled the inse-
curities I felt as a young woman. Would I have been ripe for recruitment by fringe elements? Remembering my fascination with edgy
activists who had inflamed the arguments about Rushdie, I could
understand how impressionable young people, especially those who
felt disenfranchised or lost, could find themselves drawn into these
kinds of movements. But there was a difference. Even when my faith
was in doubt, I had had my family. I knew I would never have crossed
that line. Still, I understood the vulnerability. Suddenly, the next step
of my mission became clear.

I realized that we were looking at the next frontier for the empowerment of Muslim women. We had been training the thought leaders and imams, reshaping the dialogue, informing communities—but we now had to look inward. The next group we needed to reach was our own rising generation of young women.

Casting around for solutions, I thought of the new WISE Up campaign that we were about to launch.

The WISE Up report would provide concrete facts about Islam and about ISIS—a good start. A vulnerable, information-seeking young woman could come upon our material or click on our website. We would provide the information, the reality check, that might make the difference in her life—that might even save her life and prevent a family's heartbreak.

THE OTHER CUPCAKE JIHAD

...

It took a large measure of talent to transform an ordinary social hall in Fort Lauderdale, Florida, into a five-star ballroom, but this Muslim women's organization had done it. In one area of the room, a Pakistani American woman displayed her red velvet cake. In another, a spread of cucumber sandwiches, cookies, and treats looked as if it would do Downton Abbey proud. In the open foyer, women browsed in pop-up boutiques featuring racks of Pakistani kameez shalwar, *traditional costume jewelry, Arab* gallabiyahs, *incense, and children's books. Presiding over it all was an artfully tiered display of cupcakes with periwinkle and pink icing. Community leaders, volunteers, and committee members manned tables while teenage girls and young women swirled through the room, which was brimming with the energy of the two hundred Muslim women who had gathered for this annual event.*

A speaker addressing this dynamic and hopeful group might have been justly proud to share the excitement of this pocket of active Muslim women who were quietly reshaping their local faith community. If—the speaker might have said—after decades of education, a challenging and rewarding career, and a busy personal life, a woman might sometimes wonder what her place is in a religious community, then this audience, with its smiles, warm embraces, and welcoming spirit, would shore up any doubts. During a discussion of women's rights mentioned in the Quran, the speaker might have noticed the audience members leaning forward. She might have sensed an instant bond, born of common experience. Who in the room had not at some time felt conflicted, or rejected, or confused by her faith—an ancient faith in modern times? If the women were surprised when the speaker pointed them to the past, where rights had been granted centuries ago, they were stunned to learn how these rights had been subverted and yet invigorated to discover how they themselves could take command of the future.

As the applause died down, two young women approached the speaker, asking how they could learn more about empowering Muslim women through the words of the scriptures. There were materials to study, websites to research, she told them. But these young women, hungry for knowledge, sought more. They asked about training sessions, which could be conducted via Skype.

A platter of periwinkle cupcakes was passed. No one could resist, especially me, the speaker. This was a cupcake jihad, of another kind. A jihad I was comfortable waging.

CHAPTER

40

HAVE BEEN INVITED THOUSANDS OF MILES FROM HOME TO ADdress a conference in Abu Dhabi on countering extremism. In the lobby of the conference facility, Muzak is playing. Research has shown that this kind of mindless music is supposed to calm boneweary, edgy travelers like us, who have weathered the rigors of long flights, lost luggage, and customs lines to assemble from so many points on the globe. We are offered cool bottles of water, cups of hot coffee, and lavish snacks. Looking around the room, I see there are dozens of women among at least a hundred people. Otherwise, we are all different, but we are also the same.

A cobra is loose in the room. It has refused to be charmed by the nice music in the lobby. It is up to us to figure out how to capture it, tame it, police it, get rid of it, or destroy it—before it finds a cozy home in our closet and strikes, perhaps when we reach out to pet it, perhaps when we bump into it in the dark, unknowing. We set out our iPhones and tablets. Our pencils are ready; our coffee is cooling.

I step up to the speaker's podium. I take the microphone.

I am in Kashmir, venturing onto the tin roof outside my window. In the distance, I see the majestic peaks of the Himalayas, rising some fourteen thousand feet toward the sky. The roof is that place that extends into the other room, the room beyond the physical world, the spiritual place—the eternal space that is beyond common human understanding.

The tin of the roof is on fire from a long day's sun. It burns, but I must trust my feet to tell me just how close to the edge I can reliably step. My eyes fix on an early star peeking through the bright blue of the lowering sky—my own true north. The wisdom of my faith anchors me as I feel my way forward. Straddling each side of the roof slope, I balance, then inch my way along to the very end. There I stand, leaning out with my arms extended. This is the cue for my mother to rush forward, arms outstretched, to catch me.

There is a jarring loudspeaker announcement. The session is about to begin, and soon it will be my turn to speak. Where am I? When did the mountains grow? How did the roof become so steep? Where is my mother to catch me? I tap the microphone. Really, I am playing for time, for a few seconds. That's about how long it takes to remember that the mountain is always moving; the sky is never still; the cobra, ISIS, today's fanatics—they are coiled, preparing to strike.

As I scanned the room, I saw people who recognized that if we did nothing to fight this threat, our next generation would be affected. I told the audience that while we didn't seem to have a clear answer, we nevertheless had a solution—knowledge! And yet I thought of what our sages had taught us: that words are so powerful they can make you believe in lies.

Karolina Dam, a New Zealander woman in her fifties who now lived in Denmark, stood at the podium. When her son was killed in Syria, she founded Sons and Daughters of the World. Her story and her ordeal were heart-wrenching. "In the beginning, I was pleased when my son converted to Islam. It gave meaning to his life," she began. "But I wish I had seen the early signs of him being recruited by extremists. If I had known the early signs, I might have been able to help. Parents need to be taught how to communicate with children who are under the influence of recruiters.

"Since I lost my son, I have had no closure. I can't bury him." She stopped speaking then and started choking, holding back her tears while trying to keep her composure. "Parents like me who lose children in Syria can't get death certificates. They can't process their grief. They can't close their child's Facebook account or their bank accounts. This is a huge problem for mothers who are grieving. Our lives are still going. Sometimes I wake up in the morning, and I wear two different pairs of socks. Sometimes it takes me one hour to get to work when it should take only ten minutes, because I can't get out of my car—I just sit and cry for an hour. I cry my eyes out, but I am still working. This is my life. This is what my day is like. And this is how it is going to be for the rest of my life."

Around the room, all eyes were fixed on her. I had to put my pen down to wipe my tears. I felt her devastation. But Karolina had an upbeat personality. Even in her grief she found a way to be hopeful; she put up a photo of her blond, blue-eyed teenage son and said, "This is my boy. This is purity. I see he is blessed. Since I can't bury my son, I have been knitting and crocheting with my tears. I chose a tree in my yard, and I covered its trunk with green crocheting. This is his tree now, and when I look at the tree, I see my son as a green bird in paradise. He will always be the most beautiful green bird in paradise. And with this tree I have brought him home, and now he can fly."

THE NEXT MORNING, SALIHA BEN ALI of an organization called SAVE Belgium took the stage. She was a woman in her forties—she was of Tunisian background and had lived her whole life in Belgium, and she too had lost her son in Syria. Her face was grief stricken, her eyes sunken, and her voice soft and measured. I felt sad for her and braced myself for what I would hear.

"My son was radicalized in only three months," she began. "He had a misconception of how he was humiliated, of how Islam was humiliated. He had an Arabic name, which was seen as a problem. The society, the neighborhood, did not provide him with hope. . . . The police provoked him sometimes, saying, 'Why haven't you gone to Syria yet?'" She paused. "The spiritual leaders, imams who were not able to express themselves in French after fifty years of living here, were unable to help him."

As I listened to her, I sensed and felt hopelessness. She was talking about deep structural and societal issues that were clearly beyond her control. "I was not able to help him; I did not even identify his hurt!" she said. "So with no one to turn to, he fell into the trap of the recruiters, who took advantage of him. When he searched for meaning and could not find it in Belgium, he decided to find it elsewhere, so he went to Syria. When I learned that he had gone there, I was devastated. I called him and pleaded with him to return. 'Why have you gone?' I asked. 'Mom, I have not been able to give my life meaning. But I will give meaning to my death,' he told me."

Just as it had when Karolina had spoken, the silent room fell into a complete stillness. I felt Saliha's grief and pain, and I was moved by her composure as she talked about her work with families whose children have gone to Syria or have been recruited by extremists. "I do this work in honor of my son, and I will spend the rest of my life making sure that not one mother more has to experience the pain of losing a child this way."

DEAR SISTER, THE LETTER BEGAN. *Do not destroy your life. . . .* The message that followed, a deconstruction of ISIS's recruiting manifesto, was sent to teachers in London for them to read to their students, after three British schoolgirls from East London left their homes and traveled to Syria to join ISIS. The letter was viewed forty thousand times within a day of its being posted online in February 2015 and was reprinted in newspapers globally. It was written by Sara Khan, a young British Muslim woman and the leader of a British women's rights group called Inspire and a British informational campaign for women called Making a Stand.

Sara had attended our 2009 WISE global conference in Kuala Lumpur, where the Global Muslim Women's Shura Council had proclaimed a "Jihad against Violence," a condemnation of domestic violence and terrorism. She had adopted the idea of a "Jihad against Violence" in the United Kingdom, and the following year, I was invited to be Inspire's keynote speaker when they announced the initiative at their conference in Hounslow, a diverse borough of West London.

When I read about those three girls, I felt the urgency behind Sara's letter. How far, after all, was the distance between any young woman searching for meaning, struggling to belong, and a one-way ticket to the so-called caliphate? Sara and I talked about the fact that these girls were part of the post-9/11 generation. They do not feel as if they belong. "That's what ISIS uses as key to their appeal," she said. "They say, 'We will treat you like a valued citizen.'" The priority now was to get to the roots of Muslim girls' alienation. While extremist recruiters tried to encourage girls to rebel against the limitations they claimed were placed on them, Sara made a point of telling them that Islam does not restrict you; it empowers you.

On October 25, 2017, I took out my biggest boxing gloves ever and gave voice to seventy-two noted scholars, using knowledge as the most powerful tool against all forms of extremism: A summit was organized in Washington, D.C., to showcase the WISE Up report. Many of the speakers were contributors to the publication, a 365-plus-page report whose Part One focuses on American Muslims—who we are; Part Two, on Islam and Islamic theology versus extremist theology; and Part Three, on preventing extremist recruitment and countering hate. The major achievement of the report was that it distilled and made accessible vast knowledge on the subject, putting it all right at our fingertips.

My friend and longtime confidante Mino was among the three hundred participants including scholars, activists, journalists, philanthropists, and imams, as well as law-enforcement professionals from the FBI, Homeland Security, etc. Mino clapped her hands to celebrate our convening power and vision to create WISE Up after years of sheer hard work and passion! As she sat in the audience, soaking it all in, she felt a strong wave of hope rise within her that "this too shall pass" and that human dignity, intelligence, and dialogue would prevail against the barrage of screaming voices that sow hate and division. She wrote, "It was a most inspiring and hopeful day for me as an American Muslim as the voices of spirituality, peace and interfaith activism ... united to speak on the topic of hate, extremism, how knowledge ends extremism as well as how social and political forces can combine to hijack faiths." She found the panels illuminating and reassuring at the same time, as they went deep to see the forces working toward hate, while spotlighting what is possible to create peace and love in the world today.

In her blog, she continued, "How lucky I am, I said to myself, to actually be in the presence of such grace, such intelligence, such patience, such vision and such hope. I promised I would take this experience with me and never let it go. It was a precious gift I received, and now my job was to pass it on. I want to tell everyone that humanity is within our reach and we can bring it back again. I want to tell others to seek knowledge and share knowledge and learn, learn, learn! I want to tell others that I always knew my faith is beautiful and deep, and no 'terrorist' or 'War on Terror' can steal that away from me! ... I want to tell others that extremists exist in all faiths, and we have to illuminate their deceit and evil."

UM "MOTHER" OF A NATION—
CHOOSE PEACE

...

I had heard news reports about young American Muslim women who had been detained for providing material support to ISIS. When I read their stories, I wondered what discontents had pushed them to make this choice.

Sara Mahmood, who worked with me on the WISE Up article "Why Daesh Recruits Women," which examined the unparalleled flow of women recruits from the West to join ISIS, had found in her research that women play an integral part in ISIS's societal structure. Unlike al-Qaeda, ISIS, by including women, symbolically elevates their status and gives them the impression that they have autonomy as rational agents. Through our research, we also know that there was no one reason why women joined ISIS. The push-and-pull factors were as complex as the women themselves; each reacted to her own set of fears, anxieties, opinions, and beliefs. For some it was social isolation; others felt constrained and frustrated that they could not shape their own destiny; some were convinced that female liberation had diverted them from their divine duty as wives and mothers; and still others wanted to inherit greatness by restoring Islam to its past glory.

The primary role for women in the so-called caliphate was to bear the children, who would not only populate the land, but also insure the survival of the group. Young women were led to feel that as mothers they were seeding a nation. Women also served as recruiters, groomers, and propagandists in the social media domain. They played an important role in attracting vulnerable young women to a romanticized notion of sisterhood in a so-called caliphate. I knew that Western women were being particularly targeted. If they could be convinced to abandon their lives in the West, they became important symbols supporting ISIS's message that Muslim women are unfairly targeted, singled out, and treated unequally because of their faith.

I wanted to meet with these young women and demystify ISIS, to tell them that for ISIS, women were just a commodity that existed for the sake of men. The functions ISIS assigned to women were solely related to the survival of the group and superseded all other considerations of women as people. But first, I had to find out how these women had been manipulated into joining ISIS's phenomenal recruiting machine, which hijacked hashtags to monitor conversations, exploited personal Twitter accounts to enable them to reach hundreds of thousands more people, and infiltrated computers to carry out campaigns via remote controls. I wanted to look them straight in the eye and explain to them that ISIS's use of social media was part of its plan to particularly target millennials, who by virtue of sharing content across various social media platforms were inadvertently acting as recruiters—inspiring others to join and risk their lives.

On May 24, 2017, I received an email from an acquaintance from D.C.: "I am writing to connect you to a respected attorney who is dealing with some of the issues that you have been focused on in your counterextremism work. I hope you will have a chance to connect, and thanks again for all of the important work you are doing," he wrote. Days later, I would get the op-

portunity to meet the client to whom my acquaintance had al-luded, a young Muslim woman who was incarcerated for her involvement with ISIS.

When I was getting ready for our first meeting, I imagined someone frail, confused, and vulnerable, who was, perhaps, a religious fanatic. Instead, she exuded warmth and confidence. She was nothing like I had imagined!

I told her that I wanted to help her but that I needed to un-derstand her motivations in order to do so. "Tell me everything about yourself. When and where were you born? What was your family like? Tell me all the good and bad that has happened in your life, and tell me how you landed here," I said. She told me she had been born in America and came from a broken home. She relayed stories of a childhood full of psychological trauma, family disaffiliation, and constant instability.

It was clear to me that many people had failed her as a child. The harshness of her life had taught her to fend for herself, but perhaps no one had told her how. Still, the question that kept swirling in my head was, how does a person like this get tangled up in ISIS? When I asked her, she told me that when a friend had shared some of ISIS's social media posts with her, she became curious and started experimenting with reposting. Adept at so-cial media, she began posting their stuff, and before she knew it, she was disseminating ISIS's propaganda.

I was upset that she had allowed herself to become an acces-sory for a terrorist group. I wanted to know what she expected to find in the so-called caliphate. I could tell that when she walked the streets in America wearing a hijab, she felt out of place, socially isolated, and not safe. She was told that in the so-called caliphate, they had law and order, security for women, jobs for women, and a sense of belonging. They told her that they would find her a good Muslim husband and that she would have children and a family of her own. For her, ISIS was not political, it was personal!

As we were concluding our talk, I showed her the WISE Up report in which we detailed ISIS's sixteen-step online recruitment process. This multifaceted approach is uniquely tailored to the recruit's personal circumstances, background, and vulnerabilities. When I asked her if she thought it could be useful in deterring other young women from joining ISIS to inform them that the organization specifically targeted individuals' discontents, she nodded. Since ISIS had not led her to happiness, I asked her if she regretted her decision. She knew she had gained nothing and had lost two precious years of her education and faced major personal setbacks.

Before I left her, I realized I hadn't earned her trust yet, and I could tell that she was trying to judge me, the same way I had done, years earlier, with my mother. So I assured her, "Through my hands and my words you will never be hurt. Can you say the same about ISIS?"

As she looked down in silence, I felt both sympathy and trepidation for her. I knew she needed a spiritual sister and a mentor. I was unsure if I was prepared to play that role. Then I wondered, if not me, then who? So when she is ready and able, I will engage her in a one-to-one dialogue. I want to teach her how to discern truths from falsehoods, to hone her ethical mores, and, most important, to reignite her spirit so she can proactively choose peace.

In things spiritual, there is no partition, no number,
no individuals. How sweet is the oneness—unearth the
treasure of Unity.

—RUMI, *translation by R. A. Nicholson*

THINK BACK TO THE 2011 WISE CONFERENCE IN ISTANBUL. THE banner on the entrance to the hotel in Istanbul read: WISE— MUSLIM WOMEN LEADERS ON THE FRONT LINES OF CHANGE. Had it been only five years since I had conceived the idea of WISE? With our team and generous supporters, we had come so far. Now, at our third global conference, we were not simply making our voices heard, but we were assuming global leadership roles that were creating history, transforming the Islamic women's empowerment movement. The Arab Spring, for instance, had been largely spearheaded by women, who led demonstrations and rallies, posted videos, and shared their opinions. Yemeni activist Tawakkol Karman, the "Mother of the Revolution," who had organized protests that culminated in the Yemeni Revolution, was awarded the 2011 Nobel Peace Prize. The two hundred women who had gathered here from forty-five countries were all at the forefront of uplifting their communities. We had chosen the theme of "women's leadership" to honor them.

As I made my way to the podium for the opening remarks, I was confronted by two secular Turkish women dressed in elegant business suits. They announced to us that they felt uncomfortable among so many women wearing headscarves. Perhaps they didn't belong here. Why had they even been invited? I told the women that we would be disappointed if they left us but that if they stayed, they might realize that they had more in common with the members of this group than they thought. The women agreed to stay on one condition. They wished to speak about Atatürk, the first president of modern Turkey, and what he had done for women. I agreed to their request. After all, we were in their home country, which was sharply divided between secular and religious populations, and their local, political view was an important representation of the regional climate. And in any case, I saw no benefit in excluding anyone, especially as one of our major goals was to unite women who were fragmented along conservative, liberal, secular, and spiritual lines.

Then, as I began to speak at the podium, I saw her—a quiet, majestic woman with a gentle smile and an aura all her own. Esin Çelebi Bayru is the twenty-second-generation great-granddaughter of my favorite poet, Rumi. His universal themes of love and unity had inspired my work and my life. Now his direct descendent was attending our event. Not only was her presence an honor, but to me it also felt like a sign of our movement toward the reclamation of women's rights that I had been seeking for so long. Bayru was on this day one in a roomful of women who were each outstanding in their own world and their own way, but only Bayru brought this unique legacy of spiritual hope. It was a moment like many others in my work, but it was one of the most extraordinary and significant moments of my life.

WHEN I THINK ABOUT working toward peace and unity, I feel as if I'm grabbing at a cloud. I can see the outlines of the formation, but the cloud itself is ephemeral, transient, and elusive. When I see women taking concrete steps, singularly and in multitudes, however, I realize that the cloud is not so amorphous after all. In fact, peace is quite possible, especially when unity is driven by women across continents and cultures. WISE is one support beam on this bridge, but there are now many others.

When I began my spiritual search, I went looking for God in all kinds of places. My quest was to define who I was in relation to my creator, to better understand what was my human identity. I discovered that I am primarily a container of the "divine breath," which allows me to easily navigate between my cultural and national identities.

In 2013, I left New York to visit my homeland. In Kashmir, I wanted to try to figure out more about my real roots. Was there something special about my birthplace and its influence upon me? Was it my DNA that was propelling me—and if so, who were all my ancestors? Did any family legends need to be explored so I could derive inspiration from them? I wanted to better understand the stories of my family, to fully comprehend their achievements and the challenges they faced. I knew I needed the stories of my ancestors to enable me to move forward.

Equipped with my smartphone, I recorded some of the family history we children had been shielded from, growing up. I was curious about my feisty grandmother Sarah and her scandalous open-toed sandals—the way she just kept walking forward, confident even in the face of social pressure and derision. I thought of myself as a newborn girl, of the perilous consequences of blind tradition that almost ended my life before it began. And yet despite the challenges that have come with asserting women's rights and with living in a divisive, fractured world, I have come to realize that I have had the key to my future in my hands all along, in the inscription in the Quran that my grandfather gave me when I first left Kashmir: *Oh Lord, increase me in knowledge*. And I understand that I, in turn, pass along these words to others—my contribution to the Daisy chain.

Then I think of Dadaji, who engineered the master plan for our family. He intuited the aptitude of each family member—his children and his grandchildren—and determined which career each one should pursue. Then he sent family members abroad to study at the best schools possible with the caveat that they return to Kashmir with their newly acquired knowledge. He was determined that the Khans be equipped to serve Kashmir and its people. Alas, it did not work out that way. As the political situation in Kashmir worsened, most of us moved to America. But I wonder how Dadaji would react if he heard that his beloved America is facing its dark days. If anyone told him that America's new immigration policy was resulting in children being separated from their parents and that those consumed with hate gave themselves the license to shoot anyone who closely resembled a Muslim, he would never believe it. In a way, I am relieved that he did not live to see this.

As I reflect on all those who have guided me throughout my life, it occurs to me that Dadaji's letter to his children, which he penned in 1982 in his book *Extracts from the Holy Quran* during his visit to Jericho, New York, was written as if he predicted that a moment in history would come when people would succumb to rage and lose their humanity. His words, written below, have a deep wisdom.

> The trials and tribulations of our daily lives are casting agony, grief, and gloom around us despite constant increases in physical comforts and rises in our standards of living. Our energies, our enterprises, our creative powers, need to be devoted to improving the texture and quality of living and being for all mankind.
>
> We must shape our lives as good human beings, adhering to principles governing social needs, human values and other duties and obligations to the creator as well as to fellow human beings.... Muslims must, individually and in cooperation with one another, do good, fight against evil, and cultivate centers of service to bring rays of hope and happiness to homes and communities infested with gloom and despair.

As I continued to explore my ancestral home, Papaji, who knew me well, showed me all of Dadaji's writings. Then he handed me a small booklet entitled *A Happy and Successful Life: Islamic View.* "Use it for yourself," he told me. As I leafed through it and his other writings, I discovered that its greatest lesson was not inside the book but inscribed in Dadaji's meticulous handwriting on the title page:

> Every Muslim grandfather considers it as his privilege to instruct his grandchildren what Islam teaches. This privilege has been denied to me because many of my grandchildren are being brought up in places far away from my residence. It is primarily for the benefit of these children that I have written this concise booklet.
>
> *—Ghulam Hassan Khan,*
> *September 25, 1984*

I immediately remembered receiving various booklets from my grandfather over the years. I had glanced through them and promptly shelved them alongside books by V. S. Naipaul, Shakespeare, Gibran, and Rumi. Now, decades later, the words inscribed in them moved me. I held the books in my hand and walked the long treelined road. I remembered merrily skipping here years ago, with an Enid Blyton novel in my hand, sporting my sixties bell-bottoms, Rocky, my Alsatian, running beside me, Dadaji smiling and carrying pruning shears in his hand, the voices of children playing hide-and-seek ringing through the fields. When I arrived at the family cemetery, I saw Mummy clearing leaves and twigs from my dadaji's gravestone.

I asked her, "Why did you plant a tree here? The leaves will keep falling."

She turned and replied, "Graveyards in Kashmir plant trees."

I wanted to know why, to which she responded, "Because every leaf prays and hallows God."

How fascinating was the cycle of life, I thought. I recalled the moment when I had wanted to know who God was and Dadaji had pointed to trees, the sky, the fruits in the orchard, the flowers in their beds. I wondered if this was why I loved lying down on the hard earth and dreaming impossible dreams underneath my favorite pomegranate tree.

I kneeled over Dadaji's grave and read aloud his very poetic words from one of his many booklets.

> *I am an old man nearing eighty*
> *And vigor departs*
> *But thousands of memories*
> *Live in my heart.*
> *Do not stand at my grave to cry or to weep.*
> *Beseech Allah to let my soul rest in peace.*
> *Thank him that he granted me all these precious years.*
> *Have faith and blot away the downtrodden tears.*

These words gave me a sense of purpose. I knew that Dadaji felt he had fulfilled his duty and it was up to the rest of his progeny to carry on—not to dream, but to act.

My origins in a land of disputed territory prepared me for my life and my mission. Because I experienced gaps between cultures first-hand, I have seen how differences between people can be a cause of uncertainty and a flash point for conflict. In my lifetime, I have had two homelands. Three wars have been fought for control over the first of my homes—during all of which my nation was largely a pawn. Now I am an American Muslim and have synthesized all my experiences. A disenfranchised birth? Life in a conflict zone? My dreams and Moji's prediction? Marriage to an imam? I know these events have prepared me for and contributed to my pursuit of social justice and women's rights—not only for Muslims, but for women throughout the world.

What the ultimate solutions are, I cannot say.

Today, I represent a challenged community in America. The reper-cussions of new wars in Muslim lands directly impact the diaspora communities. Muslims must articulate and identify with their Amer-icanness, because their loyalties are being questioned. The civil liber-ties violations against them, which stem from the Patriot Act, have increased, and workplace discrimination, school harassment, and hate crimes are underreported. There are those who still propagate a clash between civilizations, who insist that Western values are inconsistent with Islamic values, and so the demand for Muslims to speak out is greater than ever. We have seen interfaith collaboration increase by 1,000 percent, and more than 80 percent of American mosques now have outreach programs and open houses for those of other faiths.

Despite the bleak news, there is a glimmer of hope. The media have realized that they need a more nuanced and sophisticated understanding of Islam and Muslims. Yet whether it's fair or not, our silence is deemed as complicity. And so Muslims have come to the sobering realization that it is our responsibility to step up and engage the media and the larger American public if perceptions are to be reversed.

On the culinary front, there is promising news. America is integrating foods from Muslim lands into its cultural fabric: Falafel has become as prevalent as pizza; hummus is the ultimate dip; kebabs are the new meatballs; biryani is as comforting as noodles and pasta.

And modest wear and emerging Islamic fashion design are prominent in the news, with Muslim models appearing on the front covers of fashion magazines. For example, Hassanah el-Yacoubi, a leading fashion and lifestyle blogger, saw the need to demonstrate that fashion, modesty, and veiling do not have to be at odds with one another. She is creating cross-cultural and religious understanding through leading a modest fashion industry. Lately, mainstream brands, including Nordstrom and Nike, have begun designing modest clothing for contemporary Muslim women. They do it simply because it makes business sense.

On a more serious note, when I see the passion and bravery of women such as Jamila in Afghanistan and the energy and commitment of young visionaries such as Sara in London, Elise in New York, and Sherin in Copenhagen, I see a new kind of partnership. I see the future of a faith. If for too long we women were not permitted at the table, we are now creating our own table. It is a long table of love, not a tall fence of hate, and as a designer, I embrace the blueprint.

CHAPTER

42

I WAS EAGER TO VISIT MY FAMILY'S ANCESTRAL HOME IN KHAN-
yar, where Moji had lived. But when I arrived in Kashmir, I realized
that many of my childhood memories were just that—memories.
Conditions had changed because of continued political strife, but
what remained of a bygone era was the stark natural beauty, snowcapped mountains, and a picture-postcard sunset on the lake. But the
loss and human struggle were difficult to digest.

I became excited when my dad and I passed Kashmir's most sacred shrine, Hazrat Sheikh Syed Abdul Qadir Jilani's resting place.
The fruit sellers were still displaying their colorful fruits in tiers; the
butcher block was still a tree trunk. Poor kids were chasing after a
metal ring, elderly men wearing *pheran* sat together sharing a hoo-
kah, and earnest-looking children with hazel eyes and rosy cheeks
wearing tattered clothes spoke volumes with their blank expressions.

Kashmiris are known for their generosity and open spirit, and
when we arrived at the gate to Moji's house, I was greeted warmly by
Shafi Uncle. He had heard that I wanted to visit Moji's house and
had made arrangements with the new owners. As we entered through
the large wrought-iron gate, I gasped to see a new brick-and-wood
house in place of our home. I was despondent. Why hadn't Mummy
told me that the house was gone? But just as I was about to complain,
a gentleman in his forties approached us and introduced himself in
fluent English. The new owner, Mr. Shah, invited me into his home.

Mr. Shah was aware that I had come to see my grandmother's home and saw the confusion in my eyes. Instead of offering me tea, he asked if I would like to go around to the back of the house. I was puzzled, but out of curiosity, I followed him. When we came around the corner, there was Moji's house! Intact and standing tall against other, newer houses. As I glanced at the vacant, bolted house, memories poured through my mind: men playing cards on Sundays while eating kebabs and drinking simmering hot *kahwa,* green tea poured from a copper samovar; kids running up and down the stairs; aromatic dishes being cooked in the kitchen . . . the stair landing where my grandmother placed me when she asked the poor to pray for me.

Mr. Shah asked me if I would like to go inside. I was thrilled. He inserted a large key in the iron padlock. We walked into the house, which was lit by dim light that came in through the windows. He led me up the narrow staircase, and as we arrived at Moji's room, I asked if I could go in by myself.

I walked in and took in the vacant room. I had goosebumps, an intense feeling of Moji's presence. I began examining every detail of the room, the bookshelves, the paint, the empty floor, the latticework windows. Why was I feeling the fullness of this room when it was so empty? I sat at the spot where Moji had held me in her lap as I dreamed of God. Then I opened the window, half expecting tens of ravens to still be there. They were all gone . . . with Moji. Uncle Shafi appeared at the door and asked if he could come in, and when he did, he said, "The blood in my veins is boiling. Did you know that Moji was the *'Taj'* [crown] of this family and that she had a 'sweet hand'?" When I inquired about his five daughters, he told me they were "well settled" and added, "Don't forget my son too!"

I asked the owner why he had not torn the house down. He smiled, closed his eyes, and said, "We know who lived here. How can we tear her home down when we are getting her blessing every day?"

Deeply touched by his spiritual wisdom, I asked if he planned to keep the house empty. He replied, *"Inshallah,* God willing, one day we hope to turn it into a heritage site so people like you can come

and see how Kashmiris lived and how a woman like your grandmother inspired so many. Are you writing a book?" he asked. I smiled
and nodded yes. He said, "Come back anytime. This is your home." I
had come to inquire about my ancestry, and much to my surprise and
joy, I discovered that a stranger was not only honoring my grandmother but also preserving our collective Kashmiri heritage. Mr.
Shah reminded me that I still had a home in Kashmir—in fact, he
gave me the blessing of a home. And although my main home is now
the United States, I carry both my homes within me—as perhaps
you do too. We are all made up of many stories, both our own and
those of our ancestors but also the stories and cultures of people
whose lives interact with ours. Mr. Shah carries a bit of Moji inside
him too, though he never knew her. The more we share our stories,
the more we open ourselves to one another, the more respect and
even love can flow between us. Once we see ourselves in the faces of
others, we can stand side by side on the basis of our human identity,
as Westerners or Easterners, as religious or not, as black, white, yellow, or brown. With layers of our identity nested within a larger sense
of identity—"out of many, one," in a single space.

ACKNOWLEDGMENTS

I HAVE A VIVID MEMORY OF WALKING INTO THE OFFICE OF LAURA Yorke and Carol Mann to seek their help in publishing a glossy book of one hundred "Heroines of Islam." My friend Nora Feller, who had made hundreds of these portraits, had connected me to them. Upon examining the photos, Laura found the kaleidoscope of women's faces truly striking, but there was a problem: The market for illustrated books was gone, she said. Then they both inquired about my work with these women. As I spoke about my passion for women's rights and the work I was undertaking around the world, their interest was piqued. Had I written a book about my life? they wanted to know. I told them I could not imagine why anyone would want to read such a book. They looked at each other and smiled, and that is when this journey began.

Along this path, I met my first fellow traveler, Cindy Spiegel, a soft-spoken, mild-mannered, kind-hearted human being. Inquisitive by nature, she listened intently to the terrains I had to navigate within my own faith, the hurdles I had to overcome with my fellow Americans, the path I had to clear within myself. She knew then that a Muslim woman's story needed to be added to the national discourse and she was glad to add my story to the stable of socially conscious books she was publishing. Traveling on the road with a novice is not easy: For one thing, I had never before undertaken this arduous journey of writing and editing. Even though we set the direction, the course was changed on numerous occasions. Cindy maintained her calm, convinced that I had a story to tell. I thank her for her patience and her astute skills to shape and polish this work.

Along the way, other travelers joined the journey. Claire Wachtel opened her home and dining table for months as we sat over kosher chocolates to rearrange, rewrite, and edit the work, and Liz Nickles continued editing even when she was recovering from surgery.

Always on this journey with me is my husband, who is my secret weapon—a warner and my enabler, who helps awaken the spiritual warrior in me.

Then there is my family, without whom I would not be here. I am grateful to my mother, who pushed me to stand on my own feet and encouraged me to move to the United States to pursue my architectural design dreams. I am lucky to have a father who not only valued me, his third daughter, but gave me the free rein to explore my creativity. I owe great thanks to my uncle Faroque; I am in his debt for taking the risk of bringing a teenager to America, and to Arfa Auntie for being my mentor and filling the void of my being without my mother in the United States.

My ancestors had set the stage already. Dadaji took the first step in leaving his home to come to America, paving the way for me to walk on the same road years later. Without his early, bold journey, I might not be here today.

There are no words to pay tribute to Moji, in whose presence I learned humility and became conscious of God. In her company, I was touched by the light; she became my guiding star. Shaykh Nur ignited the spirit and breathed new life into me.

To the nuns of the Presentation Convent School in Kashmir, the education you imparted in me lives on. To all my friends from there, Halima, Anjum, Muz, and my other classmates, your friendship has enriched me in ways you never imagined. To the American Muslim communities and its scores of women warriors, I hope my narrative provides clarity to the intractable issues we are trying to overcome.

To the women whose photos I could not publish, my story is your story. I dedicate this to all of you, who are working tirelessly and risking your lives to uplift women and girls. To shaykhas around the world, including Maryam, CemalNur, Aisha, Fariha, Seemi, and Camille: Your spiritual wisdom is greatly needed today. To my friends and fellow spiritual activists Laleh, Mino, Yasemin, Latifa, Fazeela, Leyla, Maria, Afra, Asmi, Naz, Mehnaz, Maha, Zeyba, Chloe, Sarah, Eileen, Joan, Maureen, Zainab: You are my torch bearers. I salute my fellow prime-mover cohorts for teaching me how to be cause-driven. I am indebted to Swanee, in whose "Teepee" company I learned important life lessons and who continues to support my growth as a leader. To Helen, Cynda, Abigail, Beverly, Lynda—your continued support and encouragement has allowed me to develop WISE as a platform for my work. To Lisa and young women like Maleeha, Erica, Gina, Nadia, and my mentees who surround me daily, your moral uprightness, care for humankind, and your ideals inspire me immensely. I look forward to watching your journey of self-discovery unfold.

My gratitude goes to my friend Rafique, and to Jesse, who helped write my early thoughts about this book. I applaud the imams, rabbis, priests, male colleagues, and philanthropists who have supported and encouraged me and many other women in our own self-empowerment, and have positively impacted our lives.

To my beloved birthplace, Kashmir, you shaped my worldview, with which I was able to embrace all cultures and religions. You are the most beautiful place on earth, and I pray you will remain so. And to my adopted country, America: Your openness made me flourish; you are the most blessed nation on earth, and I hope you will continue to live up to your ideals.

To my Creator, I am blessed to have been given the opportunity to discharge my duties as a human being and, especially, a woman on this earth. I hope the next part of my journey is as rewarding as the previous one.

DAISY KHAN is the founder and executive director of the Women's Islamic Initiative in Spirituality and Equality (WISE), a global organization that works on behalf of women's rights in Islam and initiated the creation of the first global women's *shura* (advisory) council, which advances women's rights through scriptural interpretation. After finding herself at the center of a national debate surrounding the Ground Zero controversy, Khan emerged as a leader in the public eye. Formerly, she served as executive director of the American Society for Muslim Advancement, where she spent eighteen years creating groundbreaking intra- and interfaith programs based on cultural and religious harmony and interfaith collaboration. She has won numerous awards for her work as an advocate for Muslim women's rights around the world and is a frequent media commentator. She lives with her husband in the New York City tri-state area.

Facebook.com/WISEMuslimWomen
Twitter: @DaisyKhan and @WISE_Leaders

This book was set in Caslon, a typeface first designed in 1722 by William Caslon (1692–1766). Its widespread use by most English printers in the early eighteenth century soon supplanted the Dutch typefaces that had formerly prevailed. The roman is considered a "workhorse" typeface due to its pleasant, open appearance, while the italic is exceedingly decorative.